CASH ON CASH

Other Books in the Musicians in Their Own Words Series

Bowie on Bowie: Interviews and Encounters with David Bowie
The Clash on the Clash: Interviews and Encounters
Cobain on Cobain: Interviews and Encounters
Coltrane on Coltrane: The John Coltrane Interviews
Dolly on Dolly: Interviews and Encounters with Dolly Parton
Dylan on Dylan: Interviews and Encounters
Fleetwood Mac on Fleetwood Mac: Interviews and Encounters
George Harrison on George Harrison: Interviews and Encounters
Hendrix on Hendrix: Interviews and Encounters with Jimi Hendrix
Joni on Joni: Interviews and Encounters with Joni Mitchell
Judy Garland on Judy Garland: Interviews and Encounters
Keith Richards on Keith Richards: Interviews and Encounters
Led Zeppelin on Led Zeppelin: Interviews and Encounters
Lennon on Lennon: Conversations with John Lennon
Leonard Cohen on Leonard Cohen: Interviews and Encounters
Miles on Miles: Interviews and Encounters with Miles Davis
Neil Young on Neil Young: Interviews and Encounters
Patti Smith on Patti Smith: Interviews and Encounters
Springsteen on Springsteen: Interviews, Speeches, and Encounters
Tom Waits on Tom Waits: Interviews and Encounters
The Who on the Who: Interviews and Encounters

CASH ON CASH

INTERVIEWS AND ENCOUNTERS WITH **JOHNNY CASH**

EDITED BY ROBERT BURKE WARREN

CHICAGO
REVIEW
PRESS

Published by Chicago Review Press Incorporated
814 North Franklin Street
Chicago, Illinois 60610

ISBN 978-1-64160-634-9

Library of Congress Cataloging-in-Publication Data
Names: Cash, Johnny, interviewee. | Warren, Robert Burke, editor.
Title: Cash on Cash : interviews and encounters with Johnny Cash / edited
    by Robert Burke Warren.
Description: Chicago : Chicago Review Press, 2022. | Series: Musicians in
    their own words | Includes index. | Summary: "A comprehensive collection
    of Johnny Cash interviews and feature stories, some widely published and
    others never previously transcribed, culled from the 1950s through the
    early days of the new millennium, offering unprecedented insight into
    one of the most significant American cultural figures of the twentieth
    century"—Provided by publisher.
Identifiers: LCCN 2022017055 (print) | LCCN 2022017056 (ebook) | ISBN
    9781641606349 (paperback) | ISBN 9781641606356 (adobe pdf) | ISBN
    9781641606363 (epub) | ISBN 9781641606370 (kindle edition)
Subjects: LCSH: Cash, Johnny. | Cash, Johnny—Interviews. | Country
    musicians—United States—Biography. | Country musicians—United
    States—Interviews.
Classification: LCC ML420.C265 A5 2022 (print) | LCC ML420.C265 (ebook) |
    DDC 782.421642092 [B]—dc23/eng/20220407
LC record available at https://lccn.loc.gov/2022017055
LC ebook record available at https://lccn.loc.gov/2022017056

A list of credits and copyright notices for the individual pieces in this collection can
be found on pages 263–265.

Cover design: Jonathan Hahn
Cover photograph: AF archive / Alamy Stock Photo
Interior layout: Nord Compo

Printed in the United States of America
5 4 3 2 1

For Holly and Jack

. . . my sun and moon

CONTENTS

Acknowledgments   ix

Preface   xiii

Johnny Cash and the Tennessee Two

November 15, 1958 | *Town Hall Party*   1

Division Street Corral Interview | RED ROBINSON

June 27, 1959 | Interview Transcript   7

Johnny and June Interview and Performance | PETE SEEGER

1966 | *Rainbow Quest*   13

The Restless Ballad of Johnny Cash | CHRISTOPHER S. WREN

April 29, 1969 | *Look*   28

G Chords and Revolutions: *The Johnny Cash Show*, 1969 | ROSANNE CASH

2015 | *Dylan, Cash, and the Nashville Cats*   36

An Interview with Johnny Cash | JACK KILLION AND PETER MCCABE

1973 | *Country Music*   41

Interview | LARRY LINDERMAN

August 1975 | *Penthouse*   56

Interview | ÁINE O'CONNOR

1975 | RTÉ Ireland   72

Cash Comes Back | PATRICK CARR

1976 | *Country Music*   77

Pacific Coliseum Interview | RED ROBINSON

August 28, 1976 | Interview Transcript   93

Johnny Cash's Freedom | PATRICK CARR

April 1979 | *Country Music* 97

Monroe County Fair Interview | DON GONYEA

August 8, 1981 | Interview Transcript 109

Norrköping, Sweden, Press Conference

November 3, 1983 | Original Transcript 116

Interview | GLENN JORGENSON

1983 | *It's Great to Be Alive* 124

Superstar Cash Still Speaks for the Hearts of Americans | ROBERT K. OERMANN

April 26, 1987 | *Nashville Tennessean* 134

"Biggest Party Ever" Opens New Cash Exhibit | ROBERT K. OERMANN

March 23, 1988 | *Nashville Tennessean* 141

Queen Elizabeth Theatre Interview | RED ROBINSON

July 9, 1988 | Interview Transcript 145

Rock & Roll Hall of Fame Induction | LYLE LOVETT

January 15, 1992 | Original Transcript......................... 148

Johnny Cash and June Carter Cash Interview | ROBERT K. OERMANN

March 1995 | Interview Transcript............................. 153

1-800-TRY-CASH | ROSANNE CASH

December 1996 | *Interview*.................................... 167

Interview | TERRY GROSS

November 4, 1997 | *Fresh Air* 173

Interview | ANTHONY DECURTIS

October 2000 and February 2002 | Interview Transcript........... 188

The Man in Black and White . . . and Every Shade In-Between |
BILL FRISKICS-WARREN

November–December 2002 | *No Depression*...................... 212

Interview with Johnny and Rosanne Cash | HOLLY GEORGE-WARREN

August 2003 | Interview Transcript 231

Sylvie Simmons Interviews Johnny Cash | SYLVIE SIMMONS

November 2003 | *MOJO*....................................... 247

About the Contributors 257

Credits 263

Index......................... 267

ACKNOWLEDGMENTS

Completing this book required the generosity and help of many people, some of whom I have yet to meet face-to-face. All interactions took place during a waxing, waning (and waxing again) pandemic. This predicament exacerbated the usual isolation of book creation, so each connection, favor, and/or kindness resonates all the more.

First and foremost, I thank my editor, Kara Rota, for the opportunity to add to Chicago Review Press's "Musicians in Their Own Words" series and for shepherding me through the process (along with copyeditor Sharon Sofinski, proofreader Allison Felus, and managing editor Devon Freeny). My faithful agent, Susan Golomb, always has my back, and I am grateful. The enthusiasm and support of Ashley Kahn, whose *George Harrison on George Harrison* inspired my proposal, was invaluable. The indispensable Brenda Colladay, vice president of Museum Services at the Country Music Hall of Fame, gave me access to a wealth of information and history. CMHOF Senior Archivist Kathleen Campbell expertly guided me through the stacks. My pal Dan Smith, a.k.a. the Woodstock MacDaddy, once again saved the day both technically and spiritually.

I cannot say enough about the power of my wife Holly George-Warren's belief in my ability to bring this book to fruition. In a very difficult year, her conviction was unwavering, her energy always available when mine flagged. Her 2003 interview with Johnny Cash—one of the last he granted, and never before published in full—is a highlight of this book. Our son, Jack, and his partner, Beatrix Herriott O'Gorman, were present during much of this book's progress, and their lively spirits helped keep everything moving. The encouragement of my mother, Mary Lucchese, and my brother, Britt Warren, is always a boon.

My friend Rosanne Cash deserves special mention not only for the two marvelous pieces she contributed, and the conversation over lunch about her father's legacy, but also for her blessing and for steadfast friendship and encouragement. Her agent, Merilee Heifetz, was very helpful, too.

The ever-hospitable Robert K. Oermann is the only writer whose name is on three chapters of this book, and they're all gold. In addition to allowing the inclusion of the work and talking freely and frankly about it, he steered me to valuable resources. He and his wife, Mary Bufwack, always make me feel at home in Nashville.

Others who contributed chapters and provided insightful context through interviews with me: Patrick Carr, Anthony DeCurtis, Sylvie Simmons, Don Gonyea, Red Robinson, and Bill Friskics-Warren. Russell Barnard was very generous with his time and with permitting the republication of three articles from his groundbreaking *Country Music* magazine. Also very helpful: Grant Alden, Kellie Robinson, *Fresh Air*'s Terry Gross, Susan Quatresols, and Amy Salit, Madeline Ticknor and Rebecca Eskildsen at Writers House, Caroline Kirkendoll of Penthouse Global Management, Kevin Rice and Joe Lauro of Historic Films, Razib Chatterjee and Breeda Brennan of RTÉ, Lindsey Meyers at Avera, Richard Weize of Bear Family Records, Tom Ritter, Phyllis Jorgenson, Terry Woster, Mari-Lynn Evans, Jeff Burger, Katy Kattelman, Curtis Hawkins, Karen Schoemer, Barbara Kopple, and Christopher S. Wren.

I appreciate Cash family historian Mark Stielper's good humor and aid. I am much obliged to Übermensch Steve Berkowitz for the loan of his trove of *The Johnny Cash Show* materials, and for the sharing of excellent intel.

Thank you to my local, the Phoenicia Library, for helping me with reference materials. Sorry for the overdue books.

Friends whose excitement over this project amplified my own: Shawn Amos; Robert George; Owen George; John, Laura, and Delilah Draper; Ernest Shaw; Mike Merenda; Greg Schweitzer and Michelle Kennedy; Amy Rosen; Mark Lerner and Nancy Howell; Josh Roy and Michele

Brown; Dennis Yerry; Ann Osmond; Martha Frankel; Richard Doll and Nancy Heidel; Nina Shengold; Jessica Miller Anna; Becca Frank; Abbe Aronson; Barbara, Phil, and Calder Mansfield; Jana Martin; Beverly Donofrio; Lisa Phillips; Katie Legnini; Andy Schwartz; Tony Fletcher; Dennis and Desiree O'Clair; Sarah Lazin; Jonathan Wasserman and Robyn-Alain Feldman; Posie Strenz; Jim Friedlich and Melissa Stern; Ellen Osgood; Sara Loughlin; Alicia Armbrester; Bennet Ratcliff and Jackie Kellechan; Edward Brinson; Kim Alexander and Mike Hood; Vic Varney; Peter McCabe and Hillary Richard. Thank you, all.

Finally, I feel deep gratitude for the man born J. R. Cash. Although I saw him in concert three times and have performed many of his songs for years, in all manner of situations, I did not get a chance to meet him. Like most people, I became a fan through his work. It occupies a special space within me. Because of this distinctive intimacy, I've *felt* like I knew him, which of course is how it goes with artists, for good and for ill. But my version of Johnny Cash is just that: a version, particular to me. Through this book, as I delved deeper into available details of his remarkable life, listened to his sprawling oeuvre, watched him onscreen, and read words spoken mostly by him, my sense of Cash broadened significantly. The sad songs feel sadder, but the raucous, joyous ones evoke even greater exuberance; the pleasure in all of it has intensified. While I can never claim to have known the man, this work has made me feel closer not only to him, but also to the millions touched by his artistry. I hope it does the same for you.

PREFACE

Nearly two decades since his 2003 passing at age seventy-one, Johnny Cash's artistry flourishes. His songs—"I Walk the Line," "Folsom Prison Blues," "Ring of Fire," "Hurt," for starters—unspool worldwide on every conceivable platform, touching an unprecedentedly broad spectrum of people: country fans, punk rockers, metalheads, rock 'n' rollers, hip-hop lovers, pop devotees, elders, and upstarts of multiple ethnicities and nationalities, political persuasions, and genders.

At this writing, almost eleven *million* Spotify users follow Johnny Cash; three hundred thousand follow him on Instagram.

Much more than his contemporaries—Elvis Presley, Carl Perkins, Jerry Lee Lewis, Roy Orbison—Johnny Cash's art feels as tailor-made for our own fraught times as for the eras in which it was created. Even in a divisive age of information overload and addling noise, Cash still *connects*. His songs cut through the din like the primitive kaiser blade with which he once cleared land on his family's Arkansas farm. Digitizing, repackaging, remixing—none of these processes diminish Johnny Cash's music, nor alter its power to move and inspire people.

Bob Dylan said of his friend and collaborator: "Johnny Cash was different than anything else you had ever heard. [He] sounded like a voice from the middle of the earth." This assessment still holds true. That otherworldly, bracingly empathetic voice—from subbasement bass, to field holler shout, to threadbare croon—harkens to the past while remaining acutely attuned to our present collective experience. As twenty-first-century troubles mount, and falsehoods gain ground, the authenticity in Cash's vocals actually resonates more than ever.

Still, although confident in many of his compositions, and secure in his prowess as a performer, Johnny Cash could be dismissive of that unusual voice. Perhaps for laughs, perhaps an expression of humility, probably both. In a 1995 *Fresh Air* interview transcribed for this book, Cash told host Terry Gross, "If I'm anything, I'm not a singer, but I'm a song stylist . . . that means I can't sing." (A stunned Gross vociferously disagreed, as would most people.) He ironically titled his twenty-eighth album *Old Golden Throat* (1968), and June Carter Cash would jokingly refer to him thus onstage for decades. Regardless, that unquantifiable trait—a legitimately golden throat, preternaturally affecting—is, in fact, just one not-so-secret ingredient in Johnny Cash's continuing relevance. And although it's less acknowledged of late, the humor with which he deflected intense attention to his artistry was an equally integral aspect of Johnny Cash's character and deserves closer attention, which this book will give.

Upon absorbing his complete works—an astonishing run of ninety-seven albums between 1954 and 2003, ninety million records sold—and the attendant press coverage and interviews (very few in the early days, myriad toward the end), one thing becomes clear: as with most icons, Johnny Cash's image, particularly his latter-day image, is built on incomplete data. Yes, his work is appreciated globally, but the reductive nature of idol making, and the journalistic mantra of "if it bleeds, it leads," have denied fans a nuanced view of the artist.

For instance, his persona "the Man in Black"—codified in his 1971 protest song of the same name—focuses on his willed familiarity with darkness, his outspoken opposition to social injustice, and his cardinal ability to help the marginalized feel seen. Titling his first bestselling autobiography *Man in Black* (1975) ensured the moniker would become interchangeable with his given name. Indeed, "the Man in Black" has stuck, even ascending to a kind of archetype. In truth, however, Cash's life and music encompass light and love as much as shadow.

But light and love don't get much traction, especially lately. Cash fans new to his oeuvre are often surprised to learn how tenderhearted he could be, and how funny. I direct them to "A Boy Named Sue," "One Piece at a Time," "Daddy Sang Bass," "I've Been Everywhere," "Dirty Old Egg-Sucking Dog," and "The One on the Right Is on the Left"; the rollicking, raw *Everybody Loves a Nut* (1966), an entire album of humorous novelty songs (sadly, never re-released); *The Johnny Cash Show*; and his many TV specials, all of which featured lots of comedy.

Drawing focus to the light is harder than one might think. I understand the temptation to explore the various levels of the blues Cash so beautifully articulated, and to reexamine the depths from which he repeatedly, miraculously emerged. Those are some jaw-dropping yarns, and Cash himself was as likely as journalists to propagate them. This book goes there, too, but my intent is also to move beyond the heaviness, the drama of his misadventures and bad decisions. I aim to brighten the corners. The interviews and features I've curated will ultimately offer a more complete version of a man who clearly sought to make people laugh as much as think, but whose most popular persona tends overwhelmingly to the saturnine.

Toward the end of his life, Cash took responsibility for folks' misunderstandings about him. In a 2002 interview with Bill Friskics-Warren, included here, Cash looked to the recent past and said, "I pigeonholed *myself* a lot . . . looking back at myself, and at what I projected out there, there seems to be a hardness and a bitterness and a coldness . . . and I'm not sure I'm too happy with that. I'm not sure that's the image I want to project, because I'm a pretty happy man."

One could also lay partial responsibility for the reductionism at the massive feet of music producer Rick Rubin and filmmaker James Mangold.

In Cash's wildly fruitful, successful fourth act with Rubin, that is, the "American Recordings Years" (1994 to the early aughts), the duo's dramatic duel with death, wrapped in captivating, raw music, seduced both younger fans and the rock literati. The former had been raised on edgy genres like metal, punk, and hip-hop/gangsta rap—all built on shadow; the latter longed for something genuinely compelling to which they could hitch their wagons. Cash-Rubin fit the bill across the board.

This was Rubin's gambit: if you build a sonic situation in which you present Cash *exactly as he is right now*—i.e., aged and ill but astoundingly driven, a walking folk music encyclopedia bravely staring into the abyss as it stares back—people will come. And they did. In the American Recordings work, Cash's ministerial gravitas, his unabashed physical frailty, his ease singing about violence, captivated boomers, Gen-Xers, and millennials alike. In short, Cash-Rubin did a fantastic job. Their penetrating art, created in the literal shadow of death, obscured much of what had come before in Cash's timeline, especially anything lighthearted. In addition to the music, arresting images from the duo's efforts linger—the Outlaw Elder, the Angry Man Giving the Finger, the Wheelchair-Bound Tortured Artist, the traumatized-but-defiant star of the "Hurt" video (currently at 134 million YouTube views and counting—far and away the most seen Johnny Cash video).

Similarly, James Mangold's 2005 hit biopic *Walk the Line* presented a riveting but somewhat joyless version of the Johnny Cash story. An unyielding emphasis on Cash's significant troubles left little room for laughter or levity. Rosanne Cash told the *Observer* that watching it was "like having a root canal without anesthetic." But it did deliver (and, via streaming, continues to deliver) Cash's music to millions more people. Despite star Joaquin Phoenix's plea to moviegoers to forego the accompanying soundtrack (on which he sang and played) and buy Cash's original recordings, that soundtrack nevertheless sold over a million copies. For her portrayal of June Carter, Reese Witherspoon took home the Oscar, the Golden Globe, and the SAG Award for Best Actress, her plucky performance inextricable from the real, complex June in many moviegoers' minds. Such is the power of a flawed but expertly crafted cinematic retelling of Cash's problematic early years. That power continues to color, and ultimately diminish, folks' ideas of who Johnny Cash was.

But stick around for a song or two, take a moderately deep dive, read his interviews—especially those from pre-Internet days—and a different, more rounded version of Johnny Cash emerges: voluble raconteur; fiercely intelligent patriot; insightful historian; ruminative thinker; patient husband; jokester; doting dad; good friend; man of faith in his God, faith in his art, and faith in his fellow humans to do the right thing. Invest a little time, and, although he may be gone from this plane, the former Arkansas farm boy will do the thing he loved most to do: he will make you *smile*.

––––––––––––

Another reason Johnny Cash hasn't ebbed into irrelevance is because he's not just a songwriter and singer. As the interviews and encounters in this book attest, Johnny Cash's artistry encompasses well-wrought, eminently repeatable *stories*. These oft-repeated tales—fictional, true, and innumerable degrees in between—also account for the continued expansion of the Cash audience.

From the days of 45 rpm singles and AM radio to the era of smartphones, social media, and particularly movies and streaming platforms, Johnny Cash stories create a lot of heat. Communicated, or miscommunicated, borne upon word-of-mouth or big-budget enterprise, the accounts inevitably morph, but they never stop.

"According to this Johnny Cash book/article . . ."

"I read this post about Johnny Cash . . ."

"I read this post about Johnny Cash's wife . . ."

"That Johnny Cash meme, though . . ."

"In that Johnny Cash movie . . ."

This millennia-old system of oral tradition is imperfect (to say the least) and is the very heart of the folk tradition from which Johnny Cash sprang. Technology has only amplified it, for better and for worse.

Since *Walk the Line*, filmmakers and playwrights continue to mine Cash's music and his life. The jukebox musical *Million Dollar Quartet*, in which the character of Johnny Cash is prominently featured, debuted on Broadway in 2010, London's West End in 2011, and tours regularly.

More recently, the 2018 Netflix documentary *Tricky Dick and the Man in Black*, co-directed by two-time Academy Award–winner Barbara Kopple, investigates Cash's controversial 1970 concert at the Nixon White House—a story covered in depth in a 1975 *Penthouse* interview reprinted here—and presents Cash at his flintiest and most progressive.

At this writing, 3.3 million people have streamed *The Gift: The Journey of Johnny Cash*, a 2019 YouTube original documentary focused on Cash's complex spiritual side. It includes the oft-told tale of his unsuccessful suicide attempt in Nickajack Cave in 1967 but barely touches on his loving friendship with politically conservative evangelist Billy Graham. Cash speaks of that friendship—a significant part of his spiritual life—in a 1973 *Country Music* magazine interview reprinted in these pages.

Needless to say, Johnny Cash couldn't weigh in on any posthumous projects, although he encouraged *Walk the Line*, which was in preproduction in his final days. To hear his unadulterated voice—the arc of his journey as told by the man himself—you go to the Cash interviews, the Q and A's and profiles. Particularly fascinating are the lengthy conversations and essays from the days when readers had much longer attention spans and editors trusted an audience could focus on thousands of words. Nuance was not so endangered then.

Cash on Cash focuses on stories from the source—both out-of-print and/or unavailable online, interviews and transcripts, often unedited, some never-before-seen. Many of these narratives were co-created and perpetuated by J. R. Cash himself, and/or his friends, collaborators, and loved ones, aided and spurred on by interlocutors.

To say "created" doesn't imply stories are untrue, although at least a few likely are. Some are certainly embellished. In some, details change over time. For instance, in a 1965 interview with Pete Seeger on the folk singer's *Rainbow Quest* TV show, Cash tells Seeger he is part Cherokee. In a 1969 profile for *Look* magazine, writer Christopher S. Wren repeats the claim of Native American lineage. Finally, when queried about his ancestry by *Penthouse* writer Larry Linderman in 1975, Cash states he has no Cherokee blood.*

Starting in the 1970s, and especially after he officially christened himself "the Man in Black," when the "why black?" question arose, he answered differently depending on the situation: To Áine O'Connor,

---

* In a 2021 episode of *Finding Your Roots*, host Henry Louis Gates revealed to Rosanne Cash that both Johnny Cash and his first wife, Rosanne's mother Vivian Liberto, had African American DNA but no Native American DNA.

in a 1975 interview for RTÉ Ireland, he said it was the only matching color of clothing he and his band had for their first gig in 1954, which was at a church. To future NPR national political correspondent Don Gonyea at the Wisconsin County Fair in 1981, Cash answered with a smile, saying, "it's a little more slimming." By 1995, in conversation with noted journalist and author Robert K. Oermann, he said, "it was really for Vietnam, for the boys and girls that were our troops in Vietnam at the time. And for the ones that we were losin'."

Whenever possible, my introductions to each piece include input from the writers themselves, memories of their time spent in the company of Johnny Cash (and a few times, June Carter Cash and Rosanne Cash). How did interviewer and interviewee, not to mention environment and situation, shape the story? What was happening in Cash's life and career at that time? My aim is to offer context and further insight into the interviews, transcripts, and features, and to showcase writers whose communication skills helped bring Cash's words and, to a certain extent, Cash himself, to life on the page.

Although it took a few years before he got the opportunity to give in-depth interviews about his work and life, Johnny Cash, recording artist, was made for the process. He hailed from storytelling stock—primarily his father, Ray Cash. The musical talent would come from his mother, Carrie Cash, who sang, played guitar, and, against her husband's wishes, purchased a battery-powered radio that would enchant their kids.

Even before the journalists came calling, Johnny Cash gamely leaned into listeners' ache for story. In the early days, the stories were in the songs, many—but not all—crafted from his life: "Hey, Porter" (his debut), "I Walk the Line," and "Five Feet High and Rising," to name a handful. "I like a song with a story and a meaning," he told the *Los Angeles Times*. "Much of the so-called country-western music that I sing is actually folk music."

Delivered with conviction, Cash's irresistible folktales-set-to-music were stunningly effective at getting through. Due credit goes to Sun Records' Sam Phillips for providing the means. In the same way he'd heard promise in a greasy-haired truck driver named Elvis, he'd intuited "something" in Cash's voice, even before hearing any of the failed appliance salesman's original material. Cash, recently arrived in Memphis from Arkansas, had come to record gospel music.

"I can't sell gospel," Phillips told him. He put Cash off not once, but twice. Cash had to essentially stalk the man on his doorstep to get Phillips to listen to him sing in late 1954. When Phillips did, both light bulbs and cash registers went off in his head. He eventually told the tall, handsome Arkansan to come back with his car mechanic friends Marshall Grant (bass) and Luther Perkins (guitar) and play some original material that was not gospel. Cash and "the Tennessee Two" (although, like Cash, neither was from Tennessee, which Cash thought was funny) soon returned with "Hey, Porter," the first of many train songs to follow.

"Hey, Porter" recounts a man returning home by rail to the American South. It's the wee small hours. Sleepless with excitement, he can't stop bothering the train workers. He pesters the porter and requests the engineer use the locomotive's whistle to help him express himself.

Hey, Porter! Hey Porter! / It's getting light outside / This old train is puffin' smoke and I have to strain my eyes / But ask that engineer if he will blow his whistle please / 'Cause I smell frost on cotton leaves and I feel that Southern breeze.

Twenty-two-year-old Cash had written "Hey, Porter" as a narrative poem, thick with imagery and sensory details, lover's mania, and locomotive-rhythm syntax. Homeward bound by train from a stint as an Air Force radio operator in Landsberg, West Germany, he'd scribbled it down, as he'd been scribbling poetic musings since childhood. He'd been in Germany three years, dreaming of starting his life as a singer and pining for Arkansas (changed to the more euphonious and rhyme-able *Tennessee* in the poem/song) and his beautiful fiancée Vivian Liberto. Once he and the Tennessee Two put the lines to music—a long, laborious process for the rank amateurs—Cash thought the tune was "OK."

Sam Phillips, however, knew he had a tiger by the tail again. He recorded the trio on March 22, 1955. With encouragement from Phillips, and liking the sound he heard on the playback, legend has it Cash went home and wrote the lyrics to the B-side, "Cry! Cry! Cry!" in one night.

The Tennessee Two helped him flesh out the music—a little quicker this time—and presto, Sam Phillips's Sun Records had a new single.

Phillips told Cash—then known as J.R.—he was renaming him Johnny, and shipped the 45. It would sell a hundred thousand copies in the South alone. Within weeks, follow-up "Folsom Prison Blues" backed with "So Doggone Lonesome" would put Johnny Cash on the Billboard charts—number four on what was then called the Top 100 Singles chart, which encompassed everything from Frank Sinatra to Nat King Cole to Pat Boone. (In 1968, the live version of "Folsom Prison Blues," recorded at Folsom Prison, would go to number one on the Hot Country Singles chart and number thirty-two on the Top 100 Singles chart.) The crossover success was a harbinger of the expansive, borderless appeal Johnny Cash would enjoy.

Sam Phillips had been correct about the inherent storytelling power of Cash's singing. Presented in a well-crafted tune, that indefinable element he'd sensed in those vocals—not unlike Hank Williams before, and Bob Dylan after—whetted Cash fans' appetites not only for more songs, but also for more detail about Cash himself. What, pray tell, is the Cash origin story featuring the hardscrabble world from which this "Johnny" sprang? That vanishing, rural landscape, integral to the mythic American experience, evoked boundless curiosity in mid-century listeners. The frontier had been brutally conquered a couple generations before, but listeners hungered to remotely experience its wildness—or rather, a sanitized, inaccurate version of its wildness—via newfangled technology like 45 rpm singles and 33⅓ rpm LPs, on "unbreakable" Vinylite.

When the media finally started asking, Cash frequently said, "I grew up under socialism." He was referring to the New Deal establishment of the Dyess Colony in Arkansas, founded in 1934 as part of Franklin Delano Roosevelt's New Deal. The government loaned the out-of-work, Depression-ravaged Ray and Carrie Cash and their five children a home, livestock, twenty acres, and a mule to get back on their feet, and out of the sharecropper's cycle of debt. (Electricity wouldn't arrive until 1942, and two more Cash children would be born in Dyess.) Thanks to the entire family, including tiny J.R., engaging in backbreaking work in their allotted fields—mostly cotton—the debt was eventually paid and the Cashes were homeowners. (When he was born, Cash's mother wanted to name him John; his father wanted to name him Ray. They compromised with "J.R.") The Dyess Colony is a vital part of Johnny Cash's genesis story, retold several times in this book.

That story includes Cash's elder brother, Jack. When Jack died after being mortally wounded by a table saw at the Dyess sawmill, the Cash family was able to fall back on their home, neighbors, and the local church for support. Fourteen-year-old Jack had been J.R.'s hero, his mentor, the golden child of the Cash progeny, bound for the ministry. Cash, twelve years old at the time, would never fully recover from his brother's grisly death, or from Jack's deathbed visions of angels singing. In time, yearning, grief, and a powerful desire for connection to his brother's spirit in heaven would inform J.R. Cash's music and his life.

Johnny Cash made no secret that government intervention had saved his family. Combined with his service as an Air Force radio operator, in which he'd spent countless hours monitoring Soviet Morse Code transmissions, the experience molded in him an ardent patriotism, inextricable with humanitarianism. (The Air Force did not permit using initials as a name, so he enlisted as "John R. Cash.") Cash's love of country was entwined with his remarkable ability to empathize with the underserved, the needy. As a successful entertainer of means, he would commit himself to those requiring a stronger force to loan—or give—bootstraps with which they could pull themselves up.

From the moment he signed his contract with Sam Phillips, Johnny Cash would endeavor to be that force. He started immediately. Upon leaving his contract signing, he gave all the money in his pockets to a hobo camped outside Sun Studio.

Cash possessed strong faith that recipients of such generosity would prevail, as his family had. But the conviction they would prevail wasn't his motive. His motive was a mixture of Christian compassion, activist righteousness, and bone-deep understanding of how to act constructively in the face of other people's need.

As fame beckoned and consumed him, Johnny Cash created a lot more stories alongside his songs. He publicly lived out a lot of exuberance, agony, and everything in between—a brazenly out-of-control addict, under the sway of his drug-enhanced Id. Not much attempt was made to conceal the ravages of his lifestyle. He often teetered quite close to death, even onstage or on camera, only to bounce back, as if charmed, anointed. All of it added to the inexhaustible canon of entertainers-as-libertines, through which fans stymied by convention live vicariously. Some of these accounts are included here, told by Cash himself, or his companions, witnesses down the decades.

Eventually, journalists recognized value in Johnny Cash's stories as well as his music. As the counterculture mushroomed, editors began granting popular artists like Cash space to share their narratives. Born raconteur Cash gamely engaged the media. From the first time he spoke before an interviewer's microphone or notepad, Johnny Cash harnessed his experiences and his gift of gab to create stories as addendums to, and extensions of, his artistic output. "Promo work" was not merely a chore; it was also in service of the songs, tours, albums, movies, and books. What we would now call "the Johnny Cash brand."

From the 1950s until just before his passing, Cash collaborated with journalists and fans on this life-as-story. The conversations also offered Cash a means of self-discovery in real time, akin to sessions with a therapist (which he also did). In some ways, Cash seemed to be mustering courage over time, and in plain sight. Although he'd often said his driven, industrious father inspired him, in later years he began to open up about the abuse he'd suffered under Ray Cash, offering more detail—often excruciating: Ray Cash had shot and killed J.R.'s beloved dog (and initially lied about it), never told him he loved him, did not support his musical ambitions, and, worst of all, blamed him for Jack Cash's death. Only in the 1990s, after Ray Cash's death, did these harsh facts begin to trickle out in public conversation.

One of Johnny Cash's only surviving audio interviews from his early days is a 1959 backstage chat with DJ Red Robinson at the Division Street Corral in Portland, Oregon. It is transcribed here. Cash is tired, but funny and friendly. His last major interview, a 2003 home studio visit with Sylvie Simmons, for *MOJO*, is also here. In it, he grieves June Carter Cash, who'd recently passed unexpectedly, but he is open—formidable, yet vulnerable.

The contrast between twenty-seven-year-old, soft-spoken, speed-taking road dog, and seventy-one-year-old, frail-but-sharp-minded artist is striking. The potent storytelling force of each version of J. R. Cash, however, is not so different.

———————

As often happens with an artist, Cash's fictional material, presented with bedrock conviction and a showman's flair, often convinced listeners he'd indeed "shot a man in Reno, just to watch him die," as the "Folsom Prison Blues" narrator moans, or indeed he'd been shackled in prisoner's chains, as in "I Got Stripes." But no, he made those up. He never pretended otherwise, but the songs had other ideas.

Cash repeatedly told interviewers that, while occasionally spending the night in the drunk tank, he'd "never been convicted of a felony." Regardless, some fans were—and remain—wedded to their belief he *was* the man in his "prison songs." The incarcerated audiences on career-defining live "prison albums"—*At Folsom Prison* (1968) and *At San Quentin* (1969)—certainly considered him one of their own.

Inviting fans—especially incarcerated men—to join in the creative process further blurred the lines between artist and listeners' lived experience. The live prison albums, released a little over a year apart, collectively comprise a watershed period, a gateway to Cash's prosperous second act. Each would yield a hit single that shaped him in the public eye: the incendiary live version of "Folsom Prison Blues" on *At Folsom Prison*, and the whimsical, Shel Silverstein–penned "A Boy Named Sue" on *At San Quentin*. Integral to each seminal recording is the audience. The spectators contribute to the narrative propelling these story songs, both of which are fictional, as if that matters. The rapturous, raucous inmates punctuate the plot points with whoops and yells, spurring the band, and Cash. Slicker recordings of the songs exist, but these are the definitive versions.

The unprecedented attention the prison albums visited on the Cash camp brought a revised narrative. Word soon leaked that Columbia Records—particularly president Clive Davis—opposed funding and releasing *At Folsom*, but Cash and noted firebrand producer Bob Johnston (who'd made a name helming classic Bob Dylan, Leonard Cohen, and

Simon & Garfunkel LPs) had plowed on regardless. Soon, an even more rebellious Cash persona began to coalesce. Needless to say, this authentic "stick it to the man" attitude endeared Cash to the rising anti-authoritarian counterculture. This faction would go mainstream in the 1970s, arguably Cash's least troubled decade, but also the one in which he became ever more preacher-like, and somewhat less an actively productive songwriter.

Throughout, Johnny Cash toured relentlessly, connecting with fans all over the world and earning his reputation as a consummate showman. These connections would at first sustain him, then wear him down, until, ironically, bad health released him from them.

Looking back over the decades, as so many stories swirl about—both within song and from Cash's offstage life—one begins to discern not only the evolution of a mutable "Johnny Cash" persona, but also the way interviewers processed the material and presented Cash to readers.

In the beginning, Johnny Cash did most of the mythmaking himself, through song. Prior to the late 1960s, substantive interviews of artists—the "tell-all," the "behind-the-scenes" scoop—were mostly focused on Hollywood. High-circulation newspapers and magazines presented splashy, superficial profiles of screen stars, and occasionally politicians and sports figures. While popular musicians received ink, no editors believed a significant readership desired *in-depth* material about rough-hewn rounders like Cash, Elvis Presley, Jerry Lee Lewis, Carl Perkins, Chuck Berry, Little Richard, and others, unhinged troubadours barnstorming the countryside with an increasingly popular but as-yet-unnamed brand of music (alternately rockabilly, hillbilly bop, folk pop, rhythm and blues, country and western). Surely this crazy fad wouldn't last long, so why bother?

It wasn't just the press missing the boat. Almost no one thought to document shows with film or audio recordings, or to ask musicians afterward how they felt about anything, and make notes for listeners, or readers, or for posterity. The few pieces herein from that mid-1950s-to-mid-'60s period find Cash still somewhat shy, fitfully adjusting to the wings his art had given him, not yet quite comfortable in his skin, even as his output was constant and frequently high quality.

By the end of the 1960s, however, culture-defining, commercially successful, revolutionary magazines like *Rolling Stone* and *Crawdaddy* were taking popular musicians much more seriously. They covered them with probing, revelatory conversations. Manager Albert Grossman had only recently insisted his number-one act, Bob Dylan, be contracted as an *artist*, and the magazines—and everyone—followed his lead, using the term going forward.

Concurrently, Cash was flying on the success of the 1968 *At Folsom Prison* album—number one on the Country chart, number thirteen on the Pop Albums chart, action he'd not seen in years. A bona fide comeback— a fresh start to coincide with a new wife, June Carter—and a semblance of sobriety. This cachet helped grant him a midseason replacement network TV program, *The Johnny Cash Show*.

Few expressed high expectations for *The Johnny Cash Show*. The one-of-a-kind ABC program—about which Cash shares details in several interviews in this book—landed Cash in millions of American homes once a week. Although it would eventually grate on him, initially, *The Johnny Cash Show* was a success. It debuted in spring of 1969—with Bob Dylan in the first episode—when Rosanne Cash was fourteen. It changed her life, and the course of American music. Her essay about that event is included in *Cash on Cash*.

The Johnny Cash Show would run for fifty-eight episodes and feature an unmatched diversity of guests including Dylan, Joni Mitchell, Jim Nabors, Bob Hope, James Taylor, Mahalia Jackson, Louis Armstrong, Linda Ronstadt, Gordon Lightfoot, Derek & the Dominoes, Merle Haggard, Kris Kristofferson, the Monkees, Neil Young, and Tammy Wynette. After three seasons, Cash and ABC would part ways in 1971, but he would return multiple times to host network shows, particularly Christmas specials, into the 1980s.

To the mainstream press, Johnny Cash was, at last, impossible to ignore. In advance of *The Johnny Cash Show*, he received extensive ink and photos in the April 29, 1969, issue of *Look*: "The Restless Ballad of Johnny Cash" by Christopher Wren, reprinted in this book. Other major publications followed suit.

Magazines featuring Johnny Cash invariably sold well, so he was asked back repeatedly. Even as he lost interest in the recording process in the 1970s and '80s and was relegated to has-been status by the Nashville establishment, he kept working, appearing on television and in movies, and the press kept tracking him down for a confab. As a live performer, he remained largely untouchable, powering through mounting health issues, financial problems, and loss. His stalwart showmanship alone was enough to justify more media coverage.

The global fan base remained interested and supportive well into the 1980s. They would pay to see him at arenas, state fairs, festivals, theaters, civic centers—all manner of venues. Through song and story, Johnny Cash had touched them at their core. Whether through his unflinching grasp of their blues, their love, their God, or their desire to act out their deepest desires, he'd immeasurably enriched their emotional and spiritual lives.

When he returned from recording exile in the early 1990s to surprise everyone (again) and make some of the best work of his career, Cash looked beyond the footlights and was delighted to see the most diverse crowd he'd ever laid eyes on: the graying fans who'd bought everything from his Sun singles to his LPs featuring Billy Graham, and young people who'd been raised on MTV and knew him through television, modern lore, and his work with Rick Rubin, with children in tow who would not recall a time without the Internet. Like Cash's original devotees, those new fans would hunger for more Johnny Cash; they would yearn to know this éminence grise beyond the music and the show. The mighty Internet can only dredge up so much for them. And while it may seem *everything* is online, it's not.

Within these pages, the voice of Johnny Cash, traversing a fascinating arc from his twenties to his seventies, offers satisfying stories, some laughs, and always interesting conversation. Reading his words, you sit ringside, ride shotgun, or commiserate over coffee. With your esteemed companion, you look to both the past and the future, but mostly you appreciate the moment with a friend who has much to give, much to sing about, and much to say.

—RBW 2022

JOHNNY CASH AND THE TENNESSEE TWO

November 15, 1958 | *Town Hall Party*

Begun as a radio program in 1951, *Town Hall Party* was broadcast live from Compton, California's Town Hall on Saturday nights over KXLA, Pasadena, California, and KFI, Los Angeles. In 1953, NBC affiliate KTTV picked it up, and the Armed Forces Television Service made 16 mm kinescopes to air throughout the world. Some of these kinescopes are viewable today on DVD and YouTube.

For the broadcasts and telecasts, organizers decorated the three-thousand-capacity Town Hall ballroom to look like a barn. *Town Hall Party* ran from 10:00 PM to 1:00 AM. Promoter William B. Wagnon Jr. booked popular country and western (C&W) artists of the day, including Lefty Frizzell, Patsy Cline, George Jones, Marty Robbins, Tex Ritter, and Gene Autry. As rockabilly arose, wilder performers like Jerry Lee Lewis, Wanda Jackson, Carl Perkins, Gene Vincent, and Johnny Cash and the Tennessee Two performed in front of thousands of sweaty spectators.

Johnny Cash and the Tennessee Two's November 15, 1958, appearance is notable for several reasons. After three years at independent Sun Records, Cash has recently signed with major label Columbia, which has promised promotional muscle and, equally important to Cash, artistic freedom. Columbia has awarded its new signing a higher royalty rate and a $10,000 bonus (almost $100,000 in 2022 dollars).

Cash, bassist Marshall Grant and guitarist Luther Perkins (the Tennessee Two), and all their families have recently moved to Los Angeles. The intent is partially to be closer to the film industry as Cash hopes to follow his peer Elvis Presley into movies. Cash would be California-based until 1965. After she divorces him in 1966, Vivian Liberto will remain

1

there to raise their four daughters, Rosanne, Tara, Cathy, and Cindy. Grant and his family, none of whom care for the Southern California lifestyle, will head back east before the end of 1959. Luther Perkins's wife, Bertie, will also return to Memphis, leaving Luther behind. Perkins will eventually follow her.

For Sun Records owner and producer Sam Phillips, the 1958 departure of Johnny Cash echoed his situation with Elvis Presley three years before. After unleashing Elvis in 1954, Phillips sold Presley's contract to RCA for $35,000 the following year (the equivalent of $300,000 in 2022). Presley left behind no product in the Sun vault.

Presley's move was a learning experience for everyone. Knowing Cash would be signing with Columbia, Phillips had instructed producer and songwriter "Cowboy" Jack Clement to record as much Cash as possible, a trove of songs to release over time. Clement and Cash obliged. Until 1961, Cash's Columbia material would occupy chart space alongside Sun releases.

One of the reasons Cash gave for his departure from Sun was Phillips's reluctance to release his beloved gospel music. By contrast, Columbia will soon release the LP *Hymns by Johnny Cash* (1959) and, eventually, *Hymns from the Heart* (1962) and many others. These albums won't sell anywhere near as much as Cash's secular material. Undaunted, he will keep recording and releasing gospel into the twenty-first century.

At the time of this *Town Hall Party* show, Cash's first Columbia album, *The Fabulous Johnny Cash*, is just out and features soon-to-be-classics "Don't Take Your Guns to Town" and "I Still Miss Someone" (cowritten by Cash's nephew, Roy), which Cash and the band perform alongside Sun singles. They also offer up two gospel numbers: "I Was There When It Happened" by Fern Jones and Cash's own "It Was Jesus." The trio delivers the gospel material with as much conviction as the sprightly rockabilly and C&W fare. The audience loves it all.

In set two, Cash gives a shout-out to rockabilly legends Lorrie and Larry Collins, a.k.a. the Collins Kids, also on the bill that night. Seventeen-year-old Lorrie and fourteen-year-old Larry often toured with Johnny Cash and the Tennessee Two.

"I Walk the Line," saved for the second set opener, brings the house down. This distinctive number—with multiple key changes and no chorus—is a two-minute-forty-five-second ode to marital fidelity, written for the right-to-be-worried Vivian Liberto. Since its rise to the number-one spot on the U.S. Country Juke Box chart in 1956 (and subsequent crossover to number seventeen on the Pop chart), the song's power has transformed Cash from shy, awkward striver to commanding performer. The opening strains, piped into the packed ballroom through a public address system, induce more excitement than anything.

Until his death, Cash will cite "I Walk the Line" as his favorite of all his compositions. —Ed.

Set 1

MC Jay Stewart: Yeah! Party time at the Town Hall, and boy, we got the wall stretchers out tonight! We got a great show planned for you in the big Town Hall. We're all out here, and I mean *all* of us are here. At 400 South Long Beach Boulevard in Compton, California, at Western Music's Hall of Fame. Town Hall Party! We got guests tonight, by golly we got the stage jam packed, and *also* we have Johnny Cash and the Tennessee Two in person as our guests here tonight! So we got a lotta folks here, a lotta folks out there, three full hours of entertainment coming your way, so stick with us, 'cause it's Town Hall Party!

This is it! This is the place—this is where you can meet all your favorite stars on Saturday nights. Don't forget that! The big Town Hall, at 400 South Long Beach Boulevard, Compton, California, it's Western Music's Hall of Fame. And here's a fella we've had the pleasure of having as our guest at the big Town Hall, adding his name to our Hall of Fame roster several times. Now that they're living out here in Los Angeles, we're hoping we can get 'em on, back here to Town Hall as often as possible, but we got 'em tonight, and we got the folks here lookin', and we got you folks out there watchin', so I know we can all get together and give a real nice hand to some great entertainers, believe you me . . . Johnny Cash and the Tennessee Two!

[Johnny Cash and the Tennessee Two play "Get Rhythm."]

Johnny Cash: Thank you, thank you very much. It's so nice to be back on Town Hall, to see such a big crowd tonight . . . I know probably all of you have all met the two fellas here . . . on the guitar, Luther Perkins, on the bass, Marshall Grant. Let's give 'em a big hand. The Tennessee Two—they come from North Carolina and Mississippi. They really do!

Luther just moved out of Mississippi. We all moved out here, oh, a few days ago. We've been moving so much, we haven't been working. This is about the first time we've played any in, oh, two or three weeks. We quit workin' for so long, we're gonna have to work up some kind of act to show the promoters what kind of work we're out of, I guess. That's the only thing we done lately . . . we rehearsed for a benefit that was canceled . . . About all, I guess.

[*To Luther*] Your wife watching tonight, Luther?

Luther Perkins: Yeah, she is.

Cash: I told 'em a while ago, Luther's wife is real pretty. She just about this high . . . layin' down. [*Laughter.*] Real pretty young lady, she really is. [*Laughter.*]

All right, let's do a couple of songs. We'd like to do one side of our latest Sun release, it's called "You're the Nearest Thing to Heaven."

[*Johnny Cash and the Tennessee Two play "You're the Nearest Thing to Heaven" and "I Was There When It Happened."*]

Cash: Thank you very much. We've got a Columbia album out this next week, and we'd like to do a couple of songs for ya, from our Columbia album. It's a got a whole variety of songs in it, some slow ones, some fast ones, some old ones, some new ones—a little bit of everything. This one here is a Western song. It's about the first real Western song I guess we ever did, we certainly hope you like it—we're kinda curious to know just what you might think about a song like this. It's called "Don't Take Your Guns to Town."

[*Johnny Cash and the Tennessee Two play "Don't Take Your Guns to Town."*]

Stewart: Johnny Cash and the Tennessee Two! Johnny, we're real glad to have you back again with us at Town Hall again. We've all been lookin' forward to it, ever since we knew you were comin' here.

Cash: I have too, Jay!

Stewart: As you can see, we've got a great turnout to come out and say howdy to ya and wanted to hear ya sing. So, we're gonna let ya mop up a little and let you do one more.

Cash: Thank you. Listen, I tell ya what . . . as we were talkin' about the album we got out next week . . . that was one of the songs from it. Here's one I know you'll recognize, a real old song called "Frankie and Johnny," except we got some brand-new 1958-style words. [*Laughs, points to crowd*] We want to do it especially for this lady right down here, this young lady. I know she's heard this song, haven't you? Good song.

[*Johnny Cash and the Tennessee Two play "Frankie's Man Johnny" and exit. Pandemonium ensues.*]

Stewart: A brand new version of "Frankie and Johnny!" Johnny Cash! The one and only Johnny Cash and the Tennessee Two!

Set Two

Stewart: It's Town Hall Party and the place is swingin' tonight! I'll tell you, we got a lotta nice folks here who are enjoyin' the evenin', and one special reason is because they get the chance to see in person one of the great entertainers of our time right now, with many, many hit records out, I want you all to welcome once again—Johnny Cash and the Tennessee Two!

[*Johnny Cash and the Tennessee Two play "I Walk the Line," "The Ways of a Woman in Love," and "Give My Love to Rose."*]

Cash: Thank you! We did a song few minutes ago, a spiritual out of our album [*Johnny Cash with His Hot and Blue Guitar*] called "I Was There When It Happened." We had a lotta calls, telephone calls on that song, people were callin' in and commentin' on it, seemed to like it very much, and also we got a call from Miss Fern Jones, who wrote the song. Very wonderful young lady, writes a lot of real fine hymns. We've got one here that I wrote, it's in our Columbia album out next week, we'd like to do it for ya. We certainly hope you like this one just half as much. It's called "It Was Jesus."

[*Johnny Cash and the Tennessee Two play "It Was Jesus" and "All Over Again." During the latter, Cash yells to Perkins "Change chord!" Afterward, he exits, again to pandemonium.*]

Stewart: [*Over sustained cheers and applause*] Thank you, gentlemen! That's Johnny Cash and the Tennessee Two! That's great! I just wanna . . . I tell ya what, I tell ya what I'm gonna do, I'll promise you this: he'll do another one. Thank you very much Luther, Luther Perkins on the guitar, Marshall Grant on the bass fiddle. Johnny of course has on several of his albums recorded some religious songs, and it's our pleasure to have him do one here before we tell him good night. Of course, we got our Town Hall Talent Time coming up in just a minute, but Johnny, come on out, let's bring him out, let's have a nice hand.

[*Cash returns.*]

Cash: Thank you. As always, it was a wonderful pleasure being on Town Hall Party, and it's going to be awful hard to quiet things down after such a wonderful job by the Collins Kids. We'd like to get the whole gang to back us up here, kinda help out, everybody that's got something to pick, pick along. We'd like to do one of our favorite songs. Jimmie Davis has got it recorded, had it out a long time and sold a lot of records. We've got it in our new album next week. Beautiful song called "Suppertime."

[*Johnny Cash, the Tennessee Two, and the Town Hall Party band perform "Suppertime."*]

DIVISION STREET CORRAL INTERVIEW

Red Robinson | June 27, 1959 | Interview Transcript

Red Robinson was the first DJ to play rock 'n' roll on a regular basis in Canada. This job, begun when he was eighteen, kickstarted a sixty-three-year career as a popular radio and television personality, frequent MC, and philanthropist. (He retired in 2017.) He's in several halls of fame (Rockabilly, Canadian Broadcast) and has received numerous awards, including the Order of British Columbia, for contributions to society.

One particularly impressive contribution is Robinson's trove of audio interviews with music stars, dating back to the 1950s.

In an era when few thought rock 'n' rollers and C&W musicians merited being archived, Robinson, barely into his twenties, had the foresight to use quality (and bulky) portable equipment—an Eicor recorder and an RCA microphone—to capture their conversations. Even more impressive, Robinson preserved his tapes. He shares meticulously digitized versions on his Soundcloud page, "Red Robinson's Legends." A short list of the icons available for anyone to hear anytime: Buddy Holly, Jerry Lee Lewis, Elvis Presley, Little Richard, Smokey Robinson, the Everly Brothers, and several versions of Johnny Cash.

Robinson first crossed paths with Cash during a brief stint at Portland, Oregon, AM station KGW in 1959. Cash and the Tennessee Two were touring with singer Lorrie Collins. On Saturday, July 16, they rolled in to Portland's Division Street Corral, a twenty-four-hundred-capacity dance hall on the outskirts of town. The "D Street" was a favorite teen hangout, frequently packed with boys in Levi's and girls in billowing skirts over stiff petticoats.

This period marks the beginning of Cash's personal life unraveling as his career sky-rockets. On this particularly demanding tour, as he mastered the stage, he suffered an unrequited attraction to then-seventeen-year-old Lorrie Collins, and the attendant guilt. He handled the difficulties by ingesting copious amounts of drugs. In *Cash: The Life*, biographer Robert Hilburn cites the summer of 1959 being "a turning point in Cash's drug use." The newly minted star was carrying several prescriptions for amphetamines and barbiturates.

Remarking on a Town Hall Party television show appearance (available to view on YouTube) three weeks after the Division Street Corral engagement, Hilburn notes Cash had "an almost glassy stare onstage and was consumed now by nervous energy. At the same time, he was reaching out aggressively to the audience with his gestures and comments, as well as doing an over-the-top parody of Elvis Presley singing 'Heartbreak Hotel.'"

That performance couldn't have been much different than the Division Street Corral gig, which included not one, not two, but three sets.

In this Red Robinson interview, Tennessee Two bass player Marshall Grant informs Robinson the crowd-pleasing Elvis impersonation is still part of the act. Cash has injured a finger doing it.

About the group's stage show, in his autobiography *I Was There When It Happened*, Grant notes: "While most country music artists at the time would just go out onstage and sing their hit songs, John believed in giving the audience something more. He did things onstage that nobody had ever done—and probably never will.

"We developed a comedy routine and did imitations of several artists, like Red Foley and Kitty Wells, but the highlight was John's impersonation of Elvis Presley. He'd shake and moan, his hair would fall down in his face, and then he'd turn to me and ask to borrow my comb. I'd pull my comb out of my back pocket, hand it to him, and he'd get it all straightened up, then hand the comb back to me.

"I'd start looking at the comb and then start acting like there was a cootie on it, then throw it on the floor. At that point, I'd pull the old muzzle-loading pistol out from under my coat, or wherever I'd kept it hidden throughout the show, and shoot the comb. Man, was that gun loud! And smoke would just billow across the stage. It would really startle people at first—they didn't know what to think. But then John would stand there and look at them without saying a word, and pretty soon the applause would start and everybody would start laughing and hollering. We got quite a few standing ovations with that routine. John loved to do things like that, things that were different. He liked to do more than just stand at the mike and sing his songs."

At the time of the Division Street Corral performance, Cash had recently purchased Johnny Carson's home in the suburb of Encino, in the San Fernando Valley. His plan to break into movies has begun to bear some fruit. He tells Robinson about his upcoming acting debut on the TV series *Wagon Train*, a bit part.

Although a fair amount of Cash's output from the late 1950s and early '60s was relatively unremarkable, the upcoming single he mentions to Robinson—"I Got Stripes" backed with "Five Feet High and Rising"—will bring two evergreen classics to his repertoire.

Robinson, who interviewed Cash again in 1976 and 1988, has fond memories of the man. Their friendship, begun in this interview, would continue for decades. "He was a good guy," Robinson says. "He had a couple personalities. You had to hit him at the right time."

The Division Street Corral was in its heyday in 1959. It boasted the second-largest dance floor in the West. Journalist Anna Prior, writing for the *Oregonian*, notes that proprietor Richard Ceciliani polished the wooden floor every day, so when the place filled up, it smelled of "perfume and wax."

Prior writes: "The decor was country-western, with bearskins on the walls and Texas Longhorns and deer heads hanging from the rafters.

"The bandstand, directly across from the entrance, was low enough that listeners could rest their arms on top of it or even reach out and touch the performers . . . Soda pop, hot dogs, candy bars and cigarettes were available, but no alcohol was served. Of course, that didn't stop some teens from slipping out to the parking lot for a sip of Olympia beer or Thunderbird wine."

Today Red Robinson remembers the Johnny Cash engagement being "packed. Sold out. You couldn't get in."

Thankfully, Red Robinson got in. He shouldered his expensive, unwieldy Eicor recorder, and sat with a sweaty, adrenalized, soft-spoken Johnny Cash, to chat between sets. —Ed.

Red Robinson: Backstage here at the Division Street Corral tonight with Mr. Johnny Cash. How do you feel after the show there?

Johnny Cash: Fine, Red.

Robinson: You look like you're sweatin' all over.

Cash: Ah well, I enjoyed it. Sweatin's good for you.

Robinson: Hey, when's the last time you were here, John?

Cash: Ah, I think it's been . . . it's been almost a year now.

Robinson: And yet the crowd here tonight seems to be bigger than last time here.

Cash: It's been . . . it's very big tonight, yes.

Robinson: You're traveling around the country, where've you been?

Cash: Well since we were here we've been, uh, touring throughout the South, we been to Australia, New Zealand, Tasmania, and Alaska.

Robinson: And you still got time to sit down and talk to a jockey here and there, who, uh . . . you look around and . . . I see you comin' in the room and you look around with a smile and then you say, "Oh no."

Cash: Well I tell ya, it's a pleasure to sit down and talk to ya, Red.

Robinson: Yeah, we're sitting right here very comfortably in a nice big easy chair—I just wanted to describe it to [the listeners]—here in the back room, beautiful room done up in a real wild décor. Where do you go from here? That's the next question.

Cash: We play Eureka tomorrow night, Lorrie Collins and myself, and then we go back to Los Angeles.

Robinson: Back to Los Angeles, California. What are you—are you living down there now? Permanently?

Cash: Yes.

Robinson: Since you signed with Columbia, is that right?

Cash: Right.

Robinson: Did you have anything to do at all with the Nashville show for the Jimmie Rodgers Memorial Day thing?

Cash: No, I was supposed to been on that show, but I had to cancel it, I did a *Wagon Train* film last week the day they had the show.*

Robinson: When is this coming out, Johnny, so we can watch it?

Cash: First week in September'll be the first *Wagon Train* show of this fall series.

Robinson: Are you singing in it, or acting in it, or both?

---

* Johnny Cash's acting debut on the popular TV series *Wagon Train* (1957–1965). The series chronicled the adventures of a wagon train crossing the West and the trials and tribulations of the series regulars. Cash portrayed cowboy Frank Hoag, and is in two scenes. —Ed.

Cash: Well I do about three songs in the background, but I have a dramatic part myself.

Robinson: How old are you right now, Johnny?

Cash: Twenty-seven.

Robinson: Twenty-seven years old. Are you married? You have a family? I always ask that for the females in the audience.

Cash: Yes. Three girls.

Robinson: Three girls! How old is the oldest?

Cash: Four, three, and one.

Robinson: What happened to your thumb there if you don't mind my asking? Seems to be a little messed up.

Cash: I cut it on a guitar string when I broke it.

Robinson: Cut it . . . oh, it looks kinda mean there, you gotta get that fixed up.

Marshall Grant: He done that when he's imitatin' Elvis out there.

Robinson: So you're doing an impersonation of Elvis out there. I got in kind of late. Are you going on again tonight?

Cash: Oh yeah. Twice more.

Robinson: Twice more? Doesn't it beat you out, traveling all over the country?

Cash: No, not really. I love it.

Robinson: Can't you think of something . . . ? Where would you like to be right now?

Cash: (quickly) Portland, Oregon!

[*Laughter.*]

Robinson: Hey, this man's a salesman! Not only a singer. All right Johnny, we'd like to thank you very much. Just one thing—I wanted to know if you had anything coming up to follow up your last big hit release.

Cash: We've got a record out in two weeks, Red, on Columbia. July 10 is the release date, called "I Got Stripes," and the other side is a novelty song about a flood, called "Five Feet High and Rising."

Robinson: You write all of this material yourself?

Cash: Most, not all.

Robinson: Where do you pick others that you don't write yourself?

Cash: Different people. A Los Angeles disc jockey was a cowriter on "I Got Stripes."

Robinson: Which one?

Cash: Charlie Williams. And Carl Perkins and I write a lot together.

Robinson: Is Carl down in L.A. permanently now, too?

Cash: No, he's in Tennessee.

Robinson: How do you collaborate? On the phone? [*Laughs.*]

Cash: We work tours together a lot, y'know.

Robinson: Tell me one thing here, in the room here I see cameras flashing all over, and of course my tape machine going, and someone else . . . doesn't this get you down after awhile?

Cash: What?

Robinson: Cameras flashing, jockey microphone . . .

Cash: Nah. Well, you know, we go out on a two weeks' tour, we expect this, we don't mind. When we get home, we rest.

Robinson: What did you do before this?

Cash: I was in the Air Force.

Robinson: You were in the Air Force. What would you rather do, be in the Air Force or do this?

Cash: [*Quickly, emphatically*] *This.*

[*Laughter.*]

Robinson: OK, thank you Johnny Cash! Short interview here backstage at the Division Street Corral.

Cash: Thank you, Red.

JOHNNY AND JUNE INTERVIEW AND PERFORMANCE

Pete Seeger | 1966 | *Rainbow Quest*

From 1965 to 1966, folk singer and activist Pete Seeger hosted *Rainbow Quest*, a TV series dedicated to American folk music. This black-and-white low-budget broadcast aired on New York City–based WNJU, UHF channel 47. The Newark, New Jersey, soundstage featured a down-home cabin set, with a rocking chair, crockery, kitchen table, and a tin coffeepot. No studio audience, and no script. Over the course of thirty-nine shows, Seeger welcomed a wide array of guests, including Buffy Sainte-Marie, Donovan, the Clancy Brothers, Judy Collins, Tom Paxton, Sonny Terry and Brownie McGhee, Reverend Gary Davis, Mississippi John Hurt, and Doc Watson. For the last episode, Seeger invited Johnny Cash and June Carter.

Rainbow Quest was Seeger's sortie into television after his 1957 indictment for refusing to name names of Communist friends to the House Un-American Activities Committee. He'd subsequently been convicted for contempt of Congress in 1961. (His ten-year prison sentence was overturned on appeal.) In the ensuing folk boom, while still blacklisted, Seeger had drawn attention to a then-unknown Bob Dylan and was responsible for bringing the song "We Shall Overcome" to the civil rights movement. His modest, under-the-radar *Rainbow Quest* is now a priceless document of mid-century American folk music.

A year and a half before Johnny and June's appearance, Columbia Records had released Cash's seminal, acclaimed concept album *Bitter Tears: Ballads of the American Indian*. It featured the soon-to-be-classic single "The Ballad of Ira Hayes," about a Native American marine who'd gained fame as one of the soldiers photographed hoisting the American flag at Iwo Jima, but who'd subsequently suffered from post-traumatic stress disorder and alcoholism, dying of exposure in 1955. Although the single sold well, radio stations' reluctance to play "The Ballad of Ira Hayes" had prompted Cash to place an angry, full-page open letter to DJs in *Billboard* magazine demanding, "Where are your *guts*?"

In *Rainbow Quest* episode 39, Seeger is eager to talk about *Bitter Tears: Ballads of the American Indian*, and about Peter LaFarge, the thirty-four-year-old Native American songwriter and nephew of Ira Hayes who'd penned "The Ballad of Ira Hayes" and four other *Bitter Tears* tunes. A Korean War vet, at the time of the *Rainbow Quest* taping, LaFarge had recently passed away from a drug overdose.

Cash is game to sing a wide variety of tunes—old folk songs, his originals, and LaFarge's tunes—and he's eager to talk about his Native American activism. But he is not well. Of the *Rainbow Quest* appearance, biographer Robert Hilburn wrote, "In a future time of more careful image control, Cash wouldn't have been allowed anywhere near a TV camera in his condition.

"From the opening moments of the show, Cash exhibited the squirming, twitching mannerisms of an addict."

Despite his condition, Cash holds his own, clearly accustomed to delivering under the influence. Although less engaged than June, and given to the occasional strange uttering and hollow-eyed expression, Cash flawlessly executes his songs. He is relishing the embrace of the rising folk community, which had begun with his triumphant appearance at the 1964 Newport Folk Festival. He begins the show in a black vest and black Cuban-heeled boots but discards them both as the cameras roll.

By 1966, Johnny Cash's touring show is an international enterprise. Cash and Carter regale Seeger with stories of playing in Korea in 1963, shortly after June joined the troupe in 1962. Tennessee Two bass player Marshall Grant writes about this trip in his autobiography *I Was There When It Happened*:

"John and some soldiers had gotten into a tank, started it up, and were driving it all over the base, poking the barrel of the main gun through windows. They even rolled over to the officers' quarters, stuck that gun through a window into a room with bunk beds, and shook it back and forth."

This prank, for which no charges were brought, goes unremarked upon on *Rainbow Quest*.

At the *Rainbow Quest* taping, June Carter and Johnny Cash are officially coworkers but secretly in love. Both of their marriages are crumbling, and their clandestine affair is fraught with drama. Although her 1963 cowrite "Ring of Fire" is a secret ode to Johnny, his addictions and out-of-control activities have led June to try to quit several times. A penitent Cash has repeatedly talked her back into the fold.

In 1966, Carter's persona is still as much self-deprecating comedienne as it is professional musician, though both her mastery of the guitar and her lovely, clear voice are undeniable. Dressed in a simple shift and pumps, she offers Seeger fascinating background on her iconic family, soaking up the spotlight while Cash looks on. It is Seeger's fascination with the Carter Family—and his confusion of the family tree, which June good-naturedly addresses—that kicks off the show.

In his introduction, Seeger assures viewers Johnny and June won't be giving "an act," but rather, they will be "singing songs they believe in and feel." Actually, they do both, which makes it a great performance. Johnny and June—and Pete Seeger—are showfolk to the bone, and this appearance is both performative and genuine, musically and interpersonally rife with subtext. In this conversation on art and life and music, a tempestuous, secret love affair is afoot; demons are held at bay, and resentments, anger, and, most of all, affection percolate beneath the repartee. —Ed.

Pete Seeger: I don't think I'll ever forget the record I heard of the song [*singing*] *You've got to walk that lonesome valley* or the song [*singing*] *John Hardy was a desperate little man*, or about two, three, four dozen other songs. And the reason 1 won't forget 'em is the same reason millions of other Americans won't forget 'em. It was wonderful music made by a group called the Carter Family. Old A. P. Carter from Virginia, his daughter Maybelle, sister Sara. And way back 'round the early 1930s, you coulda heard their records on all kinds of country music programs around this country, north and south. And me, I was just one of millions that thought it was the most wonderful music I heard.

Well, I sing it by way of introducing the person who's gonna be on our program, this *Rainbow Quest* today, who's come around. We're very fortunate to have Mother Maybelle's daughter, June, June Carter. She's traveling through town and she said she'd like to drop over and sing a few songs with us. And with her is another fella, well, let me tell you a little bit about him, too, 'cause he's kinda interesting. You know, people like me up north, we sang songs about what it was like to be a farmer down south like [*sings*] *Seven cent cotton and forty cent meat / How in the world can a poor man eat? / Flour up high and cotton down low / How in the world can we raise the dough?* Coming out of my mouth, a song like that sounded kinda funny and silly. I was never a cotton farmer, I never walked behind a mule. Never drove a truck either, except just my own little pickup truck. This fella who's gonna drop 'round to our program—in just a few minutes you'll meet him—came out of a family of hardworkin' people in Arkansas. Done a lotta hard work himself. He also liked to pick a guitar and he liked to make up songs, and his songs touched the heartstrings of all kinds of people around the country, back in the years, the 1950s, if you remember them [*sings*] *I walk the line.* And a whole batch of other ones.

Instead of me talkin' about him, I think you ought to meet him yourself. His name is Johnny Cash. Now of course he and June Carter and some other musicians, they've been touring around the world, they just got back from overseas, they have a whole big show. And normally it's a little unfair to ask them to perform without their whole show here, because it's a wonderful show, but I asked them if they'd come around, just the two of 'em, so we could get a chance to talk a little, and if we kind of improvise our way through a program, I think maybe you'll get to know 'em better. It won't be an act or anything like that. Because they're singing songs that they believe in and they feel.

June Carter and Johnny Cash, just a moment.

Johnny Cash: [*Sings, plays*] *I am a pilgrim, and a stranger / Just travelin' through this wearisome land / I've got a home in that yonder city, good Lord / And it's not, not made by hand / I'm-a goin' down to the river of Jordan / Just to bathe my weary soul / If I could touch but the hem of his garment, good Lord / Well I know it'd make me whole.*

Seeger: Oh, Johnny. Y'know, you know so many thousands of different songs, I know we're not gonna get time to do more than a few of 'em on this program, but I hope you sing a couple that you made up, and a couple old ones.

Cash: Well thank you, Pete. Love to. That song there [*"I Am a Pilgrim"*], that is the first time I think I ever sang that song. I sang *at* it. Thanks to June Carter and yourself.

Seeger: June, whatcha doin' with a banjo in your hand?

June Carter: I'm holdin' it! [*Laughter.*] No, Pete, I tell ya I'm not a banjo player, especially around you. I've listened to you play for so many years. I pluck on one a little bit sometime, and listen to my mother play the ol' drop thumb lick. I've listened to good banjo players, and that's about as close as I am to bein' a banjo player. I just hit a lick here and there.

Cash: She's a clever thief. [*Laughter.*] Pickin' up the licks. No, she's very good, Pete. I'm very proud of her. In Korea, we went for the armed forces—Korea, Japan, and all over the Far East, about three years ago, and it's the first tour she ever played the banjo, and the troops just loved her for it.

Carter: I had to, I didn't have a front tooth! [*Laughter.*] That's a story all its own. Would you like to hear it?

Seeger: Sure.

Carter: We were playin' at a place back up in Korea called Camp Howard, way back up in behind Seoul up there in the mountains, and so many of the boys hadn't been home in so long y'know and hadn't seen an American girl I don't know when, and I'm in there with a whole mouth fulla teeth and grinnin' and smilin', and I do the first tune on the stage, and I had this cute little trick where I used to take the microphone and sing this little song and throw the mic into the footlights and yank it back real quick. Well it always came back, and that day it *really* came back. It hit me right in the mouth and knocked teeth everywhere, and I'm standing there with my head down and my teeth—I'm pickin' 'em up off the floor and I didn't know what to do, I didn't know whether to sing, cry, or what to do. At any rate, I sang with my teeth out. Because they were lined up for like miles to get to the show, and I thought, well, even without a tooth I think maybe they'd like to hear a good ol' girl from home, so I stood up there and propped my foot on that chair and picked the banjo and picked the guitar and just grinned like I had a tooth. [*Laughter.*]

Cash: She came downstairs for breakfast at Seoul, Korea, and she's so homesick, I guess, or she's thinkin' 'bout home, she says, first thing she says, "I know where there's a whole bunch of huckleberries."

Carter: [*Laughs.*] There wasn't in Korea!

Cash: I says, "Where's that, June? In Seoul, Korea?"

Carter: But that wasn't where the huckleberries were.

Cash: I know. But I said, "Where's that, June?" She said, "Well, you know where Grandma Carter lives? Well, go over the knob and then go up Clinch Mountain about two hundred feet there's a whole bunch of huckleberries." Nobody else said a word.

Carter: It was about that time for the huckleberries. I was wantin' some huckleberries. Speaking of Grandma Carter, Pete you were talkin' 'bout the Carter Family a minute ago and I'm afraid you're just a little bit confused about something. Do you mind if I tell you the whole story?

Seeger: Please set me straight.

Carter: All right. [*Laughs.*] Well, there was the old original Carter Family—A.P., Sara, and Maybelle. That you know, but you've got their relationships mixed up.

Seeger: Wasn't Maybelle A.P.'s daughter?

Carter: No, she was A.P.'s sister-in-law. She's my daddy's wife, and he was A.P.'s brother, and Aunt Sara was not his sister, but his wife. And she and mother were first cousins, so that makes you your own grandpa. [*Laughs.*]

Cash: One thing here June, real quick. Aunt Sara Carter is coming to Nashville. She's there today. She arrived today. For the first time in twenty years I suppose, Sara Carter is going to record with Maybelle. The two of them. Just the two of them. It should be a real collector's item. She sings great.

Carter: Well, this is the first time that Mother and Aunt Sara—they cut their last recording in 1941. You see, A.P.'s been dead quite a while. [*Died November 7, 1960. —Ed.*] He's been gone quite a while, and that's all of the old original sound that's left—Mother and Aunt Sara. We're real happy about it. She just didn't have anything to do with the music business. She really didn't care, y'know, too much. Except we got to sendin' her tapes, talkin' to her, and she got to sendin' us tapes of songs that she had sung. She has the greatest voice, Pete. It's just as strong and as vibrant as it can be. And she sent cold chills all over us with those ol' tapes that she sent, so John and Mommy and Daddy and the girls and I sent her a tape and begged her to come, and so she's comin'!

Seeger: Oh, wonderful.

Carter: And we're just thrilled to death about it.

Cash: It'll be a real collector's item. Sara and Maybelle Carter singin' the old songs, their style, nobody else in the background, y'know, she's pure as the driven snow, or her voice is anyway, I don't know much about her background, June probably does [*June laughs nervously.*] but she is a great lady and she got a fabulous voice.

Seeger: What would be one of those songs we could sing together?

Carter: You mean an old Carter Family song? Well, do you have any preference? Do you ever sing the "Worried Man Blues"?

Seeger: Oh, I sing it all the time.

Carter: Do you really? John, do you mind giving me the guitar, and we'll take it from there and see where we go. Going way back on this one.

[*All sing "Worried Man Blues."*]

Cash: My favorite [Carter Family song] is "Keep on the Sunny Side." June, and Marshall Grant my bass player, and I do it onstage sometimes. I'll tell ya real quickly, a story, why that song impressed me so. June asked me to go up see her old home place up at Maces Springs, Virginia. You know where that is, of course. Maces Springs. That's near Hiltons. Anyway, at . . . what's the name of the cemetery?

Carter: Mount Vernon.

Cash: Mount Vernon Cemetery. We drove up this winding gravel road, and the tall pines all the way around, and there was one little spot of sunlight way down at the end, and the sun was shinin' on a rose marble monument. Well, we walked right straight to it. And the writing was on the other side. And I said, "That's it, June." She'd never seen it, either. She'd heard about it, she knew about it. I walked around and right where the sun was streamin' down, on this rose marble, the words said A. P. CARTER and a gold record under that, and under that: KEEP ON THE SUNNY SIDE. And he was on the sunny side. They buried him where the sun would shine on him it seemed more hours in the day than anywhere else.

Carter: Did you ever know him, Pete?

Seeger: No. Just heard his records, that's all.

Carter: Would you like me to tell you a little something about him?

Cash: I will, too. [*June laughs nervously.*]

Carter: Well, my Uncle A. P. Carter, 'course that's my daddy's brother, he was a tall man, he was about six two-and-a-half, six three, something like that, he was quite tall and he was quite handsome when he was young. Dark and, I mean, y'know, darker hair, and some of the people may have seen his pictures, I don't know. He walked like a giant, I don't know how to explain, how to justify that, other than the fact that when he walked onto a stage, years and years ago the old Carter Family did concerts without even realizing that they did. He walked out on that stage and there was something about that man that just *demanded* attention, and got it. He stood and Mother and Aunt Sara used to sit down with their guitars, and the old lamps would be lined across the front of the stage.

Cash: No microphones.

Carter: No mics at all. But he would tell a story about the songs, where he got it, where it came from, if they wrote it, or where he got the song. And how come them to do the song. And so many of the particular songs they did, like "The Cyclone of Rye Cove," which was written about the disaster of the Rye Cove schoolhouse, he told why, where it came from, "The Fate of Dewey Lee," so many of those old ones, the songs from the Spanish-American War, and things like that. He would just say he got this down on the river, y'know, such-and-such's house, but where it came from, y'know? There was just something about the man that made him great. And Mother and Aunt Sara had the same thing, I don't know what it was. But it just demanded respect, they got it, and the country people used to come and listen to them, and I remember one story that was told by Mr. J. L. Frank, who used to do all the shows out of the Grand Ole Opry. He said, "Without the Carter Family, we might have gone under." Now this is years ago, y'know. He said that when Pee Wee King and Eddy Arnold, and all of 'em, Minnie Pearl, started from the Grand Ole Opry, they'd play tours, and he said, "We'd go out and we'd do enough to barely get by, and then we'd be starving," and then he'd say, "I'll have to see if I can just get hold of A. P. Carter." [*Laughter.*] And he said they'd call somebody in the hills and somebody'd go up the valley, and they'd leave the mountain there and come out, and he said, "Then we'd have a whole week of good dates if we could just get the Carter Family." [*Laughs.*] And so that's the way it was back then. But he was quite a man.

Seeger: [*To camera*] It's this tradition, you know, of singing the old songs, and also making up new ones, which is the wonderful thing which the Carter Family taught to me and many other people. Woody Guthrie got it from them. The idea that folk music wasn't just old music and it wasn't just new music, it was a combination of the old and new, all mixed up together. And no two people sang 'em exactly the same. That's the wonderful thing about it. You get hold of an old song and you kind of wear it a little bit until finally after you've sung it a few years it's like a good ol' pair of shoes, it just fits your feet.

[*Johnny Cash has removed his Cuban-heeled boots and sits in his black socks.*]

Seeger: Johnny, I want you to sing some of your songs, too.

Cash: Pete, when I was a kid, say one, two, three, four, five years old, my dad hopped freight trains, rode the rods, boxcars, on top of 'em, to wherever he could get work, y'know. He always sent the money back home. And that left—except the kids in school—my mother and I. She played the guitar, and she has, uh [*he strums*], like that. And I just loved it. And the first song I ever learned was one that she sang. She might've been thinking of my dad who was away working for a livin' to send money home, when she sang, so often, *There's a mother always waiting you at home* . . . It's the very first song I ever [*inaudible*] . . .

Carter: Why don't you sing it?

[*Johnny Cash sings "There's a Mother Always Waiting."*]

Seeger: Was that back in the '30s? The Depression?

Cash: I was born '32, so I guess '35, '36. 1935, I remember my mother playin' the guitar and singin'.

Seeger: When did you first start making up songs?

Cash: Not long after that, but I hid 'em, burned 'em, threw 'em away, y'know. But the first one that I kept I was twelve years old. And I wrote poems, short stories, drew pictures, a little of everything to keep my grades way down to C and D, till they clamped down on me. But I went to the Air Force after graduation from high school. It was in Germany in the Air Force. And a bitter winter, in January, a blizzard was ragin', I had five dollars in my pocket, I walked five miles to Landsberg and bought a five-dollar German guitar. It had no name, but that's how I got my start. I was twenty-one. I'd written several, countless songs up till then, but I had the tunes here, y'know [*points to head*]. No accompaniment.

Seeger: You were singing one back there in the dressing room about the Mississippi Flood, was it, 1937? That you wrote?

Cash: Oh, we were in that.

Seeger: Sing just a little bit of that.

Cash: All right. My daddy sat on the front steps of the house, watched the water risin' from the levee breakin', five steps, and every day he would say, "Well it's over another step." And Mama'd say, "How high's the water?" And he'd say, "Well, it's two, three, four, five feet high and risin'." When it was five, he had to get out. Swam to the road. [*Sings*] *How high's the water Mama?* I wrote this twenty-five years later. [*Twenty-two, actually. —Ed.*]

[*Cash sings "Five Feet High and Rising."*]

Cash: That was in '37, and in '38 there was a good cotton crop, and pickin' time was real good.

Seeger: Sing that.

Cash: I'm, I'm, I'm, I'm sorry, I wasn't asking to do another song. [*Laughter.*]

Seeger: I wanna hear it!

Cash: But it was. It was a bumper crop that year. And this, this song came from thinkin' about the crops in '38, '39, '40, '41 in the Delta land in northeast Arkansas.

[*Cash sings "Pickin' Time."*]

Seeger: Johnny, you and I and June too we had a very dear friend who's not with us anymore, and I'd like to sing a song of his. I don't know if you know . . .

Cash: You talkin' about Peter LaFarge.

Seeger: Pete LaFarge, Indian, proud of it . . .

Cash: I am too.

Seeger: You're part Indian?

Cash: I'm proud of Peter. And yes, I'm part Cherokee.

Seeger: No foolin'.

Cash: Yeah. Peter was Hopi, I understand. Full-blooded.

Seeger: Well, Pete came to New York, I met him about four, five years ago. He helped me build a chimney back at our house.

Cash: He told me about that.

Carter: We saw the chimney! [*Laughs.*]

Seeger: Great big stone! I thought it was gonna break through the floor before we got it up!

Cash: He was a great man.

Seeger: Well, he was a very thoughtful guy, and I think in many ways one of the most thoughtful people I ever knew. He told me how Indian people had a feeling for the world and nature that he found missing in a lot of city people. He told me about the little coyote, for example, and as far as the ranchers were concerned they just wanted to poison him out of existence. But the Indians' name for the coyote was "Little Brother" and he had a song about it.

[*Seeger sings "Coyote, My Little Brother."*]

Cash: Y'know in '57 I wrote a song called "Old Apache Squaw," and then forgot the Indian so-called protest for a while, nobody else seemed to speak up with any volume of voice, then not long before I met Peter, I wrote a thing called "Apache Tears," y'know the stone out West, in souvenir shops that they smooth in a tumbler in Arizona 'specially, it's black and looks like a tear. I wrote a song called "Apache Tears," and I wrote one called "The Ballad of the Talking Leaves," the story of the creation of the Cherokee alphabet.

Seeger: Hey, no foolin'! I wanna learn that.

Cash: Well I'll give ya seven hundred thousand copies. Anyway—

Seeger: I just read about Sequoia a few weeks ago.

Cash: Did ya?

Seeger: Tremendous guy. Without any formal education he decided that the Cherokee should have their own written language, that they had to organize themselves if they were going to withstand the approaching settlers.

Cash: In my album [*Bitter Tears: Ballads of the American Indian*] there's a little story that tells how he came to do this. He was fifteen years old. He was following his father across a battlefield where they'd been fighting the white man, and some officer's notebook had scattered in the wind, the pages, and Sequoia had never seen paper. Never, never seen printed word on paper. And he picked 'em up as he was runnin' along and he ran to his father and he said, "What is this father, these strange squares with such beautiful bird track marks on them?" He said, "Not even the owl could put these there." And his father grabbed them from him, said, "That's the white man's talking leaves." And he said, "Talking leaves, what do you mean?" He said, "Just forget it." Well, he followed him, finally got it out of him, said, "That is how they communicate. They make bird track marks on these snow-white leaves and they send it to their brother, and his brother knows what's in his heart, what he's thinking." So I wrote the thing about—

Seeger: —how Sequoia made up the Cherokee alphabet.

Cash: Which is, as you know, the most complicated alphabet in, I suppose, in the history of the world. Something like seventy-eight letters—

Seeger: —at the same time it was so simple for Cherokees that within a few weeks a Cherokee boy could be writing letters to his own family. That's what I understood. That within three years the entire Cherokee nation was reading and writing.

Cash: Right. Because . . . I mean . . . they were a great and noble race, and they said, the white man can talk on leaves, why not the Cherokee? And they studied it, it was pounded into their heads, they wanted to learn it, and they did. And there's a newspaper published now, in Phoenix, in Cherokee.

Seeger: Johnny, just a minute, I want you to sing one of these songs. Either one of yours, or one Pete wrote, telling the story of the American Indian people. OK?

Cash: Yes, Peter LaFarge was an Indian who loved his heritage, his country, and also, well not most of all, but he did love his music, but he used it not as a vicious tool, but as a great . . . as a voice for the American Indian. And we were very proud he came down from New York City and he brought us five songs to do on this *Bitter Tears* album. Protest songs for the American Indian, which I think was long overdue. Here's our favorite. June, would you help me on this one?

Carter: Sure.

Cash: Our favorite Peter LaFarge Indian song.

[*They sing "As Long as the Grass Shall Grow."*]

Seeger: Johnny and June, I'm mighty glad that America has people like you traveling around, flying around. I know you keep on the run more than almost anybody I know. Every time I see you, you're just kinda zippin' through. Let me sing this song for you both as you fly around. One of my favorite old banjo tunes. I don't know if you've heard it before—

Cash: Hey, after you do this one, would you do me a special request? We came to New York just to get you to do this special request. [*Laughter.*] Will you play just a little bit of "Cripple Creek" on the fretless banjo?

Seeger: All right.

Cash: Go right ahead, Pete.

[*Seeger plays "Little Birdy" on the five-string banjo.*]

> *Little birdie, little birdie,*
> *What makes you fly so high?*
> *It's because I'm a true little bird*
> *And I do not fear to die.*

> *Little birdie, little birdie,*
> *What makes your wings so blue?*
> *It's because I been a-grievin',*
> *Grievin' after you.*

> *Little birdie, little birdie,*
> *Come sing to me your song;*
> *Got a short while to be here*
> *And a long time to be gone.*

> *Little birdie, little birdie,*
> *What makes you fly so high?*
> *It's because I'm a true little bird*
> *And I do not fear to die.*

Cash: [*Marveling at Seeger's banjo technique*] I wish I could do that, but you know I picked cotton for so many years, that's a different lick, pickin' cotton.

Carter: That's right!

Seeger: You wanted me to do something on the fretless banjo? [*He gets fretless banjo.*]

Carter: Yeah! Go get it!

Cash: If you don't mind, I'd love to hear ya.

Seeger: Well, this is the banjo you gave me, Bob Johnston gave it to you, and you brought it up to me.

Cash: 1855. That's older than June.

[*June laughs nervously.*]

[*Seeger plays "Cripple Creek" on the fretless banjo.*]

Cash: [*Clapping.*] That's good, Pete.

Seeger: [*To camera*] How many more minutes do we have, Mr. Man? Four minutes more? I want June to sing a song. [*Sings*] *I'm thinking tonight of my blue eyes.*

Carter: I've never sung it as many times as the Carter Family did, but I'd try it for you, Pete, if you wanted to.

Seeger: Might say this song doesn't have but about two or three verses, but it's a lotta fun to sing, a lotta fun to harmonize on, too. Any of you out there . . . [*To camera*] Y'know, that's a main reason for this *Rainbow Quest* show, is not just to show what we can do but show how you can have a lot of fun yourself making music. I mean it, I hope that you all out there, young and old, tall, short, fat or thin, quick or slow, no matter what kind of color or shape of person you are, if you like to make music, go ahead. Don't let the microphones and loudspeakers faze you—

Cash: Take your shoes off!

[*Laughter.*]

Seeger: And this would be a good song to try if you want to. [*He tunes his banjo.*]

Carter: That takes a while to tune. That's like Mother Maybelle, she'd stop and tune if the world come to an end. That's the only thing to do.

Cash: But she does get it tuned before she plays it.

[*All play "I'm Thinking of My Blue Eyes."*]

THE RESTLESS BALLAD
OF JOHNNY CASH

Christopher S. Wren | April 29, 1969 | *Look*

Author and former *New York Times* editor/foreign correspondent Christopher S. Wren's association with Johnny Cash is unique. For starters, he enjoys the distinction of having two of his songs recorded by Cash—"The Gospel Road" from the concept double album of the same name (1973), and "Jesus Was a Carpenter," on albums *Hello, I'm Johnny Cash* (1970) and *The Gospel Road*, plus live versions on *At Madison Square Garden* (2002) and *Bootleg Vol. III: Live Around the World* (2011). He also wrote the first Johnny Cash biography, *Winners Got Scars Too: The Life and Legends of Johnny Cash* (1971), *and* he penned one of the first significant profiles of Cash, for the April 29, 1969, edition of biweekly *Look* magazine, reprinted here.

In the prologue to *Winners Got Scars Too*, Wren explains the seismic changes in mid/late 1960s country music: "Nothing encourages progress like money, and the country market, not taken seriously before, [has] quietly boomed. In the 1960s, country records started outselling classical or jazz. From Wheeling, West Virginia, to Bakersfield, California, the industry grew nationwide until it grossed over $100 million a year. Artists from Ray Charles to Bob Dylan caught the new wave of country music popularity. Whatever happened to the gap-toothed hillbilly stereotype? A Grand Ole Opry veteran reportedly quipped with a toss of her blue mink stole: 'Hillbilly becomes country when you can wear one of these.'"

Of Cash specifically, Wren writes: "Country music has matured from back-porch enter-tainment into a sleek showbiz culture, and at the top of its pecking order of stars is Johnny Cash, a slab-shouldered six-foot-two-inch sharecropper's son from Arkansas, the big daddy of Nashville with a drifting, compelling baritone and an income that tops several million dollars a year. Cash has sold more records in a year than any other single entertainer—six and a half million in 1969 . . . He has sold nearly thirty million LPs and singles, and well over a million prerecorded tapes. The awards he has to show for it, including seven Golden Record awards for six LPs and a single that each grossed over a million dollars, clutter his home on Old Hickory Lake outside of Nashville; on one occasion they piled up on the back seat of his Cadillac because he didn't quite know where to stash them. He carted off five Country Music Association awards in 1969, a feat that remains unduplicated."

That memorable night would transpire six months after this *Look* feature. Cash would take home Album of the Year for *At San Quentin*; Single of the Year for "A Boy Named Sue"; Vocal Group of the Year, with June; Male Vocalist of the Year; and the night's highest honor: Entertainer of the Year. Cash was actually nominated *six* times, but winning all six trophies was not possible. His "Daddy Sang Bass"—by Carl Perkins—had also been nominated for Single of the Year. He would not win another CMA award in his lifetime. In 2003, two months after his death, he would receive Album of the Year for *American IV: The Man Comes Around* and Single of the Year and Music Video of the Year for "Hurt."

Wren concludes his prologue with an anecdote that rang true in 1971 but would become less true as the 1970s unfolded: "he has never been driven to explain himself, a lapse among celebrities. His monosyllabic but polite response to interviewers usually sends reporters frustrated to their typewriters, but the indifference extends to other trappings of success that envelop him. When he swept the CMA Awards several years ago, Columbia Records hired an airplane to pull a banner of congratulations back and forth over his stone mansion on Old Hickory Lake. Cash shrugged when asked about it later. 'I didn't see it. Yeah, I knew they did it, but I was busy inside. I didn't see it.'" —Ed.

"It's amazing that such a nothing looking place could mean so much to you."

John R. Cash squinted across the cotton fields that defined the horizons of his boyhood home in Dyess, Ark. It was his third trip home in ten years. A cotton stalk with a ragged boll that the picking machine had missed snapped under his soft black boot. "I can remember my mother chopping cotton out there in that field when she didn't feel like it. I could pick 200 pounds of cotton right now, not that I want to. It's something you don't forget."

As a teenager 20 years ago—they called him J. R. back then—he picked 350 pounds a day, dragging a nine-foot-long sack down the tangled rows. Today, at 37, Johnny Cash is a superstar firmly embedded in the firmament of country music. Hillbilly no longer, it's become a confident $100 million industry, and this year, Cash will carve a gross of nearly $2 million from it.

His rock-steady baritone fills more than 12 million records—LP albums and singles—and almost a million tapes. Three albums sold over 1 million each. Technically a country artist, Cash swept the charts with a pop hit like *Ballad of a Teenage Queen*, and still got invited to sing at the purist Newport Folk Festival.

Country music was spawned in the rural poverty of the white South. It is Cash's world. Even in foreign fields (at the London Palladium last fall, he broke all attendance records), Cash paces his show like a backwoods revival. Clad in black, his favorite color, he fills the stage—a towering circuit rider selling salvation. He scratches his D-28 Martin guitar high across the inlaid neck, flings it across his back, pulls two harmonicas from his swallowtailed preacher's coat. Guitar, bass and drum behind him amplify the tempo. Converts not mesmerized in their seats walk forward in steady procession, each to pop a flashbulb of a tiny plastic camera at his sweating face.

Though he needs two corporations to handle his business—they make him possibly the only executive to crack walnuts with his teeth—Johnny Cash can't really remember how many shows he does a year ("a couple hundred, at least"), how many songs he's written, how many awards they've racked up. He is driven by darker recollections: when he was young, it took hours and nearly 80 pounds of cotton to fill that nine-foot sack.

Johnny Cash performs the midwifery on his uncommon songs in pencil across long yellow paper, then tucks the finished lyrics inside a black folder "to give them an air of mystery." They hit with the blunt, sometimes violent imagery of a tale told firsthand. Cash conjures up the delirium of an escaped convict dying in the desert: *Then up jumped the Devil and ran away laughing. He drank all the waterholes dry.* He crams a simple declaration with protest: *I'd sing about more of this land, but all God's children ain't free.* Most often, the words disclose a plain-style Faulknerian pre-occupation with his rural South.

Country music, if it meets any definition, tells a story. Johnny Cash, who finds hard times something to sing about, has a lot of stories to tell. In the winter of 1935, Ray Cash, a farmer busted by the Depression, put his wife, six kids and a few belongings in an old truck. Franklin Delano Roosevelt had opened Dyess Colony, 14,000 scrub acres up in northeast Arkansas. A man who cleared the land would get 20 acres with a house, barn and mule.

"I was almost four," Johnny Cash remembers, "but I remember the ice hanging off the trees. It was raining and freezing all the way up. We found house No. 266 and moved in. All us kids slept on the floor that night."

His father and oldest brother hacked out ten acres the first year and planted cotton. They killed water moccasins and a wildcat big enough for three cash children to lie down on the hide. A good crop brought two bales to the acre. "Dyess Colony was our salvation," says Cash. "I don't know what we would have done otherwise. Probably been following the wheat crop and going to the dogs like the others."

If FDR brought Johnny Cash to Dyess, country music pulled him away. At 14, he was hauling two five-gallon water jugs for the work gangs along the Tyronza River. He earned two and a half dollars a day: "They kept me running as fast as I could. I'd turn on the radios in the workmen's cars when I was getting the water, and slip in and listen to the country songs."

He even answered music-magazine ads that promised to publish the songs he had been writing. Sure, he was naïve, he says. "They didn't get any of my money because I couldn't raise it. That's the only reason, though."

One July morning in 1950, Johnny Cash—still plowing with two mules—worked in the cotton fields. That afternoon, he joined the Air Force. He was trained as a radio intercept operator and sent to Germany, where he bought his first guitar. After four years, he got out as a staff sergeant.

The way he figured it, he could get into country music as a disc jockey. Heading for Memphis, he enrolled in a radio-announcing course. To support himself, he sold appliances door to door. Cash recalls that he wasn't any good: "I hated every minute. Once in a while, down in the poorest sections of town, I'd sell a used washing machine."

He also hunted the chance to sing. Three times, he asked Sun Records in Memphis for a tryout. He waited six months for one audition, arrived to find it cancelled. Finally, after a year, he was given a few minutes. His songs clicked, were recorded, and sold well. A low-key ode to fidelity, *I Walk the Line*, shot him into the major leagues. Cash has pulled big at record shop and box office ever since. His mileage spans 24 LP albums for Columbia.

A complex spirit who finds the entire world a little claustrophobic, Cash was stretched tighter by the demands of his success. About 1961, he turned to a stimulant, Dexedrine, to keep up. To relax, then, he needed a tranquilizer. He was soon locked into the cruel cycle of "nice" drugs. In 1965, he was arrested returning from Mexico with 1,143 pills, and spent a night in the El Paso jail. Ironically, the pills that put him there were legally available on any doctor's prescription.

By 1967, Cash had run through his first marriage. He estimates that he used up to a hundred stimulants, plus tranquilizers, to get through a day. "I don't know why it didn't kill me," he says now. "I started missing dates and dressing like a sharecropper."

One night stopped him cold. "I woke up in jail in Georgia and didn't know how I got there." A policeman had found him wandering the streets and brought him in to sleep it off. Cash quit pills then and there, outlasting the chill sweats and nightmares. "I had no trouble straightening up," he insists. "I was ready for the gutter, you know. Now I consider myself a good man. I don't make excuses. I guess this is the first time I've talked about it."

His ordeal was private, because the country-music business is still wholesome enough to worry over its own. "The guy has so much good in him," says one Nashville writer who admires Cash, "that none of his friends deserted him. John's got a miracle pulling for him, and that's June Carter."

Cash married June Carter in March, 1968. "I couldn't be happy with her if I hadn't started living right," he says. June, with the kind of scrubbed good looks that college girls used to have, is full of old-fangled femininity. She rises at 5:30 a.m. to cook the family breakfast. A large Bible sits in their living room, another in the dining room. Naturally, June delivers the impromptu grace before meals. She cuts John's hair, presses his pants, serves up the squirrels that he sometimes shoots for dinner, and bakes fresh biscuits in the tiny galley of their tour bus. At the hint of criticism, she rushes to defend her man ("He's done a lot that other men would like to do if they had the guts!").

She herself is an impressive talent, bred to the country sound. An offspring of the Carter Family of folk-music legend, June picked guitar and sang on Nashville's Grand Ole Opry for 17 years. She wrote John's big hit *Ring of Fire*, and has sung with him in the Cash show since 1961.

They spend two-thirds of the year on the road, playing mostly one-night stands. Half the time, when the audiences are small, they must piggyback two shows. The troupe often arrives without any notion of where to spend the night. In New York's Carnegie Hall and high school gymnasiums alike, Cash belts out of the right side of his mouth whatever songs come to mind onstage. June, when she isn't singing, works with the lighting man; her guesses are the cue sheet.

Cash is most at peace when he can sprawl out in his oval living room or walk the woods nearby. On tour, he walls himself behind a screen of antic restlessness. The long airport waits nearly drive him crazy. He gobbles hot dogs, buys and flips though a half-dozen magazines and books at a single sitting. When he loses sight of June, he yells whatever pet name comes to mind until she rushes up while onlookers stare.

June started filling a black "couth" book with suggestions for John: *Do not sing bluegrass songs in airports; do not eat sardines and crackers on airplanes.* Her hopes have not been particularly rewarded.

Small-boy mischief masks his fascination with her. "I like you better'n my first bicycle," he tells her solemnly, "or watermelon, or—hell, I dunno—a new pair of shoes on a rocky road."

A broad 6'2" with plow-scarred hands, Johnny Cash looks tough. He is. As a boy, he swam across the Mississippi River below Memphis. More recently, he bushwhacked his jeep up and over Tennessee's 2,126-foot Lookout Mountain in a four-hour grind. But he isn't hard. Cash's parents now run a trailer park he set up for them near Ventura, Calif. Driving home from Florida, he picked up a hitchhiker who wanted to become a singer, and gave the young man a valuable 12-string guitar when he let him out. When the local high school band in Hendersonville, Tenn., was invited to the Orange Bowl, Cash put on a show and raised the travel expenses. "I'm not that damn noble," he says defensively, "but you've got to do *something*."

The Ku Klux Klan went after him three years ago, spreading the rumor, untrue, through his loyal Southern audience that he was "married to a nigger." A few less-loyal fans spat in his face. Cash remarks icily that Klansmen are the only people not welcome in his home: "I'd like to see them all get 40 lashes with a snake whip."

Cash has ridden causes that are intensely personal. Quarter-Cherokee himself, he has long battled for the neglected American Indian. His bitter protest songs fill an entire album. When he can, he puts on benefits at the reservations to raise money.

Another compassion, for convicts, haunts his songs. He has played many of the big penitentiaries, with repeats at San Quentin and Folsom. At the Texas State Prison in Huntsville, he stood singing in the driving rain, after the wet amplifiers had shorted out.

"I don't see anything good come out of a prison," he argues. "You put them in like animals and tear the souls and guts out of them, and let them out worse than they went in."

The new country sound of popular music is not new to Cash. All along, he has been country, pop and folk. Now, he ranks among the top singers in any music, but he's not overly impressed.

On a recent tour, the red-and-white Cash bus was parked outside a lunch joint in southern Virginia. Inside, Johnny Cash had just swallowed a ham and egg sandwich and a bacon and tomato, ordered and eaten a steak sandwich "like that one" at the next booth, and tried a bite of June's butterscotch pie, liked it, and finished the whole wedge. He'd buy a ten-cent chocolate bar on the way out.

At another table, some teen-agers dropped a dime into the jukebox. *Folsom Prison Blues* filled the room: *I shot a man in Reno, just to watch him die*. Cash hummed along a little with himself, got bored, and chewed up the ice in his glass. Slouched in the booth, he stared out the window. Abruptly, he turned to his wife to share with her what had become the most wondrous thing in the world: "Just look at those clouds rolling the other side of that mountain, June love."

G CHORDS AND REVOLUTIONS:
THE JOHNNY CASH SHOW, 1969

Rosanne Cash | 2015 | *Dylan, Cash, and the Nashville Cats*

In her 2010 memoir, *Composed*, Rosanne Cash wrote of a happy time in her youth:

"In my early teens a great, gray fog seemed to lift from my family for a few years. My dad was at a peak of success and health. He was gaining in physical and artistic power, and his television show was a huge hit. After Bob Dylan or Joni Mitchell or any of the icons of my youth were guests on his show, I went to school the next day with great confidence and pride. I basked in that reflected glory. Both of my parents were flush with romance and exuberance in their new marriages [*Johnny with June, Vivian with police officer Dick Distin —Ed.*], and I was feeling the first stirrings of my independence. I went to high school at St. Bonaventure in Ventura and wore my Catholic uniform skirt very short. I had my first boyfriend, and I fell in with a small group of classmates who were a little left of center, like me. We called ourselves the 'Anarchy Society.'"

The new stability in Rosanne's father's life coincided with a significant rise in Johnny Cash activity, including two back-to-back, career-defining hit albums: *At Folsom Prison* (1968) and *At San Quentin* (1969), both produced by maverick Bob Johnston (Leonard Cohen, Bob Dylan, Simon & Garfunkel) and both successful commercially and critically. The former brought the song "Folsom Prison Blues" back to the top of the charts (a live, amped-up version that would also net Cash the Best Country Vocalist Grammy); the latter introduced Shel Silverstein's "A Boy Named Sue" to Cash's repertoire. It would reach number one on the Hot Country Singles chart *and* ascend to number two on the Hot 100 (a.k.a. Pop) chart, Cash's only time in that particular Top Ten (held from number one by "Honky Tonk Women"). Bob Johnston, sonic architect of it all, and thorn in the side of

Columbia Records for his anti-authoritarian modus operandi, would play a significant role in getting *The Johnny Cash Show* off on the right foot.

Cash's manager, Saul Holiff, had been trying to get his client on television since the mid-1960s. Cash, however, was leery of how he might come across in a less spontaneous setting, paired with unsympathetic artists. But Holiff persisted, enthusiastically sharing his vision of Cash as a TV star. He asserted that Cash would be the boss.

Variety shows were the rage in 1960s American culture. Joining established icon Ed Sullivan in the "TV host" ranks were Jim Nabors, Tom Jones, Carol Burnett, the Smothers Brothers, Rowan & Martin (*Laugh-In*), and Glen Campbell, to name a few. Campbell, another country crossover artist, was riding particularly high. *The Glen Campbell Goodtime Hour* was a big success on CBS, the top U.S. network. Struggling rival ABC saw similar promise in Cash, particularly with rural viewers, whose numbers were on the rise. Both ABC and Holiff talked Cash into filming six episodes of *The Johnny Cash Show*, to air in the summer of 1969 as a summer replacement for another variety program, *Hollywood Palace*. It was, essentially, a tryout.

Going in, Cash was adamant about several aspects: No "Johnny Cash Dancers"; rather than Los Angeles, taping would take place at the Ryman Auditorium in Nashville, a.k.a. "the Mother Church of Country Music" (much to the chagrin of the crew, who found it primitive and unreasonably hot); Cash would have control over who was invited to perform (this would not pan out); and, crucially, his friend Bob Dylan would appear on the first episode—June 7, 1969. If he could achieve that coup, Cash knew his show would be a hit. Dylan would need some convincing.

Bob Dylan had largely been out of the public eye since his motorcycle accident in 1966. But he'd fallen for Nashville. He'd begun recording there with Bob Johnston, turning out classics *Blonde on Blonde* (1966), *John Wesley Harding* (1967), and *Nashville Skyline* (1968), on which he duetted with Cash on album opener "Girl from the North Country." Under the aegis of Bob Johnston, Cash and Dylan had even recorded some loose, unwieldy-but-spirited jamming during the *Nashville Skyline* sessions, which Columbia had refused to release. (The tracks would circulate as bootlegs for decades.)

Still, despite their solid friendship and mutual respect as singing-songwriting masters, Dylan was not enthusiastic about *The Johnny Cash Show*. Cash enlisted Bob Johnston to work his wiles to convince him, which Johnston did. Dylan told Johnston he had "nothing to wear," so Johnston bought him two suits, a white and a black one. He would wear neither, but he would show up.

Upon arriving to the Ryman, Dylan recoiled at the barnyard set. Cash arranged for it to be changed to a simple rock wall, and taping commenced. Even as Dylan grappled with nerves and insecurity, his music, enmeshed with Johnny Cash's for a reprise of "Girl from the North Country," would enrapture attendees, reach millions in one fell swoop, and alter the fabric of American music.

Forty-six years later, for the *Dylan, Cash, and the Nashville Cats* exhibit at the Country Music Hall of Fame, Rosanne Cash wrote about this historic confluence for the exhibit's accompanying book. Her essay follows. —Ed.

On June 8, 1969, I walked into St. Bonaventure High School in Ventura, California, on one of the last days of my freshman year, newly fashioned as the coolest kid in the entire school. Bob Dylan had appeared the night before on the very first episode of my dad's new television show, *The Johnny Cash Show*, and a nuclear reaction had occurred in the musical foundations and entrenched loyalties of the entire country. It was a cultural event akin to the crumbling of the Berlin Wall.

My dad, thirty-seven years old, freshly clean from drugs, handsome, authoritative, already an Elder Statesmen of Cool, and Bob Dylan, twenty-eight, edgy and nervous as a schoolboy, but clearly the very same Bob Dylan who was to make the American musical landscape untenable without his presence, sat next to each other, with their guitars, in front of a rough-hewn rock wall and sang "Girl from the North Country," the opening track on Bob's album *Nashville Skyline*. They had recorded the song in Nashville as a duet and released it a few weeks before the show. (Dad wrote the album's liner notes, for which he won a Grammy.) Earlier in the show, Dylan had performed a vulnerable version of "I Threw It All Away," also from *Nashville Skyline*. But the duet is what seared itself into the minds of my generation. The sum of the parts of the two artistically voracious and already iconic young men on "North Country" was so great that it exploded off the little screen and, it is not an overstatement to say, changed the course of American musical history. For those of us who witnessed the moment live on television, it was almost too much to bear. (Three thousand miles away, in New York City, my future husband, John Leventhal, was also watching that performance, and had an epiphany that changed the course of his own musical life.)

Nashville Skyline was not the first time Dylan had recorded in Nashville. Dylan and Cash had been circling around each other for years. Dylan said of my dad: "Of course, I knew of him before he ever heard of me. [He] was different than anything else you had ever heard. [He] sounded like a voice from the middle of the earth."

Reciprocally, my dad had a portable record player that he took on the road to play *The Freewheelin' Bob Dylan* when it came out in 1963. He said he listened to the record in his dressing room every night, went out and did his show, and came off and listened to it again. Cash wrote Dylan a fan letter, and they began corresponding in 1963. They finally met in 1964, at the Newport Folk Festival. Dad gave Dylan his guitar during the festival, an important symbolic gesture and a tradition in country music—if an older, established musician (in this case, thirty-two years old) gave a younger musician his guitar, it was an act of supreme respect, admiration, and an initiation into the inner circle.

Two years after Newport, in D.A. Pennebaker's rarely seen documentary of Dylan's 1966 tour of the UK, *Eat the Document*, there is a brief scene of Dad and Dylan at a piano, in an unspecified location, fumbling their way through a version of "I Still Miss Someone." I've seen *Eat the Document* many times, and I have to squeeze my eyes shut during that scene. Dad is shockingly gaunt, dark of spirit, jumpy, exhausted, and straining to reach the notes in one of his best-known songs, which apparently Dylan knew better than he at that moment.

But by the time of the Johnny Cash television show, three years later, my dad was clean, healthy, strong, and settled back into his own body. The impact of the television show, in which he pushed aside every possible musical boundary to showcase some of the most potent musicians alive in the great heyday of rock and country music of the late '60s and early '70s—Dylan, Joni Mitchell, Ray Charles, Judy Collins, Creedence Clearwater Revival, Merle Haggard, Neil Diamond, Neil Young, and many, many more—cannot be separated from his very personal transformation.

From *Nashville Skyline* and its tremendous success, in part because of Dylan's appearance on the television show, an entire era of music was birthed. The Byrds' seminal album *Sweetheart of the Rodeo* preceded the show by ten months, but in the years following the Dylan appearance, dozens of rock and pop artists flocked to Nashville and created a stagger-ing catalog of work, often with the premier Nashville session players. Neil Young, Simon & Garfunkel, Linda Ronstadt, Ringo Starr, Leon Russell, George Harrison, Joan Baez, the Byrds, and many more artists con-nected the dots between roots and pop, and the work that came from that symbiosis defined the era in popular music. Recordings essential to the American canon exist solely because of the collaboration, synergy, and mutual love between those creating traditional and new folk, rock & roll, country, and pop music.

For me, the essential records in my collection were the ones that came directly from that communion: Neil Young's *Harvest*, Steve Goodman's eponymous record, George Harrison's *All Things Must Pass*, Simon & Garfunkel's *Bridge Over Troubled Water*, the Nitty Gritty Dirt Band's *Will the Circle Be Unbroken*, and albums by Ian & Sylvia, Eric Andersen, Leon Russell, Steve Miller Band, and of course, my dad and Dylan.

I have a triptych of photos of Cash and Dylan backstage at Carnegie Hall at Dad's 1968 show, taken by photographer Jill Krementz. In the first photo, Dylan asks Dad to sign his program, and Dad feels his vest pocket for a pen, and clearly doesn't have one. In the second panel, Dylan hands Dad a pen, and in the third, Dad signs the program. Dad looks good. This was post-Newport and *Eat the Document*, pre-television show, by less than a year, and four months before he and Dylan would record "Girl from the North Country" together. It was all there—Dylan appropriately respectful, Dad genuinely humbled, two great artists in awe of each other and inspired by the other's very presence. How lucky we are that we were able to witness the result of that mutual inspiration, in an electrifying moment, on June 7, 1969. The reverberations from that time linger. There is a visceral quality to the feeling and sound and images of those few years, and particularly of those two men together, that has not receded, but continually renews itself, still provides inspiration for those of us who create roots music.

My dad said, years after the show aired, that he didn't realize how important the Cash-Dylan televised duet was at the time. He said, "All I did was just sit there hitting G chords."

From modest G chords, mighty revolutions grow.

AN INTERVIEW WITH JOHNNY CASH

Jack Killion and Peter McCabe | 1973 | *Country Music*

In the spring of 1971, ABC canceled *The Johnny Cash Show*. The third and final season had been a mixed bag for Cash. While he'd been thrilled to host several "History of Country Music" nights (featuring Tammy Wynette, Webb Pierce, Faron Young, et al.), he'd also reluctantly agreed to allow a circus—with clowns, animals, acrobats—to take over an episode, and he'd bemoaned the need to still tour on weekends to meet the significant overhead of his payroll and expenses. *The Johnny Cash Show* was also taking up time he'd much rather spend with his and June's infant son, John Carter Cash, born March 3, 1970. By all accounts, John Carter was as much an agent of change in his life as June had become.

Despite some continued impressive bookings—James Taylor, Mahalia Jackson, the Staple Singers—viewership declined sharply in late 1970 and early '71. ABC executives blamed the loss on Cash speaking to the audience ever more stridently and frequently of his Christian faith. Cash blamed waning audience interest on the network's interference and lack of imagination.

In any event, variety shows were falling from favor. While the format would continue into the 1970s, the mid/late '60s variety show boom was quieting down; many productions were cancelled in the infamous "rural purge" of 1970-71, an attempt by networks to launch programming that appealed to wealthier demographics.

After being cut loose, Cash would grumble in retrospect about *The Johnny Cash Show*, but he never apologized for any aspect of it, or for using the platform to talk frankly about his spiritual devotion. Since a 1970 dinner over which they'd struck up a friendship with evangelist Billy Graham—about which Cash speaks in this 1973 *Country Music* article—Johnny and June had become ever more demonstrative of their faith. Now, with the show over, they were looking for ways to express that faith, to spread the Good News without the meddling of bottom-line-watchers.

Rather than deal with an opinionated financier and other outside influences, when he and June hatched their idea to create some devotional art, Cash chose to self-finance and completely control his only foray into movie production: *The Gospel Road: A Story of Jesus*.

To direct, and to star as Jesus, Cash picked Robert Elfstrom, who'd helmed the acclaimed 1969 documentary *Johnny Cash! The Man, His World, His Music*. That cinema verité film, made for public television, had coincided with the dizzying confluence of Cash's career-rejuvenating prison albums, the network show, and his sudden superstar status in Nashville. Most important, working on *Johnny Cash! The Man, His World, His Music* had deeply endeared Elfstrom to Cash. According to Cash biographer Robert Hilburn, when asked by the film's producers if he'd captured any incidences of Cash's drug abuse, Elfstrom said no. "I wasn't interested in that kind of shotgun journalism," he says. "I didn't care about the music world or any drugs or promiscuity unless I came across it, and the only thing I saw him drink was a bottle of beer or a glass of wine. Drugs were simply not part of his life when I was with him. In the end, I wanted to show what I was seeing: John was a poet, an artist, and a wonderful, spiritual person."

When time came to put that spirituality onto celluloid, Cash reached out to his trusted friend, and they got to work. They cast non-actors—including June as Mary Magdalene—and headed to the Holy Land. —Ed.

When did you first get the idea to make the film "Gospel Road?"

It began about six years ago with a dream June had. We were in Israel for the first time and she said, "I dreamed I saw you on a mountain with a book in your hand talking about Jesus." At that time I didn't want to hear anything like that. It sounded too much like preaching.

We went up into Galilee and we saw the mountain up at the north end of the Sea of Galilee. We didn't know what mountain it was, but we found out later it was Mount Arabel. And all around this area is the land that Jesus lived and walked—Magdala where Mary Magdalene lived, the place of the Sermon on the Mount, the mountain where He fed the multitude. June said that was the mountain she dreamed about. So we came back two years later and I brought a recorder, and the result of that trip was the *Johnny Cash And The Holy Land* album. We decided then that some day we'd come back and do a film.

You see, for somebody like me, who grew up singing Jesus songs all his life and who was raised up in the Baptist Church, going to Israel is like going home. You see the things you've been singing about all your life. You sing about the old oak tree at home all your life and you go home and there it is. You want to hug it.

Was that your only motivation?

Another thing that happened about three years ago; I met Billy Graham for the first time. He called and he said he wanted to come to Nashville to see me. I never had met him. He came down, we had a big meal and we sat around and talked a long time. I kept waiting for him to say what he came to see me about. Finally I asked him. He said he just wanted to meet me and talk to me about music, but another thing he wanted was to talk to me about gospel songs, Christian songs and songs about Jesus. This was just before the big Jesus song thing came along. He said the kids were not going to church, that they were losing interest in religion, and he said he thought that the music had a lot to do with it, because there was nothing in the church house that they heard that they liked. The latest thing that the kids hear in church is "Bringing In The Sheaves" and "How Great Thou Art," and those are not the kind of things going on in religion that makes kids say, "Hey, I like that. Let's go hear some more." There's nothing that they can relate to.

So he talked to me about myself and other songwriters like Kris (Kristofferson), who think along that line, and he kinda challenged me to challenge others, to try to use what talent we have to write something inspiring, that would inspire people to sit up and take notice of religion and Jesus.

Well, first thing that happened, the night after he left, I wrote "What Is Truth." Just him coming to the house inspired me to write that, if you want to call it inspiration. But June and I also got to talking about the thing we'd talked about doing in Israel. We'd thought about making a kind of travelog, walking the steps that Jesus walked and telling His story, and then we talked about taking some contemporary, country-style Jesus songs, having songwriters write them and telling His story with them. As it turned out, that was a rough concept of what the film was actually going to be. We didn't know it at the time. When we went to Israel we had two songs that we thought would probably be in the film. We had gone through all the church hymns, discarded them, not because they weren't any good, but because they didn't say anything to people today. We had "Jesus Was A Carpenter" and another Christopher Wren song called "Gospel Road."

We hired an Israeli film crew to supplement our crew that we took over there, and we decided since we'd gone to all the expense to take a bunch of people to Israel that we were gonna shoot the moon, and we were gonna make as good a film and spend whatever it took for the month that we had to spend over there. And that's what we did. We hired extras. We didn't try to make a little big movie. We didn't try to make a Cecil B. DeMille film. We used as few extras as we could, and at the times when there should have been a multitude of people, we didn't use anybody. We used sound effects, to try to make it seem like there was a multitude of people. Well, when we came back and started editing the film and putting it together, we saw the need of a song to help tell the story here and there. So a boy named Larry Gatlin came along, who wrote a song called "Help Me." Kris has recorded it now—Kris and Rita Coolidge. And it fit so well in the scene about Nicodemus that we used Kris' recording of it in that scene. We had Gatlin write two more songs, I wrote two or three for the film, and we got Joe South's "Children" for the sequence where Jesus is playing with the little children on the beach. We spent a year picking songs and fittin' them in the film, and that's what we've got now, a musical drama with a bunch of good, new songs that I think people will enjoy hearing if they can stand my voice. One prerequisite for seeing this film is you've got to be able to stand Johnny Cash for 90 minutes. If you can't, then you don't need to go. But if you can stand me for 90 minutes, then you're gonna enjoy it because it's an excellent film as movies go. If it wasn't, 20th Century Fox wouldn't be spending a half a million dollars to promote it and make prints like they are.

Let me ask you about the financial side of it. Tucked away in a Newsweek *report was a suggestion that you consciously went out and raised a lot of money to make this film.*

No, I didn't go out and raise it. I had it. I guess it cost half to three quarters of a million dollars, somewhere in that area. I don't know what the cost is gonna be when they tally it up. But it was the first time anybody was ever stupid enough, if you want to call it that, to put up all their own money to make a movie. But that's what we did, and we did it for a very good reason. If we hadn't put up our own money, we couldn't have done it exactly the way we felt like we wanted to do it. We would have had to do it the way the financier wanted it done. And we could have taken somebody's money. We could've had it financed. We could've had our bank put up the entire amount, because we have a good reputation with our bank, and we had no doubt that we could've got the money. But we wouldn't have had the say and it wouldn't have been our personal film. And this is. This film has our personal feelings in it, and it's got our believability because we believe in what we're saying and what we're doing.

I think I understand the effect that you hope this film will have on other people—but what effects has the actual making of the movie had on you, your circle of friends and your family?

Well, it's had a great effect on a lot of people that have been associated with it, like the little crew that Robert Elfstrom (director) brought over. He referred to them as a bunch of blackguards, as a bunch of profane outlaws. The first day on the set, when they realized we were serious about the subject that we were making the film about, all the profanities stopped, and I think most of the drugs stopped—I'm not sure about that—and if there was any wenching going on, it was on the sly.

I had about a 30-minute meeting with this crew the evening that we got to Tiberius, Israel. We sat around on the floor, and I told them that whatever they'd done before, it didn't make any difference to me. Some of them had pretty tough reputations; they'd been in the riots in Mississippi; some of the people that worked on this film had been in

South American revolutions. I said, "We're beginning a film about a man that is my Lord, and you're working for me, and that's all I want you to remember, that we're making a film about my Lord. There's not gonna be any preaching; there's not gonna be any orders given; there's not gonna be any rules laid down." And I said after the first day of filming, "I think you're all gonna get into the spirit of the thing and believe in what we're doing." And the second day of filming, everybody was up at 3:30 a.m. cleaning equipment. We drove 20 miles and were on location when the sun came up ready to start shooting. It was that way every morning. This was the most devoted bunch of people that anybody could ever hope to have.

Will you make other movies after this one?

This is probably the first and last film I'll ever want to produce because I don't want to be a film producer, if you want to call it producer, 'cause that's what I was on this. This is my life's proudest work that I wanted to produce, to lay down a story and put it on the screen, have people go and sit and enjoy it, and when they walk out of the theater, feel good about it. Not walk out of the theater saying, "Oh me, I'm a sinner. I've got to run and do something quick, to get right." It's the kind of thing that will make you think about your religion, but it's a beautiful film.

When Jack Hurst spoke to you last Fall for a story in Country Music, *he asked when religion became important in your life. You said you didn't know, but you said you felt it had something to do with when John Carter came along and you and June "realized that you weren't children any-more." Could you talk a little more about that now?*

Well, for seven years I tried about every dirty rotten thing there is. I took all the drugs there are to take, and I drank, and then when I married June, I decided that was all no good, that I'd run through every evil, dirty thing there is, and I didn't like it. I wanted to live, I saw a chance to find a little peace within myself. Everybody had written me off. Everybody said that Johnny Cash was through, 'cause I was walkin' around town, 150 pounds. I looked like walking death and they were turning and laughing at me. I saw it myself, many times, people saying, "Oh man, he's gone."

Well, it didn't take too much of that for me to say, I'll show you, that ain't all of me. I had June to hold onto, and my religion helped. My religion now is no different than it was when I was a kid, it's just that after a few years of adult life, I went down the wayward path.

Do you feel any sense of accomplishment from those years? I'm thinking particularly about the songs that you wrote.

Yes, there's a lot of things I wrote that I'm proud of through those years. And I feel that everytime I went onstage, I tried to do a good job. There were some shows I missed, and some bad shows I probably did, but I'm not ashamed of it. Right now I'm not ashamed of a thing I did because when God forgave me, I forgave myself, see. That's one thing that people like me have to learn to do, that after you've straightened up and stopped all that, and you know that God forgave you, then the big sin would be not to forgive yourself. So I'm not ashamed of all that rot that I did. I don't like to think about it. Some of it I've erased from my mind, so I don't think about it, and some of it I refuse to admit that I remember.

Do you think your audience has changed since you've moved more toward gospel music? I know many people found it easy to identify with what you were singing, and your songs appealed to anybody who had even the slightest troubled frame of mind.

You know, the accent is not all that much on gospel music. It's just that when I sing gospel music or record gospel music, I'm serious about it, whereas a lot of artists I know, every three or four years, or at one point in their career they say, "Well I think I'll record a gospel album now because it would be the right thing to do and it would show the people that deep down I'm a religious person." That's the way I used to think about it, too. Now my last record was *Any Old Wind That Blows*, and the one before that was *Oney*. You know I'm still the same person that I always was. It's just that I'm serious about the gospel songs when I do sing them. I'm serious about this film, but there's a good chance that

I might star in a film called "Old Fishhawk," a story about an Indian. 20th Century is now trying to buy the rights for me to do that film, and it's got nothing to do with religion.

I guess there are two things that have really influenced your life and career over the last few years. One, the fact that you stopped taking drugs, and two, the arrival of your son, John Carter.

Yes, John Carter's got a lot to do with it. You know, I used to go rabbit hunting and squirrel hunting, and killing all kinds of animals. But John Carter's almost three years old now. He's got all these animal books, and I tell him stories about animals, and I can't go killing any animals now. John Carter has had a lot to do with the change in me. I'm 40 years old, and all of a sudden this little redheaded boy comes along. Everybody thought it was going to be a black-haired boy, but this little redheaded boy comes along who looks like June Carter and follows me everywhere I go. I can't go anywhere in this house without him being right at my heels, and I enjoy all the quiet, nice, little things that three year old boys do. There's something strengthening about that. He's had a lot to do with it all right.

Did giving up drugs make you feel that this was the first time you'd stood up to something and really come through it?

There's been a lot of us that was on drugs and quit. There's been a lot of us who had the problem with alcohol and quit it. It takes a real man to be able to do it. It really does. But the toughest thing I ever did was to quit smoking. I can say that, and maybe I don't really mean that, because I made myself forget all those nightmares I had when I was trying to come off barbiturates. Before I married June and lived out here on this house on the lake, I used to get those pills by the hundreds or thousands, and I used to put a hundred of them in a sock and hide them between the boards in the floor, or in the ceiling in the bathroom, or behind the light or something. Last week I found a box full of pills! They were not in a sock, but in a matchbox. Merle Haggard incidentally knows where I used to hide my pills sometimes. I told Haggard where I hid 'em and

I'm not going to tell you, but Haggard knows where I used to hide my pills when I wanted to carry 'em on me. But I found a box full of pills under the washbasin and I almost broke my arm to get to 'em. I knew that I had hidden some pills five years ago under that washbasin. I got down on the floor and I stuck my arm under there and the tips of my fingers touched a little box. It slid around a little bit, and I kept straining and skinned my arm to get to 'em, pulled them out and there was that box of little yellow pills. Half yellow pills and half tranquilizers because I'd hide both kinds, so I could go up and come back down, too. I pulled this box of pills out and looked at 'em. Smelled 'em, that weird sticky smell they have, and I thought of a bunch of things I'd done while I was on 'em. I took them up to the bedroom and June and John Carter was laying on the bed. And I opened up that box of pills and said, "June, look what I found." I emptied them on the bed, and she said, "Oh my God, no," 'cause she remembered a bunch of bad things, too. And I said, "Don't worry, let's go in here and flush 'em," and June and John Carter and I went into the bathroom and John Carter said, "What are you doing that for daddy?" And I said, "Because it's the thing to do, son." I said, "That was bad stuff daddy flushed—bad stuff." So we got rid of the pills. There may be some more pills at the house, but if I ever find 'em, I'll flush them too.

To change the subject a little, what do you think is happening in country music now? Probably you, more than anybody, in the last ten years have broadened the scope of country music, popularized it for a much wider audience.

That's happened, and will probably continue to happen, but when it's broadened, it can spread pretty thin. But I think better songs are being written than ever before. Tom T. Hall's "Watermelon Wine" is one of the greatest things ever written in country music. This is the kind of thing I love. It's philosophy, it's life, it's real—and those are the kind of songs that are going to stay, no matter how wide the spectrum spreads. Songs like that are gonna make it. So I think that so long as people come along like Tom T. Hall writing great stuff like that, then country music is here to stay. Well it's here to stay anyway, but I mean in a big way, 'cause there's some really good talents around. There's a young writer that we've got here named Dick Feller, who has just recorded for United Artists. He's going to be a big artist. I recorded a song of his, one called "Orphan Of The Road." I think as long as people like him are coming along, country music's got a great future.

Do you see yourself moving more toward producing?

No, not at all. We've got the best studio at House of Cash, the finest one in Nashville. The feeling here is great. People love to record here, but I don't want to produce. I don't want to produce records. I want to do my own records, and that's it. I don't want to get involved in a bunch of business ends of the business. That's one reason why I'm still around and going, because I haven't stuck myself behind a desk. Although I've got a nice desk here, you won't find me behind it once a month. I don't like the business end of the business.

There was some talk recently that you were going to play more small halls. Is there anything to that?

Well, I'm not only playing small halls. I'm still playing the big halls, but I enjoy going to a town that I've never been in before, like a 100,000 population town. I just looked at the map and made up a list of towns that I gave to my manager last week, for him to check out. I like to play a smaller hall because the audience response is better in an auditorium of 3000 or 4000 people.

What effect, if any, has working with companies like American Oil and Lionel had on your career and your audience?

It hasn't had any effect on me. Those commercials I do for American Oil about every six months take three days of work and then I forget about it. Of course then my fans see me on TV. I don't really know what effect it has on them, except I get a few letters. I haven't had a half a dozen letters in two years offering any harsh criticism on those commercials. I really do use American Oil, up here at the station in Hendersonville, and I try to be realistic about things. I like to sing about trains and the old times and the good old days and all that business, but if my boy gets sick and I need a doctor, I don't want him to walk 15 miles. I want him to burn some gasoline to get out there.

I think there's always two or three ways to look at everything. The commercials I did for American Oil helped pay for things like the film, or part of it. So I use the money that I make to do a little good now and then. We're very active in a lot of charities, in mental health and boys' homes, so I don't have apologies to make for anything that I do to earn income. I employ a lot of people here and feed a lot of children and I'm very proud of all the work that I do because there's a lot of thought and careful consideration that goes into all of it. It doesn't mean I don't make mistakes because I know I do. I've seen them. I do just about as many things wrong as I do right, but at least I'm doing what I feel is right at the time.

You pledged to support President Nixon and his policies in Indochina toward the end of the Vietnam War. Do you feel you were right now that the war has ended?

The only thing I know about is what I've read. One thing, *Country Music* Magazine said something about me refusing to endorse the President. What was that headline?

"Cash Is Cool To The Republicans?"

Well, I guess you *could* say that, but all I said was that I didn't feel that an entertainer had any business going to political conventions. I still feel that way. It had nothing to do with Republicans or Democrats, or the President. I think the dignity of the office of President of the United States should be maintained and respected no matter who is our President. He is our President, and we the people have elected him whether you or I voted for him or not. As far as the war in Vietnam is concerned, that war just made me sick. I'm not supporting that war or any other war and whether or not Nixon did his best, I don't know, because I don't know that much about his job. I have to assume that he did because we believed in him enough to re-elect him.

Do you think there's been a big change in the American way of life since the sixties? Do you think we're going back to the fifties way of thinking?

No, I don't think so. Change is the whole process of life. Change is for the most part healthy, of course. We made a lot of mistakes in the sixties. We'd like to just erase that whole war from our history books. That would really be nice, except you can't forget the ones that died and every time the war is brought up, you think of something that brings it home.

Maybe Vietnam has taught us a hard lesson to not be involved in foreign wars. Maybe that's the lesson we've learned. I hope we have. Then all those things that happened in the sixties were solidifying and strengthening for this country. The riots, the campus riots—I was just reading a copy of *The New York Times* I have at home from 1873, and in Washington D.C. in 1873 there was a student riot, and there were burnings in effigy and bonfires out in front of the Capitol and students singing and dancing and drinking all night. Kids want to get out roaring, and get organized in their roaring and march while they're roaring. I don't think that's gonna stop. They're gonna let off steam however they want to. And sometimes they get serious about it and sometimes some-body gets hurt. I think we've learned a lot of lessons from the sixties.

What happened to your testimony on prison reform last Fall?

I guess because I got a lot of attention from prison shows and albums, I get a lot of requests from people who want me to be involved in this or that program. One thing I did, I went with Senator Brock to Wash-ington to testify before the Senate Sub-Committee On Prison Reform for some bills he was trying to get through. I told how I felt about prison reform and such, and about some things I had seen or knew about that go on in prisons. People say, "well, what about the victims, the people that suffer—you're always talking about the prisoners; what about the victims?" Well, the point I want to make is that's what I've always been concerned about—the victims. If we make better men out of the men in prison, then we've got less crime on the streets, and my family and yours is safer when they come out. If the prison system is reformed, if the men are reformed, if they are rehabilitated, then there's less crime and there's less victims.

Ever since I've been in the entertainment business, from the very first prison I played in 1957—Huntsville Texas State Prison—I found that a concert is a tension reliever. A prison is always full of tension, but sometimes it gets to the breaking point and there's trouble. I'm not saying our concerts have prevented trouble, but who knows? They may have, because I've been called on by a warden here or there to do a concert when they've had trouble, and we've done it, and there's not been trouble. Here at Tennessee State Prison, I had a man come up to me and say, "I believe I can make it another five years. I know somebody out there cares, cares enough to come in here and sing for us." A concert does relieve a lot of tension because it makes them forget, it makes them happy, it makes them applaud, it makes them laugh, they tap their feet to the music. That's our purpose, to give them a little relief.

You seem to have acquired a great deal of tolerance and you seem to have mellowed a great deal. How do you see your life moving now?

I think I feel better onstage now than I ever did in my life. I worked a concert in Fargo, North Dakota recently, and I never felt so good on stage as I did that night. I see myself onstage, if God lets me live, 20 or 30 more years. It's what I feed on, the performance and the audience reaction. It's what I love and that's all I want to do. I want to try to write and record better country songs. I've got my own studio here and just because it's the biggest and prettiest in town doesn't mean I'm going to fill it full of fiddles every time I record. I spend a lot of time in there with just my flat top guitar. And another thing, talking about the future, I want to try to become a musician. I started taking piano lessons at the age of 40. I just had my first piano lesson about two months ago and I already know C, F and G7. That's one of the proudest accomplishments of my life is to learn those three chords on the piano, and I've got another lesson tomorrow afternoon, my third lesson. I'm trying to learn to finger pick on guitar. Red Lane will laugh at this, but I'm trying to learn some finger picking. I learned my guitar lick from Norman Blake and Red Lane. I've been working on it. They don't know how good I'm gettin'. I'm gonna show 'em some day. Then I took my first piano lesson. I learned three chords and I practice them. And then Walt Cunningham, a young man that's been playing piano for us on some of our concerts, taught me how to vamp in 4/4 rhythm and everyday I practice on that. That's something I've never done in my life, sit down and play something. Strumming is all I ever did before.

Is John Carter interested in music?

Yes, he is very much interested in it. June and I did a show at a handicapped children's school last week. We took him with us because there's little kids there. I was right in the middle of a song when he bounded onto the stage and said, "I want to sing." I stopped the song and said, "What do you want to sing?" and he said, "I wanna sing 'The Cowboys And The Indians And The Sheep'." So he started singing, and when he got through that I said, "okay son, let's hear another," and he said, "Oh, The Wind Blows On The Cows." That's the name of another one that he made up. And the kids loved it.

But last week in Fargo, I brought him out on stage because he told me—now I know that people won't realize that John Carter is old enough to think like this, but he's 3 years old now—he said, "Daddy, I'm going to sing tonight." I said, "What are you gonna sing, son?" And he said, "Peace In the Valley." So in the show when I got ready to do "Peace In the Valley," I called him out on stage and he sang the chorus with me. At the end of the song, he took a bow and went off, and they kept applauding, and he came back and took another bow.

When someone interviews you and you talk about your personal life, do you think that serves a purpose to cut through the stage image which I guess all performers have?

Well, when I'm onstage I feel like I'm really a complete person because that's what I feel like I do best and that's what I'm most alive and happy doing, performing. Any other part of me might be interesting to the people that like that image on the stage. Yes, I think it's realistic;

it's justifiable, the interviews, the pictures of the life of the man that lives off stage. And I think in most cases it's an honest picture, like right here, because it's really the way I feel about things; when I sit down and talk to you and tell you these things, it's the way I feel.

INTERVIEW

Larry Linderman | August 1975 | *Penthouse*

In 1975, Johnny Cash released four albums: *The Johnny Cash Children's Album*, *Johnny Cash Sings Precious Memories*, *John R. Cash*, and *Look at Them Beans*. In this expansive interview with Larry Linderman for *Penthouse* magazine from that year, neither Cash nor Linderman mention any of them, or the accompanying singles, by name.

Also telling is the setting: the Imperial Suite at the Las Vegas Hilton. The Johnny Cash Show is in the middle of a weeklong engagement, playing to packed houses of high rollers and tourists, night after night. These audiences are decidedly different from Grand Ole Opry fans, and evidence of Cash's continuing, and unmatched, boundary-defying appeal. Despite releasing many albums that don't do well commercially or critically, and despite a dearth of Johnny Cash on the radio, in 1975, Cash is still King of the Road, the biggest country star on the planet.

Even though the Christopher S. Wren–penned Cash biography *Winners Got Scars Too: The Life and Legends of Johnny Cash* was only four years out at the time of this interview, at the urging of Billy Graham, Cash had just written his first autobiography: *Man in Black: His Own Story in His Own Words*, published by Zondervan Christian Publishing. At the time of this conversation, it had just landed in bookstores. In it, Cash details his drug-induced dark nights of the soul and his return to the Christian faith of his youth.

Cash's unsatisfying recording output and lack of radio presence did not affect his autobiography's success. *Man in Black* would sell over a million copies and go a long way toward establishing the public perception of Johnny Cash as a man whose addictions and trespasses had been redeemed by a reaffirmation of his faith, shared with his similarly devout spouse.

Perhaps most striking in his conversation with Linderman is Cash's recounting of his and June's attendance at the Watergate hearings, where they had coffee with Nixon cabinet members H. R. Haldeman (talkative) and John Ehrlichman (not so much), both of whom were convicted of conspiracy, perjury, obstruction of justice, and other crimes. Although President Gerald Ford would pardon their boss, Haldeman and Ehrlichman will do eighteen months of prison time each.

What is not mentioned in this interview is how the early to mid-1970s were a period of healing in the Cash family, a long-hoped-for rapprochement. Cash was clean and sober, likely as physically healthy as he ever would be, miraculously intact after a long period of drug abuse and many accidents. He and June were then engaged in rigorous Bible study through correspondence courses. He was actively attempting to make amends for abandoning daughters Cindy, Tara, Kathy, and Rosanne in 1967. They, in turn, were in the process of building solid relationships with him. One by one, the Cash daughters had been leaving California to come live near him, June, John Carter, and Cash's parents.

Rosanne had already been on the road with the Johnny Cash Show, mainly in the wardrobe department, since graduating from high school in 1973. She would credit this time not only with reuniting her with her father, but also with introducing her to country music and sparking her desire to become a songwriter, an artist.

Flush with pleasure at these newly healthy aspects of his life, in 1975, Johnny Cash was optimistic about where he and his beloved nation were heading. He saw good things ahead for his government, and his hopes for prison reform were not yet dashed. If he was concerned about record sales and critics, he did not let on. —Ed.

It has now been twenty years since Johnny Cash first surfaced as a singer, and in the course of establishing himself as the unquestioned king of country music he has recorded nearly 350 songs, sold more than 30 million records, and currently earns more than $3 million a year.

Almost equally pleasing to Cash is the increased acceptance he's won for country music. Prior to his emergence, such fabled Southern troubadours as the late Jimmie Rodgers and Hank Williams could win followings only along the corn pone circuit. Cash, as welcome at Carnegie Hall as he is at the Grand Ole Opry, brought country music to the cities. And also to the young—pop idols Bob Dylan and Kris Kristofferson are among the many youthful singer-composers strongly influenced by the Nashville-based balladeer. As we head into the second half of the seventies, Johnny Cash seems a sure bet to become the most dominant figure in the entire history of U.S. country music. For a man who was a failure as an appliance salesman at twenty-three, Cash has clearly come a long way since those early lean years.

Born in Kingsland, Arkansas, on February 26, 1932, John R. Cash, at the age of three, was brought by his parents to Dyess, Arkansas, where the Roosevelt administration had established a federally financed farm settlement to aid depression-poor families. Cash's hardworking father was given a twenty-acre farm, a small house, a barn, a mule, a cow, and a plow—and eventually paid back the government for everything it had advanced him. One of seven children, John (which is what his friends call him) grew up on a steady diet of fatback, turnip greens, and hard work—he was picking 350 pounds of cotton a day by the time he was fourteen. Following his high school graduation in 1950, Cash worked for two weeks on a Detroit automobile assembly line and then enlisted in the air force. After a four-year stint in Germany—where he learned to play the guitar—John returned to Memphis and a job selling appliances.

Cash was a lamentably bad salesman. "Maybe that was because I hated every minute of it," he recalls. To supplement his meager income, John formed a trio with local auto mechanics Luther Perkins and Marshall Grant, and they were soon playing church socials and county fairs. After doing a series of fifteen-minute Saturday afternoon radio shows in Memphis, Cash decided they ought to audition for Sun Records. In early 1955, their first recording, [*"Hey Porter" backed with*] "Cry, Cry, Cry," sold 100,000 records across the South. "Folsom Prison Blues" came next, and when it rose to the top of the country music charts Cash quit his job—and has been singing country music ever since.

Johnny Cash is much larger up close than he appears to be onstage. A big, barrel-chested man whose face looks like it crashed into a wall, Cash looks raw, speaks plain—and is surprisingly gentle. At the same time, however, the passivity seems tightly controlled: Cash has an enormously strong personality that he underplays. His sidemen are more than suitably impressed by their boss and talk of him in terms approaching sainthood. And it often seems that's what he's aiming at.

In addition to being a remarkable singer and songwriter, Cash is also a consummate performer. Several times a year he plays week-long engagements at the Las Vegas Hilton (which has that gambling town's biggest showroom), and his usual complement of two SRO crowds a night don't leave disappointed. Cash is often onstage for one and a half hours, and virtually every song he performs has won him a gold record. June Carter, his wife of seven years, joins him for several songs about midway through the proceedings, and occasionally their four-year-old son, John Carter Cash, also gets into the act. (John and June have both been married before, which accounts for their six daughters.) Cash knows how to bend a lyric just so, and his gravelly, slightly off-key baritone seems able to dive into bottomless pits. Unlike a number of performers these days, Cash is better in person than on his records. And his records are superb.

After catching one of his midnight performances, the author met Cash the next morning in the Hilton's Imperial Suite, a spacious and dandy refuge reserved for whichever entertainer (Ann-Margret, Tony Bennett, Barbra Streisand, Bill Cosby, etc.) is currently headlining downstairs. Cash was stretched out on the carpet, dressed in one of the black shirt-and-slacks outfits he performs in (and apparently lives in as well). He quickly bounded up, got coffee, and then sat down to talk. Cash really can't abide Las Vegas—he doesn't gamble and the desert air never fails to play havoc with his throat—yet there are at least a couple of reasons he keeps playing the town. One is the six-figure weekly salary he draws from the Hilton. Another is the rousing reception he gets from high-rolling crowds who aren't country music buffs. Cash's singular ability to turn virtually any audience on to his brand of music provided a logical opening for the interview.

Penthouse: Although the music scene seems to be composed of enemy camps, you've somehow become a superstar not only to country music fans, but also to folk, rock, and gospel followers. What accounts for that?

Cash: Well, to start with, I have no illusions as to who Johnny Cash is: I'm a country boy and I'm a country singer. But I've always felt that the country songs—especially the ballads—have something to say to everybody. It finally just gets down to how they're presented; are you gonna present a song to people that'll get them feeling the same way *you* feel about it, or will you do it in such a way that people will end up thinking, "Nope, that's not for me." I think I was aware of this as early as 1956 when a song I wrote called "I Walk the Line" was one of the first so-called country songs to become a pop hit as well.

Penthouse: Musical innovations aside, what do you think your songs communicate to people?

Cash: Love. I sincerely love people. And I especially love children. Now that I have six daughters and a little boy and I'm forty-three years old, I've learned to appreciate children. So I have them in mind when I make my records, and I also have the church people in mind, because that's part of my life now, too. And I also have convicts in mind. I try to remember that the airwaves belong to everybody—*anybody* can turn on a radio—so I try not to put my music into a bag.

The same is true of myself, 'cause I've never wanted to be put in a bag either. You know, even in the fifties, people in the country music business in Nashville considered me some kind of unorthodox left fielder, mostly because I came down from Memphis, where Elvis and Carl Perkins and Jerry Lee Lewis and I had been putting out all that strange stuff on Sun Records. I thought a lot about being considered weird—and it was all right with me. I bought it. It's still all right with me, 'cause I still don't want to be put in a bag. And because of that, I'll continue playing to different kinds of audiences. Like prisoners—I just played an Oklahoma state prison and a Mississippi state prison. And before that, I played a Billy Graham crusade and a Sunday school class. I just think it's fascinating for a man to spread himself around, to walk through different doors, see different groups of people, and understand and feel what they react to. You learn a lot.

Penthouse: You've been extremely critical of how prisons are run, and once said, "I don't see anything good coming out of prisons. You put men in like animals and tear the souls and guts out of them—and let them out worse than they came in." Exactly what did you mean by that?

Cash: I've got a good friend named Glen Sherley, who wrote "Greystone Chapel" on my *Folsom Prison* album. He's been out of San Quentin for three and one half years now, and he'll tell you—and I've seen it—that the prison system, like it was and probably still is at San Quentin and Folsom and some of the other big hellholes, is just a school for crime. On top of that, prisons are terribly overcrowded. Tennessee State Prison, right in my hometown of Nashville, has about 5,000 inmates—and at night there's only thirty people that take care of the needs of all those guys. They don't even have a *doctor* assigned to the prison. Can you imagine that many people with no doctor on call? Listen, that's just an example of the lack of concern people have for prisoners. And we keep putting men into settings like that. It's as if we're all saying, "Okay, let's send this man who's offended society to the school for crime that we call our state joint." The result is that when the guy comes out he'll be able to pull off a bigger-and-better robbery, or kill somebody, and that's what's been happening.

Penthouse: Do you see any signs of change in the penal system?

Cash: Well, decent things are in the works in different places. Tennessee, for example, is trying to build about seven different regional facilities around the state—farms where first offenders and nonviolent criminals are sent. Some of these prisons-without-walls even have work-release programs—prisoners are allowed to go home on the weekends if they're sent to the facility that's in their area. A lot of these prisoners in these places have been convicted of marijuana charges, and I personally don't think they should be in prison in the first place. But so long as the law stands against them, they should at least be put in a place where they can improve their lot and be trained towards going along with those laws.

Penthouse: Would you like to see all marijuana legislation abolished?

Cash: Well, I just think there's a lot of money spent on enforcing marijuana laws that could be spent for better causes. As to whether it's harmful or not: I smoked grass for a seven-year-period during which I did everything. I was on amphetamines, barbiturates—and I smoked a *lot* of grass. But when I smoked it, I was usually on amphetamines, so I can't really say whether marijuana ever did me any good or any harm.

Penthouse: What first got you into drugs?

Cash: The same thing that gets anybody into drugs: they make you feel good. It was a thing I did gradually, and it felt so good when I started taking pills in '58 that I just kept trying things that felt better. Drugs were an escape for me, a crutch—a substitute for what I now feel. I was looking for a spiritual high to put myself above my problems, and I guess I was running from a lot of things. I was running from family, I was running from God, and from everything I knew I should be doing but wasn't. I was rebelling, and really for no reason. So I was living from high to high, and the highs got higher—but the lows got lower. *So* low, sometimes, that I realized I was at the bottom, and that if I didn't stop I would die.

Penthouse: A lot of people who knew you then are still surprised that you *didn't* die.

Cash: Yeah, all my friends had me written off, and I think some of 'em are still mad at me 'cause I rewrote the script. But I almost accommodated them, that's for sure. My first marriage was in trouble when I lived in California, and I have to take the blame for that—because no woman can live with a man who's strung out on amphetamines. My first wife put up with me for years after I was hooked, but I'd go home and try to put all the blame for it on her, and then I'd get into my jeep or camper truck and head for the mountains. And I'd get so stoned every time I'd leave home to go into the desert or the mountains that I'd wreck whatever I was driving. I totalled a lot of vehicles, and I guess I must've broken twenty bones in my body—my toes, my jawbone, my nose, my fingers, my elbow, my foot, my kneecap. I don't know why I didn't kill myself then. I think it was because God was really good to me, which is why I'm where I am now spiritually.

Penthouse: During that seven-year period—from 1961 through 1967—what was your life like?

Cash: It was like I was living with a bunch of demons. I don't want to get deep into demons 'cause I don't know that much about demonology, but I used to get into the desert, and I'd start talking to them. I'd talk to the demons and they'd talk back to me—and I could *hear* them. I mean, they'd say, "Go on, John, take twenty more milligrams of Dexedrine, you'll be all right." And I'd say, "Yeah, but I've already had forty today." And they'd answer, "Take twenty more, it'll be good for you, it'll make you feel just fine." So I'd take 'em and continue talking back and forth to the demons inside me.

Penthouse: That doesn't sound too healthy, John. How did you feel about it at the time?

Cash: I felt completely crazy—and I *was*. Really, I was *completely* crazy. One time I remember going into my camper truck and looking at myself in the mirror. I put my hand over my face and peeped through my fingers at myself and said, "Let's kill us." And then I said, "I *can't* be killed. I'm indestructible." Well, I looked myself right in the eye and said, "I dare you to try." So I got in that camper truck and started driving down a mountain. The truck turned upside down twice, but the only thing I broke was my jawbone, which still gives me a pain now and then. It was really a battle that raged within me for a long time—but somehow I survived.

Penthouse: What finally caused you to give up drugs?

Cash: God. The times when I was so down and out of it were also the times when I felt the presence of God, or whatever you want to call it in whatever religion you might follow. I felt that presence, that positive power saying to me, "I'm still here, Cash, to draw on whenever you're ready to straighten up and come back to life." Well, that's what finally happened, and I'm not playing church now. I was brought up in the church when I was a boy, and I didn't play church *then*. The spiritual strength I have is real, it's solid, and I don't compromise it. It's something within me that nobody can argue about with me, because it's a very personal strength that I feel and that I draw on. That's what pulled me out of it. But there are people I used—like June Carter, who stuck by me all those years while I was on drugs and fought me, to the point of stealing my pills and destroying 'em whenever she could. And then feeding me and trying to get me back on my feet. Strangers were also used, like the sheriff in the last jail I was in.

Penthouse: Why had you been arrested?

Cash: I didn't really find out until the sheriff told me, 'cause I'd been so high at the time that I didn't know *what* I was doing. I'd been out banging on somebody's door, trying to get in to use the telephone after wrecking my jeep in the woods in north Georgia—I had no idea where. The next day I woke up in the Lafayette jail, and the sheriff there unlocked my cell and led me out to his desk. He put a tray on his desk and said, "Here's your money—and here's your dope . . . Now get out of here and go kill yourself." I said, "What? What do you *mean*, 'go kill myself'?" And he told me, "You got the power to do it and you're trying to, so go ahead and finish the job. You don't have far to go." I said, "I don't *want* to kill myself." And he answered, "Of course you do. You almost *did*. When we brought you in here I called a doctor and he gave you a shot and put you to sleep. But he said you evidently want to kill yourself, so there's your dope—go ahead and do it." That was the turning point.

Penthouse: Are the religious songs you now sing in your shows a result of your giving up drugs?

Cash: No, I always sang those songs—but I never did sing them with the feeling and the free spirit I have since I quit the dope. You know, I used to sing "Were You There When They Crucified My Lord?" while I was stoned on amphetamines. I used to sing all those gospel songs, but I never really felt them. And maybe I was a little bit ashamed of it at the time because of the hypocrisy of it all: there I was, singing the praises of the Lord and singing about the beauty and peace you can find in Him—and I was stoned. And, miserable; I was climbing the walls. But regardless of how I felt inside, those songs have always been a part of me. They're the first songs I ever heard—and I know this sounds corny, but they're the first songs my mother sang to me. Gospel songs are the ones I love the most, and I can never wait for the part of my show when I sing them.

Penthouse: Is that the high point of a night's work for you?

Cash: It's just *one* of the high points, because I really brighten up when my wife June comes out to sing with me. She's my spotlight, and there's a magic to her that just fires me up about the time I really start getting tired onstage. And I also enjoy singing things like "The Ballad of Ira Hayes," which is one of four Peter La Farge songs about American Indians that I've recorded. Peter is a great writer and through him I came to love the American Indian. We were very close just before he died about ten years ago, and I just sat up a lot of long nights listening to his songs and stories about his people. I've always loved Indian legends, and by now I've got about a thousand books on the subject.

Penthouse: A number of press reports have stated that you're part Cherokee. Are you?

Cash: No. I have no Indian ancestry. Some folks have said I do, but *I* can't find it anywhere—and I've got my family tree. Of course, when I used to get high, well, the higher I got, the more Indian blood I thought I had in me. And a lot of people wanted me to be part Indian, especially after I recorded the *Bitter Tears* album.

Penthouse: Have you performed those songs before Indian audiences?

Cash: I sang 'em at Wounded Knee eight years ago. I went there to help the Sioux raise money to build a school; back then Indians hadn't started to speak out for themselves, and neither had any national figures.

Penthouse: In view of your efforts on behalf of prisoners and Indians, a number of people were surprised when, after returning from a tour through Vietnam, you declared yourself "a dove with claws."

Cash: I thought that was *awful* clever of me at the time—and now I wonder where I ever got that stupid line. My thoughts about Vietnam really had to do with our boys over there. Like one night at Long Binh air base, a Pima Indian boy—crying, and with a beer in his hand—came up to the stage while I was singing "The Ballad of Ira Hayes," which is about the Pima Indian marine who helped raise our flag at Iwo Jima. At the end of the song, that young Indian asked me to take a drink of his beer, and with the tears running off his chin, he said, "I may die tomorrow, but I want you to know I ain't never been so alive as I am tonight."

Things like that made me want to support our guys, because I loved them so much. I knew they didn't want to be there, which is why I went over myself. I was asked to come to Vietnam and I was paid well, but right away we all got caught up in the whole thing. Pretty soon June,

Carl Perkins, and I were doing seven and eight shows a day, sometimes for only ten people in a hospital ward. Anyway, please forgive me for saying I'm "a dove with claws."

Penthouse: Not long after your return from Vietnam you were invited to perform at the White House and created a stir when you refused to sing the two songs President Nixon had reportedly requested—"Okie from Muscogee," which puts down longhairs, and "Welfare Cadillac," which characterizes welfare recipients as cheats growing affluent on the public dole.

Cash: I think everybody got that whole thing wrong, because the president didn't ask me to do those songs—one of his secretaries did. I think they wanted me to believe President Nixon was familiar with my music, but evidently they'd just picked up a copy of *Billboard*, found a couple of songs in the Top Ten—and then took it from there. I simply told them, "Look, 'Okie from Muscogee' is Merle Haggard's song, it's identified with him, and I won't do it because it wouldn't be proper. As for 'Welfare Cadillac,' well, I've heard the song once, I don't like it, and it doesn't say anything I want to say. If the request actually does come from the president, tell him that our program is already planned and that I certainly hope he'll be pleased with what we do."

Incidentally, I took my daddy with me to the White House that night, which is one of the main reasons I went. He was a soldier in World War I, and in 1916 he served with General Pershing's forces and helped chase Pancho Villa back across the Mexican border after Villa had burned down Columbus, New Mexico. My daddy's a patriot and gave me a sense of history and a strong love for my country. And I really enjoyed walking around the White House, seeing the paintings and other things—like the room where Andrew Jackson's mountaineers came and swung on the curtains and poured their moonshine on the carpets.

Anyway, the White House performance took place in 1970, and at the time President Nixon was very popular, but it probably wouldn't have mattered if I'd been asked during the start of the scandals—I would've gone, because it was a performance at the White House. I was glad to go.

Penthouse: Did Watergate upset you?

Cash: Yeah, it really made me sick—sick and ashamed. But Watergate is just another growing pain, another lesson for us, and I think eventually we'll be a greater country because of it. Right now, you're watching a housecleaning going on. You know, even though we're set up on a capitalistic system, Congress picked Rockefeller to pieces during the vice-presidential hearings; they really put him down, because of all of his money. In a way, they were putting down the very system the government stands for, and I think that's some much-needed housecleaning right there. There are going to be quite a few changes made because of Watergate.

In time, we're going to see that the whole Watergate mess was one of the best things that ever happened in the U.S. I may be dead wrong, of course, but I think Watergate is gonna make us a better democracy: the people are going to rule. That's really what I say in "Ragged Old Flag." We've had some hellish wars that have just about torn the country apart, and now we've had these scandals. Well, the flag is symbolic of the spirit of the people and of the way of life we've cut out for ourselves. Sure, our flag may have holes in it, and it may be ragged and tattered and torn—but it's still waving. It's going to overcome. The *people* will overcome—and our government will be set up the way the people want it to be set up. That's going on *now*; it may not look like it, but that's just because we're housecleaning.

Penthouse: And apparently—judging by your attendance this fall at the trial of Haldeman, Ehrlichman, et al.—you don't wish to see any dust swept under the rug. What prompted you to show up in the courtroom?

Cash: James Neal, the government's prosecuting attorney in the Watergate trial, is also my attorney, and he invited June and me to sit in on our way back from an afternoon with Billy Graham in Norfolk, Virginia. So we went, and we heard the tape of Nixon talking to Haldeman on June 23, 1972, which was a cover-up conversation.

I had a chance to talk to Haldeman. As a matter of fact, he was the first man I saw when I walked into the courtroom, and his mouth dropped open and mine did, too. He immediately turned to someone else and then looked back at me with an expression on his face like, "What the hell is *he* doing here?" When the court took a recess I walked over to him and introduced myself and he said, "I tell you, James Neal is really giving me a lick today. Not only is he on the other side, but he's got my favorite entertainer on the other side with him." I told Haldeman, "Wait a minute. I'm not on any side. I'm here as a spectator. You're a piece of American history, whether you like it or not, and I'm just here to witness it."

He asked if we could go have a cup of coffee together, so June and I went out with him and Ehrlichman, who never *did* say anything except hello. At the table, the first thing Haldeman asked was, "You've been on the hot seat, haven't you?" And I told him I sure had been—he was talking about the couple of times I'd been before a judge on pill busts. He said, "You know how it feels?" And I said, "Yeah, it don't feel good, does it?" Then he started to say, "Look, I just want you to know—" and I interrupted him and told him, "Wait a minute, you don't have to explain anything to *me*. I'm not here to decide what side I'm on. I'm only here to witness." He went on, though, and said, "I just want you to know that I did what I thought was right at the time. I was only trying to do my job." I told him I wasn't questioning that, and then we talked about the music business.

After we left Washington, June and I talked about Haldeman a lot. I really liked him as a person, and he seemed exactly what the president of the U.S. needed for that job. I think he was doing what he was told to do, and also making recommendations on his own that he thought were right. And the whole thing still makes me sick.

Penthouse: Do you think you're becoming something of a political radical?

Cash: No, I sure don't. I look at it the other way: I'm just trying to be a good Christian. You know, there's three different kinds of Christians. There's preaching Christians, church-playing Christians, and there's practicing Christians—and I'm trying very hard to be a practicing Christian. If you take the words of Jesus literally and apply them to your everyday life, you discover that the greatest fulfillment you'll ever find really does lie in giving. And that's why I do things like prison concerts. Compared to that, projects like the television series I did, for example, have very little meaning for me.

Penthouse: Did you enjoy weekly TV?

Cash: It was all right the first year, but I soon came to realize I was just another piece of merchandise to the network, a cog in their wheel, and when the wheel started squeaking and wobbling, they'd replace me with another cog. Besides that, I began to feel as if every part of my personal and family life was being merchandised and exploited; I felt as if they were stealing my soul. To get ratings, they immediately started putting guests on my show that I couldn't—if you'll pardon the expression—relate to. People about whom I felt nothing, and that just made me uncomfortable. Eventually I was walking around thinking, "I don't have to do this. What am I doing this for?"

Penthouse: If weekly television was such a bummer for you, why have you agreed to do a new series next fall?

Cash: Because it's a dramatic show that won't give me the same problems. I'm going to play a character named John Andrew Jackson Stone, a country boy who's been through Vanderbilt Law School and who's a detective in the Nashville police department. Actually, I'm playing Johnny Cash as a policeman. The character has always wanted to be a singer, and the Nashville music scene will be part of the show. The whole thing grew out of a guest shot I did on "Columbo" last year.

Penthouse: What kind of acting ambitions do you have?

Cash: None. I've never had any ambition to become an actor, because I love music much, much more than I could ever love acting. But I think I'll enjoy playing myself in the series, and another good thing about it is that it'll keep me home for five months—we're gonna be filming in and around Nashville. That'll give me a lot of time to sit around and talk to songwriters, and that's important.

Penthouse: Why?

Cash: Because it winds up with me writing songs. Like, if I'm around Bob Dylan, well, he doesn't talk much. He's a very quiet, kind person who loves his wife and children very much. We're in different worlds—he's a few years younger than I am and from Minnesota, and to him, Johnny Cash was always somebody from the South who sang those country songs. I think he has a great respect for my work and I certainly have a great respect for *his*, but it's not like we can't wait to get together to sit down and write a song. Actually, we *did* write a song together once when he visited me at home. We were fishing at my boat dock and when we sat down to eat lunch we wrote "Wanted Man"—and we could hardly wait to get through with that song so we could go back to fishing. What I get from him is the same thing I get from all great songwriters: inspiration. It's like, I'll hear something they've written and think, "Why couldn't I write that—that's the way *I* think, too." Maybe it's more like a challenge than an inspiration, because after I've sat around with guys like Dylan or Kris Kristofferson and they've gone, I'll think, "Yeah, that's a good song he wrote, but maybe I can do better." And at that point I'll start writing.

Penthouse: Do you have the same effect on other songwriters?

Cash: I think so. Especially when I have the songwriters' parties at my house, which is every three or four months or so. We'll sit in the living room and pass the guitar around, and anybody there who sings and writes knows they're going to have to come up with something. That sure motivates *me* to write, because I know I'll be in the hot seat sometime during the night, so I've got to have a song good enough to compete with what these other people will present. It's really a thing we all look forward to, and sometimes those nights have been memorable.

Penthouse: One final question: The people who know you best seem to think you have a mystic destiny. Do you feel that way, too?

Cash: I don't know what's in store for me, but I know there's things I'm going to do that I haven't touched on yet. I don't know what they are, but I feel it. It's almost like when I was seventeen years old and my mother heard me sing for the first time after my voice had dropped. She said, "God's hand is on you, you're going to be a well-known singer." I smiled at her and said, "Oh, momma." But I knew it myself. Back then, the big deal was singing on the radio—and when I was seventeen years old, I *knew* that I'd be singing on the radio. And that people would know my name. So yes, I feel there are things I'm going to do, but I don't know what they are. I'm writing a book about my experiences and beliefs, but that's not it. And the TV series may work out, but *that's* not it either. I'm not yet sure what's meant for me, but I believe I've got a lot to do—and whatever it is, I hope it's worthwhile.

INTERVIEW

Áine O'Connor | 1975 | RTÉ Ireland

As Johnny Cash told Áine O'Connor in this 1975 interview for RTÉ Ireland, he first came to Ireland on vacation at the start of his Columbia recording career, circa 1958. That trip birthed a notable Cash song about Ireland: "Forty Shades of Green." He would later say, "I was in a car with a road map of Ireland in my lap rhyming the names, the names in Ireland just beg to be sung anyway. To get the title, I guess I just looked out the window and there they were, the 'Forty Shades of Green.'"

Columbia first released "Forty Shades of Green" as the B-side to Cash's 1961 single "The Rebel—Johnny Yuma," the theme song to the hit television series of the same name. In 1963, it was included on *Ring of Fire: The Best of Johnny Cash*, although not released as a single. Despite the lack of promotion, over the years "Forty Shades of Green" would develop into something of a standard in Ireland, with Cash becoming increasingly beloved in both The Republic and the North. According to Cash biographer Robert Hilburn, four years after this RTÉ interview, "battling factions in the ongoing Catholic-Protestant conflict called a truce to allow [Cash's] performance in a Belfast church to proceed. Leaders of the opposing factions even sat across the aisle from each other."

In conversation with Áine O'Connor, Cash did not directly speak about the four Columbia albums he released that year. Nor did O'Connor inquire. But she did ask, and he answered, about material from his recently published bestselling autobiography, *Man in Black*. He made clear the increasing role his faith was playing in his life. He reiterated the dangers of the addictions he was working to manage and offered yet another answer to the question of why he always dressed in black. —Ed.

[**Áine O'Connor:** Why do you dress in black?]

Johnny Cash: In '55, when I started with the Tennessee Two, our first public concert was in a church. And we were looking around for shirts and clothes that matched, y'know, some kind of uniform look that we could wear, and the only thing we had alike was black, and I said, "Black would be better for church." So we wore black that night, and it became a kind of trademark. I got away from it for a couple of years, but we got back to it, and it's what I've always felt comfortable in, so it's what I've continued to wear.

O'Connor: When did you start songwriting?

Cash: As long as I can remember I've been writing songs. Poems. I didn't call them songs when I was a kid. I called them song poems. I never did write music, but it's something I've always done.

O'Connor: Are you from a musical background yourself?

Cash: Not a professional musical background. My mother played piano and guitar, and so did her sisters. There's a lot of music in the family, all right.

O'Connor: Has your wife influenced your music?

Cash: I think so. You know, June's mother started recording in 1927. Mother Maybelle Carter. And she's still very active. She's with us on most of our concerts, though she was not able to come to Europe this time. But on June's side of the family, the country music roots go way back to the '20s. And I've always loved the Carter Family songs. I know many, many of them. And I think probably in a way the Carter family style of songs influenced me, yes.

O'Connor: You only took up music seriously when you came back after the war.

Cash: Right.

O'Connor: Did the war affect you very much, in the kind of things you started writing when you came back?

Cash: No, you see, I wasn't in the Korean War. I was in the Air Force at that time, but I was not in the war. I was in Germany. I was there for three years. I think it's during that three years of semi-isolation, so far as friends, family, and home is concerned, that I really began seriously thinking about a career in the music business. 'Cause it's really all I lived for. And when I got back to the United States, I knew that sooner or later I would be in the music business, because it's what I had to do.

O'Connor: Did you see yourself then as being a big star at that time, or did you merely want to earn a living out of playing music?

Cash: No. Becoming a big star never entered my mind. The thing I always thought about was back then, you have to remember, it was just radio. I wanted to be a radio star. Wanted to be a radio singer, and I thought if I sang on the radio station in Memphis, Tennessee, that'd be about as big as you could get. Because that's the station I listened to. A little station. Well, not a little station, a big station really—WMPS, Memphis. And when we worked in the fields, we'd come in for the noonday meal and we'd listen to WMPS, to the country music shows and the gospel music shows, and I always thought that if I could ever sing on that noonday show on WMPS, that would be as high as you could get.

O'Connor: Were you ever a tenor? I'd heard that you were a tenor one time.

Cash: Mm-hmm. I was. Up until I was seventeen. [*Laughter.*] When I cut wood all day with my dad—we'd cut wood for the winter's fire, you know. And I think that hard work that day is what made the voice drop, because I came in singing that night from the woods and it was very low. My mother noticed it.

O'Connor: So you never looked back after that? [*Laughs.*]

Cash: No.

O'Connor: Who influenced you the most in your music, do you think?

Cash: Whoever was popular. The first ones I remember were the Carter Family, Jimmie Rodgers, then later on there was Ernest Tubb and Hank Snow, the Louvin Brothers, who were very popular in Memphis. Smilin' Eddie Hill, all the local singers.

O'Connor: Do your songs express your attitudes to life, would you say?

Cash: In a lot of ways, yes. You know, sometimes it's pretty hard to separate a man from his—I like to call it *art*—when it's so much a part of him, you know. Like my faith is part of me, and that shines through in some of the songs. I've always sung gospel, spirituals, and I've always enjoyed it because it's a part of me, and I still do a lot of that, especially in the concerts. A lot of the songs are from true experiences, a lot are from imaginary tales that I've dreamed up, but a lot of them—like, for instance, "Five Feet High and Rising" is really a slice of life the way I knew it, about a flood I was in. And a song like "Pickin' Time" tells about life on the cotton farm the way I remember it.

O'Connor: You said in your book that . . . part of it was about avoiding the pitfalls of the entertainment world. What kind of pitfalls?

Cash: Well, I was talking about the things that caused my heartache and pain in the first place. I was talking about the pills and the booze. The dope.

O'Connor: What was the situation, do you think, gave rise to you having that problem? Was it the strain of having to . . . ?

Cash: Yes. I think so. I was very vulnerable because at the time—this was like fifteen years ago—I was, y'know, trying everything. I was a rambler, I was a rounder, I'd gotten away from the faith that I had as a child. And I was trying everything that came along. Whatever was going around, I was having some.

O'Connor: Would you have any advice to give to a young country music singer, say, starting off in this country? It's very popular here, as you know.

Cash: Well, I would just say: be sure you know that it's what you want to do. And then don't stop trying. Because it might be the ninety-second time you tried that you finally make it.

[**O'Connor:** When did you first come to Ireland?]

Cash: The first time I was in Ireland was 1957 or '58. I came here on vacation. Spent ten days here. It was on the way home from that vacation that I wrote "Forty Shades of Green." Because we loved the country, and I wanted to say that in a song. How much we did love it.

O'Connor: No Irish grannies tucked away anywhere, no?

Cash: [*Laughs.*] I don't think so, no.

CASH COMES BACK

Patrick Carr | 1976 | *Country Music*

Patrick Carr met Johnny Cash in 1972. In time, Carr would be the writer with whom Cash spoke on record the most.

Carr had been a Cash fan since his 1950s childhood in Hull, East Yorkshire, England, when his elder brother got his hands on the Sun singles. Of his relationship with Cash, Carr says, "It was not exactly a friendship. It was a beast of its own color. But with some people you have some sort of bond. That was true with Cash and me from the start. We shared an interest in a lot of stuff. There's even a vague possibility we were related genetically. My wife and June were certainly related. Cash's people came from an area in the eastern highlands of Scotland, and so did my mother's people. My mother's people came from the glen next door to the glen Cash's people came from. We were both amateur historians. That's what we read. We shared books. Of all of the people with whom I dealt, he was probably the one with whom I had the firmest bond."

The occasion of this 1976 *Country Music* magazine piece was Cash's "comeback" album *One Piece at a Time*, featuring the Wayne Kemp–penned number-one single of the same name. It was Cash's fifty-fourth LP.

A novelty song about a GM factory worker who steals car parts piece by piece over several years to assemble his own vehicle, "One Piece at a Time" almost didn't happen. Despite what Cash says in this interview, according to bassist and longtime road manager Marshall Grant, and biographer Robert Hilburn, Cash wasn't impressed with a demo of the song. Grant heard potential but had to talk his boss into recording it. It would be Cash's first hit since 1971.

Since the dawn of the 1970s, Cash's recorded output had steadily lost focus, and sales slumped. His contemporaries Willie Nelson and Waylon Jennings—inspired in part by

Cash's raw 1960s work—had turned their backs on Nashville to spearhead the "Outlaw" movement, releasing critically acclaimed, seminal albums that sold well. Cash, meanwhile, had remained within the strictures of the Nashville country music establishment, relinquishing control, offering inconsistent fare.

Patrick Carr maintains the diffuse nature of Cash's early 1970s work was due in part to fallout from *The Johnny Cash Show*. Of the television series, Carr says, "[Cash] said it flat out: TV killed his recording career. I think it's a syndrome. The same thing happened to Glen Campbell. This person is a musician, and people are not used to seeing him or her as a person, and can imagine all manner of things about him or her. This character on vinyl exists in people's imaginations much more than it does in real life. Television destroys that. This person is now a character, another character on TV, a person one can like or dislike. The mystery is gone. The magic is gone."

Carr thinks politics also adversely affected Cash's sales. In all their published conversations, Carr insistently seeks Cash's political opinions. Cash protests, but never holds back.

"His politics set him apart," Carr says. "Most of the people working in the country music industry did not share his political beliefs. I asked Cash about politics because of a couple very public things he'd done. One was when he went to Vietnam with June to see for himself. He did shows for the troops in Vietnam, and came back, and made a public declaration that he thought that war was immoral and unwinnable. He and June were shocked and horrified by what they saw, specifically the choppers unloading the corpses, for instance. What the soldiers themselves told them about how it was, and how it all worked. The other thing was that famous thing with him and Richard Nixon. When he was invited to the White House to perform [in 1970] and Nixon asked him to sing Merle Haggard's 'Okie from Muskogee' and Guy Drake's 'Welfare Cadillac.' [Both songs play on Conservative Republican sympathies.] And he refused. He did 'Man in Black' and 'What Is Truth' and 'The Ballad of Ira Hayes' [songs that do *not* play on Conservative Republican sympathies] instead."

In one of the more compelling dichotomies of Cash's life, despite his leftward politics, his and June's alliance with deeply conservative evangelist Billy Graham strengthened through the 1970s.

Throughout, Cash was touring consistently, keeping a sizable retinue employed. The road, not record sales income, was his bread and butter, and would be until the 1990s. Marshall Grant writes about this early to mid-1970s period in his autobiography *I Was There When It Happened*. Cash would book studio time, but Grant says, "When he did [show up], his mind often wasn't on recording. We'd had so much success with our records it just wasn't important to him anymore; he seemed content to just sit back and enjoy life." Even after Cash had purchased the Plantation Dinner Theater near his Hendersonville home in 1969 and transformed it into a state-of-the-art studio, the House of Cash, he had little enthusiasm for recording.

Yet he was obliged to deliver product to Columbia Records.

With the happy accident that was the "One Piece at a Time" single, the accompanying LP was seen as a comeback and energized him. The back-to-basics affair harkened to the sonics of Cash and the Tennessee Three's classics. It all grew from the debut single, for which Cash and producer Charlie Bragg employed old hands W. S. "Fluke" Holland (drums), Marshall Grant, and Bob Wootton (guitar). Cash credited everything to "Johnny Cash and the Tennessee Three," a moniker he'd not used since the early 1960s. In addition to the titular single, the album offered Cash's underrated "Committed to Parkview," convincingly sung from the point of view of a mental patient. In 1985, he would re-record it with the Highwaymen—Willie Nelson, Kris Kristofferson, and Waylon Jennings—for their hit debut album. *One Piece at a Time* also included "Love Has Lost Again" by Cash's twenty-one-year-old daughter, Rosanne.

"One Piece at a Time" was Johnny Cash's last number one. —Ed.

When *One Piece At A Time* went to Number One on the country singles charts it was plain that Cash was back, and this time in high style. Since the late Sixties, Cash's records have been rather strange—more the recorded evidence of a great artist floundering in confusion than the masterful products of Cash's own unique mold. The hardness, the humor, the songwriting genius, that rockabilly "magic thumb," were hard to find on those records, and most of them failed to reach the top.

Meanwhile, however, Cash was still a major force. His charisma continued to make him the most respected and perhaps the most interesting country singer of our time, and it seemed that even if he never produced any more music from the top of his form, he'd still be The Man. But it also seemed that in place of John R. Cash the musician, we might have to settle for Johnny Cash the public figure—author, folklorist, preacher, patriot, figurehead and moral backbone.

Two years ago, when I interviewed him in New York, it seemed that Cash was aware of this theme, and didn't like it. We discussed his plans to return to the old Sun Records sound by recording with the

Tennessee Three, producer/songwriter Jack Clement, and Waylon Jennings—his old colleagues from the crazy days which produced most of his strongest material and just about all of his big hits. My impression then was that some sort of life cycle had ended for Cash; that he was through re-adjusting himself to pill-less reality, finding his sanity and accomplishing the kind of goals represented by his religion, his family life, and the House of Cash, and that now he might be secure enough to begin playing again.

It was encouraging to watch Cash put his plan into action at the House of Cash with Waylon, Jack and company. Though no tracks from these sessions have been released, the music was legitimately great (if a disk ever surfaces, get it) and the event re-established Cash's links with the musical world he helped create back in '56 (which is no small point; scratch today's Waylon Sound and you'll find the Cash/Clement style of the late Fifties).

The end result of Cash's decision was *One Piece At A Time* and the album named after that superb, funny, slapback single. The album definitely recalls the "old" Cash. The production is a rockabilly's joy, the singing *there*, in tune with the spirit, and the inclusion of hard-edged songs like *Committed To Parkview* and *Daughter Of A Railroad Man* does a lot to destroy the often saccharine, musically unimpressive memory of Cash's last cycle. The album stands, in 1976, as a decent example of the state of the art, and Cash is planning to follow it with more of the same, plus another delightful wrinkle—duet work with Waylon.

This time I talked to Cash on August 10th in Valley Forge, Pa. He was, as usual, frank about his music, himself, and his politics.

CARR: *When I interviewed you two years ago, you said, "It's apparent that what I've been doing is not really what the people want to hear, so I'm going to try to do something that they want to hear . . ." It strikes me, after listening to the* One Piece At A Time *album, that you've done just that.*

CASH: I meant what I said, see . . . right? I think that I did something they wanted to hear, and what they wanted to hear was what I've done best all along—and that's the three-chord ballad with the Tennessee Three. I'm glad that's what they want because I know how to do that.

CARR: *Is that what you enjoy doing most?*

CASH: Yes, it really is. It's what I enjoy most. I'm getting such a kick out of it, feeling the same things I was feeling twenty years ago in my music. It's a whole new discovery for me, y'know—like, "Hey, I remember how good this felt, and I remember when I did it like this, and *this* is the way it feels best." Y'know? I just recorded a song I wrote 18 years ago and forgot about. A song called *It's All Over.* It sounds like the things I was doing eighteen years ago, and that's the way I recorded it, with the Tennessee Three. It's a weeper, a love song. It's kind of like being reborn again. I started out with the old simple sound on Sun Records, and I enjoyed it, and the people enjoyed it. But then I went through kind of a period there. Y'know, the real problem was not that I wasn't enjoying what I was doing; it was just that I was looking for something new, seeing if there was a new way for me to do it. As it turns out, what I think I discovered was that the way I started with it, the old way I've always done it, is the way I really enjoy it.

You'd feel the atmosphere in the studio now . . . There's a lot of laughter at my sessions. There's a lot of horsing around, joking, kidding each other. It used to be like pulling teeth, like, "OK, let's get *this* over with." It's not that way anymore. It's joy, it's fun.

CARR: *During that whole period when you were messing around with arrangements and so on, were you in control? Was all that stuff your doing?*

CASH: Well, I agreed to it. That came out of a meeting I had with some Columbia Records people. They came out to my concert in Las Vegas, and they talked about, "Let's try something. Let's try this arranger. Let's try recording with the Big Sound."

CARR: *Was the arranger Gary Klein?*

CASH: Yes. For that kind of stuff, Gary is the best there is. He really knows what he's doing . . . They thought it was the way to go, and *I* didn't know for sure at the time. So I went along with it, and I let them select most of the songs—which was a mistake, because if I'm not personally involved in the music, it ain't going to be right. I'm not going to have a feeling for it when I go into the studio. So all that whole scene, as capable as Gary Klein is, was a wrong scene for me.

But I learned a lot, and somewhere along the line Gary and I will do something—something that requires the kind of taste and artistry he's got. But it's like, ah—please pardon me for getting into politics—it's like we learned from the Vietnam war not to send troops to Africa, y'know? (laughs) And by the same token, I learned from those production days with Gary Klein that *I* shouldn't do it that way any more.

CARR: *These days you're choosing your own material, right?*

CASH: Yeah. That's the big thing, too. These days I'm totally involved with it from the time I choose the songs until the thing is finished in the mix. That's another thing I didn't use to get involved in. After the session, I'd never be there for the mix. I threw a lot of good sounds away because I didn't give 'em my ideas, y'know?

Charlie Bragg works with me in the studio, and he's the one who harped on me about, "Go back to the old sound, go back to the old sound." My attitude was, "Oh, I can *always* do *that*. I want to do something else." So he mixed it the way I wanted him to. I'd tell him how I wanted it, and that's the way he'd do it—under protest. He was a mighty happy man when I got into the studio with him when he'd called a session for mixing, and I said, "Let's put the slapback on there. Let's put the old Sun slapback on there and forget about quadrophonic sound and stereo and everything, and make it sound like 1957." And I enjoyed it! I didn't think I'd enjoy it, but I did, and I got to thinking . . . "Cash, you got involved in selecting the song; you put it down the way you wanted it; you saw it through the session. It would be stupid now to stay out of the mixing—like getting a ship almost to shore, then turning it over to somebody else in the middle of a storm." So now I go in with Charlie on the mixing, and I tell him how I want it. We have some disagreements, but it always comes out the way I want it (laughs).

I'm really enjoying it. I guess that's the whole key to it. If I don't enjoy it, somehow the people out there know it. For some reason, they know it.

CARR: *Well, they usually do, don't they? That's what most of these producers forget. But how did you come by* One Piece At A Time, *John?*

CASH: Don Davis found it, and called me. Wayne Kemp was going to record it himself, but Don asked him to let me have it. They agreed, and Don brought it out to me.

CARR: *Did you know it was the one when you heard it?*

CASH: Yeah, I knew it. I knew that was it.

CARR: *That's your first Number One single in . . . oh, how long now?*

CASH: I guess since *Man in Black* . . . No, since *Flesh and Blood*, 1971. Five years.

CARR: It must feel kinda good.

CASH: It really does. It really does. It's a joy, y'know? I dunno, maybe it's 'cause I'm older now. I used to take those hit records for granted. Back when everything I was releasing was going to Number One or up in the tops, I kinda took it for granted. Like, I would never look at the trade magazines. People would say, "Congratulations on your Number One record," and I wouldn't even know it was Number One. But it's like everyone shared in the excitement of *One Piece At A Time* being Number One. Everybody in town would be calling the office or the studio, saying "It's number seven this week," and somebody would get a tip that it was going to be number four next week, and they'd call. So I started looking at the trade magazines. I still don't read 'em, but I look at the charts and see who's doing what and what's happening in the business . . . who's selling, who's not. It's kinda interesting—again.

See, I had a couple of side involvements that took a lot of time and energy—but they were awfully important to me, and they were what I wanted them to be. That was my movie and my book. And you've only got so much energy. Right now I'm putting my energy into my music.

CARR: *What about Jack Clement? Anything doing there? Are you doing any work with him?*

CASH: Well, Jack Clement is always around, and I feel like I am, too, and sooner or later Jack Clement and I will do something together again.

We didn't do too bad on *Ring Of Fire* and *Ballad Of A Teenage Queen* and *Guess Things Happen That Way*, some of those—and we'll have some ideas that gel perfectly sometime, and we'll get back in the studio together eventually.

CARR: *Is anything going to happen to those tracks you recorded with Clement and Waylon a couple years ago—the first cut on* Committed To Parkview, You're So Heavenly Minded You're No Earthly Good—*all those?*

CASH: Ah . . . We had one I really like, *Someday My Ship Will Sail.* I think Waylon and I are going to get that one out and listen to it again and see if we need to do anything to it. Waylon and I just did another session, did you know that?

CARR: *Yeah. Just this past Monday, right?*

CASH: Yeah. We cut two tracks for a single together, *I Wish I Was Crazy Again* and *There Ain't No Good Chain Gang.* I guess we're just going to call the record companies' bluff. They say we can't record an album together, but I think we're going to do it anyway, and then say "Here it is. Work something out." I guess we both could get in trouble, but I tell you what: I respect Waylon as an artist, and I think he respects me. We've been friends for 15 years and we always did enjoy working together, and just because we both happen to be professionals and make a lot of money for other people doing it, I really don't see where that should hold us back artistically. If we want to get back in the studio together, we're going to do it. I think these record companies ought to set up a subsidiary amongst them for people like us, 'cause we're going to cut an album together. No doubt. We might do some country classics like *Lost Highway*, some of those old heavy things. And we'll *do* it.

CARR: *You were talking about taking more control over your music. Did the* One Piece At A Time *album really satisfy you on that level?*

CASH: No, it just kinda got me primed and cocked for more and better to come. Like, it slipped me back into a whole new world of music and directions . . . like, I just recorded an old Presley song, *You're Right, I'm Left, She's Gone,* and I did it with trumpets like I had on *Ring Of Fire,* and

I've kind of got a sneaky feeling about that one. I *really* like the sound on it. I've always loved that song . . . so we're going to do an album of the old Sun things, the old Memphis stuff, '53 to '56. That's my next album project, the second one after *One Piece At A Time*. Some of my songs, a couple of Presley's, maybe a Carl Perkins song, a Roy Orbison song. It's not just an attempt to re-create the sound. I think we can make it sound like today's market, like today's thing, y'know? 'Cause I really enjoy it, and I search my conscience, and if I sing something I really enjoy, then that's what I ought to do. It's not always commercial, but it's what I ought to do. It's like *One Piece At A Time*. It was really what I wanted to do. I couldn't have been happier, unless it had been a song of mine.

CARR: *That song was—well, not exactly socially acceptable, you know what I mean? I mean, it was really nice to hear you sticking it to the car companies.*

CASH: Well, it's maybe back a little more towards a more realistic outlook on life, y'know? There's so many people that would like to rip off the factory. It's not a statement that's totally far out for me, because I worked at Fisher Body Company making 1951 Pontiacs in 1950. I worked as a punch press operator in Pontiac, Michigan in the factory—so I kinda had an understanding about what I was singing.

CARR: *Would you say the sentiments of the song echoed your own feelings, then?*

CASH: Probably did so. I was eighteen years old, broke, hitch-hiked to Pontiac, Michigan, got a job in the car factory and there was all this wealth of car parts rolling down the assembly line and these brand new '51 Pontiacs coming off the other end . . . I guess every one of us in that place had thoughts about driving home one of those things. Or someday owning this construction company. Y'know, everybody that's ever worked cleaning up trash for a construction company has had these thoughts in the back of his mind . . . "One of these days, I'm gonna *own* this construction company!" Well, I felt that way about Fisher Body Company. So when the song came along, it was like memory time for me.

CARR: *There was a lot of pretty hot picking on the album—a touch of the old boogie-woogie there. Are we likely to be hearing more of that from you? It's not something you've done much of in the past.*

CASH: Yeah, I think so. *City Jail*, a song I just wrote for the next album, has that boogie-woogie in there. Jerry (Hensley) is on all my sessions now, so you'll be hearing more from him.

CARR: *Have you been writing much lately?*

CASH: Ah—I haven't written anything in the last month or so, but I write in cycles, y'know. Like, when I was getting ready to do this last album, I wrote like a house on fire. And when I get ready to work on the next album, *that'll* inspire me to write some more. Yeah, I have some ideas that I'll be working on.

CARR: *You know, there's an awful lot of emotional range between a song like* Sold Out Of Flagpoles *and one like* Committed To Parkview.

CASH: Well, they're from two different slices of life, and life is made up of *all* kinds of highs and lows, ups and downs—emotions. *Sold Out Of Flagpoles* is the light, up side, and *Committed To Parkview* was somewhere . . . I've been. I still write about things I remember. I still sing *Sunday Morning Coming Down* 'cause it's something you don't shake in seven years, that kind of life. You might have become a different person, you don't live that way anymore, but it's sure not easy to forget the bad times. For the time I was singing *Committed To Parkview* I was *there*.

CARR: *Do you still have a bad time sometimes? Temptation? Despair?*

CASH: No, I'm never in despair. I'm never depressed. I got a lot on my mind sometimes, and it might seem like I'm depressed, but I never am. Temptation, yeah. I haven't fallen for it, but it still gnaws at me. It's a daily fight. But I can't afford the luxury of taking a drink or taking a pill because I'd have to have another one if I did. I *know* that. 'Cause you see, even after I quit in '67, I goofed up a few times. Several times. Nobody read about it in the papers, but I did, like when I went to the Far East in '69 and when I was in California cutting the San Quentin album. There were three or four times when I had to keep re-learning my lesson that I can't mess with it, or I'm dead. And I know that's where I'd be if I got back into that stuff. It's either a matter of life or death with me. I either don't do it and live, or I do it and die. That's the way it is.

CARR: *Is it a hard fight?*

CASH: No, it's not really, because I got it all together family-wise, love affair-wise, and everything else. I'm very much in love with my wife. I don't have any desire to fool around, and I really don't like liquor anyway. I know I'd really get a kick out of the pills for a while, but I can't do that. No, I'm really happy. I really think I'm a well-adjusted man.

CARR: *You carry a lot of responsibility. . . .*

CASH: Oh-*huh*. You bet.

CARR: *You're a figurehead, a target . . . does that bother you?*

CASH: Being a figurehead and a target and carrying a lot of responsibility? Yeah, I get, er, I really get tired of the responsibility I have to bear. But being what I am, and with the success that's come my way, that's all a part of it.

Sometimes I get *really* tired of it. Sometimes I really want to shake it all off and go sit under a tree all day and forget who I am and where I am. That doesn't happen very often, you know, I *enjoy* being Johnny Cash. I really do. Today at that press conference—all that attention—anybody would have to be crazy not to like being admired and respected that much, to have all these people fly in from all over the country just to talk to *me*. I enjoy being Johnny Cash most of the time. The only thing that really irritates me—and it really irritates me *badly*, to where I might use a little force—is these people . . . I've seen them at my office all day long, and I've seen them on the road between my office and my house, I've waited while they get out of the way so I can drive out of my driveway, I've stopped to take the pictures and sign autographs and talk to them (and I talk to them every time). And yet, when I get ready for bed and I bed down with my family for the night, they come knocking at my door. *That . . . really . . . irritates . . . me.* And I'm not gonna be responsible for what I say and do. I'm sorry to say I've been really rude to a few people. I just explode, y'know, when they come knocking at ten o'clock and say "I've driven a thousand miles, and you gotta talk to me."

But the responsibility of living up to people's expectations about what they want me to be—being a figurehead—I don't mind that. I got a lot of self-confidence. I can handle any situation I've been faced with in that line.

CARR: *What kind of feeling do you get about the industry these days, John? You know, about how music's going, how the controls are operating . . . the Outlaws thing, for instance?*

CASH: I think all of that's good, y'know. And it's nothing new. The more change there is, the healthier the whole picture is. We can't lay back on our accomplishments and achievements . . . you know, "when this runs out I'll just quit."

Now, so far as the directions in the business, the Outlaws, I think that's just another way of saying "new direction." Waylon, Willie, Tompall, all of them are saying the same things, but they're saying them differently, and as an artist I really appreciate that. Y'know, myself, back in '56, *I* had a hard time breaking into the country community in Nashville. I came up to the Grand Ole Opry to talk to Jim Denny, who was the manager of the Opry. *I Walk The Line* was Number One. I had an appointment—finally, my manger had gotten me an appointment—but I sat in his outer office for two hours before he ever saw me. Finally he let me come in, and the very first question was, "What makes you think you belong on the Grand Ole Opry?" See, I was one of those Memphis rockabillies—had sideburns—from that Memphis school of Presley and Perkins and Lewis and Orbison and Cash. It was a wonder they even let us in the city limits, the way they looked down at us at the time. Elvis had a bad experience there—a very disappointing, unsettling experience. But Jim Denny asked me that question. I believe I'd just read Dale Carnegie's "How To Win Friends And Influence People" or some such thing, so I sat back and collected my thoughts after such a brusque, abrupt invitation to conversation, and I said, "Well, I love country music—always sung it—and besides that, I have a Number One country record."

He sat and looked at me for five minutes before he ever answered me, and then he said, "When do you think you can come up here?"

But that first night, I got the feeling backstage at the Opry that there were a few of them weren't too happy to have me there. A few of them were maybe afraid of the competition (something I've really learned to appreciate is competition), but there were some of them like June Carter who really made me feel welcome. She'd worked shows with Elvis, you know, knew the Memphis scene. Then there was Minnie Pearl, and Roy Acuff, Hank Snow . . . y'see, guys like Acuff and Hank Snow are smart enough to know that people's tastes change. How many decades had they been singing, even in 1956? Acuff's smart enough to know that new people are gonna come along and be accepted, but that doesn't necessarily mean the old ones have to go cut their throats. Hank Snow had befriended Elvis. There were a few small minds who wouldn't talk to us as we walked by, but I made it. It took a while, though.

But back to your question. Rebels are going to come along and if they're not accepted they're gonna rebel until somebody notices them. But the thing that has been noticed about some of these rebels like Waylon is the *talent*. Who's going to deny Waylon's *talent*?

CARR: *You have any gripes about the industry?*

CASH: Well, the record companies in our business are all looking for the "crossover" record, and the Nashville hype is the big thing going around. These radio stations all over the country get a call from a promoter or publicist or public relations person in Nashville, saying, "jump on this one, it's a crossover record." The whole deal is trying to cut a country song with a crossover sound, a crossover feel, so it'll get on the pop stations. My friend Hugh Cherry talks about us standing in danger of country music losing its identity or its net worth, maybe, by concentrating on crossover and *not* concentrating on good country, and I think there's a lot in what he has to say.

I'm proud of the fact that my big crossover songs—*I Walk the Line* or *Folsom Prison Blues*—were *country*. In no way were they an attempt to cut a crossover song. They made it over into the other markets on their own merits.

The whole big thing now is to cut a record that'll blanket all the stations across the board, right off, and I think the music, the songs, the records are suffering. A lot of songs that could've been good country records aren't anything, because such an attempt was made to make them crossovers.

You know, take Waylon. I can't remember a record Waylon cut that sounded anything like an obvious attempt to put out a crossover record. Every record I've heard of Waylon has just been Waylon.

CARR: *John, who would you pick for the CMA Awards this year?*

CASH: Male Vocalist, Waylon. Female Vocalist? Looks like Tanya Tucker. Country Music Hall of Fame—Merle Travis. Merle Travis or Kitty Wells. They both deserve it, even though *I'm* one of the finalists. I was really surprised when I was on the list . . . really felt twenty years older.

CARR: *John, what do you think of Jimmy Carter?*

CASH: I *knew* you were gonna get around to this. How many political questions you got there, Patrick? Looks like a *bunch*.

CARR: *C'mon, John, you worry too much. That's my shopping list. There's only one question. Really, now—what do you think of him?*

CASH: Well, I think Jimmy Carter is part of the whole air of positivity in politics that has come around recently in healing this country's experience from Watergate and Vietnam. Now, Jimmy Carter—some of those who say they're voting for him are doing it because they believe what he believes, and some of them are voting for him because he believes in *something*. Whether *they* do or not, they're voting for him because *he* believes in something. "I'm not sure *I* do, but I know *he* does, so I'll vote for him . . ." That's the feeling I get from people.

I think he'll probably be the next President, and I think everything's gonna be all right. On the other side . . . well, you didn't ask me that, so I ain't gonna tell you.

CARR: *Mr. Ford?*

CASH: Looks like he's done a pretty good job.

JUNE CARTER: I like Jimmy Carter the best 'cause of family ties.

CASH: Jimmy Carter's June's fourth cousin, I believe it is. Yeah, they're cousins. *He* brought it up. He's the one who told her where the family ties lie. She was really surprised. He'd told her that before, kidding, y'know, but recently he told her the names—how they're related.

But I really think he will be the next President, and I guess that would be all right.

CARR: *You feel OK about that, huh?*

CASH: Yeah I *think* I'm going to vote for him. I think I am. I'm not gonna say for sure, but I *told* him I was gonna vote for him. That was about three months ago, and I haven't changed my mind yet.

CARR: *Has he asked you to work for him?*

CASH: Yes, he did. I haven't replied to that request, except . . . Well, I don't think it would be fair for me to *campaign* for a Presidential candidate and try to influence people that way. That's important stuff and big stuff, and I don't think I've got a right to exercise any such control over people. Voting is kind of a sacred, precious thing in this country . . . You're the first person in the press I've ever told about voting for Carter. I'm not recommending that anyone else vote for him; I just think *I'm* going to.

I didn't *refuse* to work for Jimmy. Jimmy just mentioned that he'd like for me to make an appearance with him later on this year in a key place, but I'm not sure I'm gonna be able to do that.

CARR: *Along with Jimmy Carter comes the whole notion that the South is going to be in the driver's seat if he gets elected. I wonder if you think that there's something about the South—some basic virtues, whatever— that might not go amiss in Washington? You know—the politics of love, the stress of family ties, all that?*

CASH: Yeah, but you know, I think that's a false impression that those kind of things like solid family ties are characteristically Southern. Or that faith in God is characteristically Southern. I think that's a misconception, an untrue philosophy about the South. I think that if it holds true there, it holds true in Michigan.

I think that probably there may be a *spiritual* strength that's stronger in the South, in what people very loosely refer to as the Bible Belt. I think that anybody with that spiritual strength would be a better President, a better leader, that that kind of mood and atmosphere and reliance upon . . . I think a man like that would do a better job. I'd feel safer with him in there, y'know . . . a man who relied upon that spiritual power to determine his decisions, that spiritual discretion, 'cause it gives him a sense of conscience, like a compass. And that really works—I know that for a fact, from personal experience. That conscience is awfully important, I think, when you're dealing with the lives of millions of people.

Again, I don't know if the South's got anything over any other part of the country along that line. They show more dirty movies in the South than they do anywhere else . . . I just don't know. All this doesn't answer your question very well, but I don't know how to.

CARR: *I think it does, y'know. You* did *raise the question of moral integrity—spiritual integrity—and that's not insignificant.*

CASH: "Integrity" I guess, is the word I'm trying to say. I feel that Jimmy Carter has that integrity. Not that Ford doesn't—he has that compass, too—but we're choosing a new man, and Jimmy's my choice of the new ones that are on the horizon and trying for the job.

PACIFIC COLISEUM INTERVIEW

Red Robinson | August 28, 1976 | Interview Transcript

After meeting Johnny Cash in 1959, Red Robinson solidified his place as a Canadian broadcasting icon. He would bring Roy Orbison to Canada for the first time, introduce the Beatles at the largest crowd of their 1964 North American tour, and befriend and promote a wide array of rising stars, from Glen Campbell to Michael Bublé.

A scene in Robinson's biography *The Last Deejay* (by Robin Brunet) illustrates how Cash and Robinson's relationship had evolved since 1959. It takes place just before the reprinted interview below:

"Even though years could elapse without the two seeing each other, Johnny Cash associated Vancouver with Robinson, as was the case in 1976 when he was booked into the Pacific Coliseum for a concert.

"That evening, a swarm of media types congregated outside the Coliseum, despite Cash specifying beforehand that no interviews would be granted. Eventually a limousine arrived, and Cash and June Carter stepped out. Cash coldly surveyed the members of the roped-off press, but when he spied Robinson amongst them, he broke into a grin. 'Red!' he shouted. 'Great to see you! Come on backstage and let's talk!' Robinson happily did so, to the irritation of the other reporters—and Cash's protective handlers."

In the years just preceding this conversation, *The Johnny Cash Show* had made Cash a superstar. Upon parting ways with ABC, under whose control he'd chafed, he'd gone fully independent with the ambitious film *The Gospel Road: A Story of Jesus*, which he cowrote and narrated with spoken word and song. Cash and his team shot it on location in Israel in 1971. An accompanying double album made it to number twelve on the Country Albums chart. Billy Graham's Worldwide Pictures eventually distributed the film in 1973.

While Cash had previously balked at the idea of being in the producer's chair for anything ever again, in this 1976 interview with Robinson, a fellow devout Christian, he speaks about possibly making another film. In his extensive studies, Cash had become fascinated, even obsessed, with the Apostle Paul a.k.a. Saint Paul. Cash identified with Paul (not to be confused with the Paul of the original twelve disciples), who had begun life in the first century CE as Saul of Tarsus, a Pharisee and persecutor of early Christians. According to the Book of Acts, while on the road from Jerusalem to Damascus, en route to arrest some "heretic" Jews (not yet called "Christians"), Saul had been struck by a blinding light coming from the resurrected Jesus, saying "Saul, Saul, why persecutest thou me?" After regaining his sight, he renamed himself Paul, accepted Jesus as the Messiah, and preached and wrote extensively about Jesus's teachings for the rest of his life, establishing Christian communities in Greece, Asia Minor, and Europe. He endured much persecution himself and, scholars believe, was ultimately beheaded and martyred by Nero-era Romans. Fourteen of the twenty-seven books of the New Testament are attributed partially or completely to him.

The movie of Paul's life would not happen, but Cash wouldn't let go of the story—or it wouldn't let go of him—and he would ultimately write a well-received novel about Paul, *Man in White*, published in 1986 by HarperCollins and brimming with the insight he'd acquired in his theological studies. It would be his only novel.

At the time of the 1976 Pacific Coliseum show, Cash was robust, with June as his almost constant companion, young son John Carter in tow. Today, Robinson recalls this Cash as significantly different from the man he'd known in the 1960s, a change he ascribes largely to June.

"He was more relaxed as a human being," Robinson says. "He didn't have to put on any airs. June did more for him than anybody had, ever. He would listen to her. That's the difference. He would listen to her. Carl Perkins said, 'When he met her, he changed.' Carl told me the story of them on the Mississippi River: they're fishing, and threw their bottles into the water and said, 'That's it.'"

Although the eighteen-thousand-capacity Pacific Coliseum was, according to Robinson, only "half full," he notes, "We had a good time." —Ed.

Red Robinson: Backstage at the Coliseum in Vancouver with Johnny Cash. Gee, we go back, I was thinking, John, look, I made a note here: back in September of 1956, your first hit, "I Walk the Line" . . . it's twenty years this month.

Johnny Cash: That's right, it is.

Robinson: Long time.

Cash: Sure is.

Robinson: You know John, I was gonna mention the fact that the Lord's been good to ya, and this is the second big go-round for Johnny Cash, if I could put it that way, isn't it?

Cash: Yeah, I guess it is. The second time is better, though. I'm enjoying it a lot more. I've looked back at where I've been, and I haven't looked back in regret, I've tried to make my mistakes stepping-stones instead of stumbling blocks, and like you said, God's been good to me, and I'm enjoying it right now.

Robinson: John, Country Music Month is the month of October, and of course all the country music stations in North America are running specials, as we are. What do you think has made country music the biggest music form in the world today? I mean when you and I were talking years ago, back in '59, country was part of pop, but today it's bigger than it's ever been. What do you think brought this about?

Cash: Well, it was always big to me. I always thought it would be accepted on a mass basis like it is. I guess it must be, being realistic about it, I guess I'd have to say it's network television, for one thing. It's programmed country music shows. For instance, next month we've got the Country Music Awards show from Nashville. Roy Clark and I are co-hosting that, and everybody in the business, just about, is on that show. They always have a big rating because I think people sense reality in the lyrics of country songs, and they're more country artists recording and more songs being written and the business is much more competitive and the best is bein' released, and it's been presented to television and more and more radio.

Robinson: Don't you think there's a swing from the '60s back to the real roots about what our North American life is all about too, by the population?

Cash: Well, I think so. I think so. I really think so. People are getting back to the country, one way or another, back to the roots, and they're finding the roots in country music.

Robinson: John, you have a television series coming up, actually a show where you're appearing again as you did on *Columbo—Little House on the Prairie.*

Cash: Mm-hmm. I believe that's October twenty-second or twenty-third, somewhere along in there. June and I both have dramatic roles in that show.

Robinson: You play husband and wife, and I was kidding, I said, "How'd they come up with *that*?" [*Laughter.*]

Cash: [*Laughter.*] Yes, we do. We play husband and wife. It's really interesting, and it was a very exciting thing for us as well. I think the people will enjoy it.

Robinson: You've gone a little bit into production, if I just may throw this in here, with your movie made in Israel. That must have been an exciting time for you.

Cash: It really was. We produced *Gospel Road*, our story of Jesus. That was in '71, finally released in '73. It's distributed now by Worldwide Pictures, and it's showing in a lot of places, in a lot of churches right now. We have in mind to possibly do another one next year—the life of the Apostle Paul.

Robinson: Beautiful.

Cash: It's a major undertaking. It'll be a slice of our life that we put into that if we can make it come about.

Robinson: I remember when I talked to you about an album series you did years ago called *Ride This Train*. The two versions are in the Library of Congress. I imagine this has got to be too.

Cash: Well, I'm not sure about that, but it was awfully important work to us.

Robinson: John, you've got to go on and do a show here. I want to thank you for taking a few moments with us. God be with you wherever you go, and have a continued tremendous career.

Cash: Thank you, Red. Good to see you again.

JOHNNY CASH'S FREEDOM

Patrick Carr | April 1979 | *Country Music*

When Patrick Carr met Johnny Cash in New York City in 1979 to discuss his latest album, *Gone Girl*—released in November of 1978—Cash was touring almost nonstop. Since his 1976 number-one single "One Piece at a Time," follow-ups "I Would Like to See You Again" and "Chain Gang" had been modest hits, yet Cash was still in a slump commercially, and his dependence issues had once again grown acute. Still, he remained largely untouchable as a live performer. Although Carr and Cash spoke enthusiastically about *Gone Girl*, none of its three singles would crack the Top 20.

Cash mentioned his annoyance with his producer Larry Butler being "busy producing some big artist" and temporarily unavailable. That artist was Kenny Rogers, whose "The Gambler" Butler had recently recorded with both Cash and Rogers. Rogers's version of the Don Schlitz song had been released before Cash's and became a Grammy-winning crossover hit, Rogers's signature song. (Bobby Bare and Schlitz himself had also released earlier versions, to little acclaim.)

Since his 1976 interview with Carr, Cash had invested significant energy outside of music. His and June's earlier career ambitions had prevented them from being present for their children by previous marriages, and they'd resolved to make up for it with their only child, John Carter, born in 1970, upon whom they doted. Cash had appeared in the hit television series *Little House on the Prairie*, starred in TV movie *Thaddeus Rose and Eddie*, engaged in more Bible study, and guested on many Billy Graham Crusades with June. (They would ultimately appear in close to forty Crusades, testifying before an estimated two million people.) He knew his public affirmations of faith could be misconstrued as proselytizing, and likely harmful to his career, but he was unfazed and unapologetic.

Although he hadn't been nominated since his historic 1969 sweep, Cash had recently hosted the Country Music Awards for the fourth and final time. (He'd MC'd in 1973, 1974, 1977, and 1978.)

They didn't speak of it directly—probably on purpose, so as not to draw focus from *Gone Girl*—but in early 1979, Cash was putting the finishing touches on a gospel double album, *A Believer Sings the Truth*, to be released later that year. While not a smash, it would be reissued in various forms into the twenty-first century. Cash had undertaken it partially in tribute to Sara Carter, the last of the original Carter Family, who had died in January of 1979. Cash also honored his favorite singer of all time, Sister Rosetta Tharpe, by recording three of her songs on *A Believer Sings the Truth*. By all accounts, he brought more enthusiasm to that endeavor than to his secular material.

In addition to the loss of Sara Carter, Mother Maybelle had passed in 1978, and her husband Ezra "Eck" Carter in 1975—all deeply beloved by Johnny Cash. And while Cash had long since fallen out of touch with his old Sun buddy, Elvis Presley's 1977 death by heart attack at age forty-two loomed large over Carr and Cash's conversation.

The 1980s were on the horizon. Within a year, the film *Urban Cowboy* would bring a new era of country/pop crossovers and even more focus on youth and newness in country music. Cash's alienation from the mainstream will deepen, Jimmy Carter and hopes of a "Christian revival in America" will be history, and the Man in Black's life will take some historically wild turns. —Ed.

His story and his accomplishments are too familiar to tell again, but the man himself is something else. Once a prisoner of fame, he travelled towards middle age as the very definition of uptown country respectability, the Country Music Association's symbol of class. In those, recent years, he seemed like a rock, immobile, dignified, and maybe also slightly bored. But now it's plain that this period, like his lost days in the early 1960's, was a phase. Today Johnny Cash has regained his freedom. His new album **Gone Girl** is a clear reflection of that freedom. In this exclusive Country Music interview, Cash speaks frankly to Patrick Carr about the change and how it feels.

Cash was not like I thought he would be. Yes, he was big and charismatic and hot with the nervous energy that is his key to other people's attention, but he was also loose, funny, and very much alive. That, the first time I met him in earnest, was four or five years ago. Maybe his mood had something to do with the fact that he was recording with his old room mate Waylon Jennings for the first time, and with his old producer/songwriter Jack "Cowboy" Clement for the first time since Sun days; certainly, it betokened something good in the wind for music fans.

This time around with Cash, it was obvious from the start that with his best album in more than a decade under his belt, he had committed himself back to fun and music with all his heart. When you think about it, you have to say that after all, he had more staying power, more strength, than any of those Sun boys.

We began, of course, by talking about music.

Carr: *The last time we talked, John, you spoke about making albums more like the old Johnny Cash . . . You know, without a lot of fancy orchestration and stuff.*

Cash: Yes, well, that's what we're trying to do. We're trying to make it sound a bit more like something that was done today, rather than back in 1955, but we had a lot of things going on with the **Gone Girl** album. First of all, we had fun making it, we enjoyed it. We had my people that I enjoy working with—The Carter Family, Jan Howard, my group—and Jack Clement came in and played rhythm guitar. He's always a ball on sessions—or usually, anyway. Yes, we enjoyed doing the album.

Larry Butler had been busy producing some big hit artist, and about the time that I wanted to do the album he was right in the middle of it. I had to wait a while, and I got a little frustrated, and he knew I got a little frustrated, and finally we got together on a date. We didn't have words or anything, but I wanted in the studio—when I wanted in, I wanted *in*.

The album came after a trip that June and Jan Howard and Jack Clement and I took to New York City. We went up and saw a couple of plays, and we sat up at night and picked and sang, and we got into some old songs like *A Bar With No Beer* and *Careless Love* and *Always Alone and Born To Lose*, all those old things. Then we got into bluegrass, uptempo stuff. Then we got to doing Jagger and Richard's song *No*

Expectations, and Jack said, "Let's do it bluegrass style." I said, "It don't quite fit bluegrass style, but let's do it uptempo," so we got to doing *No Expectations*. Jan Howard knew it—she'd sung it before on the Grand Ole Opry—so she gave us the words for it. So we sang *No Expectations* perhaps forty times during the whole evening, and when we quit singing it the people next door called the room and said, "Please play some more!" We thought we'd been keeping everybody up.

That's the kind of spirit we had in the studio when we recorded the album—you know, we were having fun.

The musicians know that too, see. It's awfully important to the musicians to feel that the artist is not acting like a star and not acting like the boss; he's acting like someone you're having fun with. That's what my guys felt in the studio that day. They were talking and laughing and cutting up and kidding Jack Clement about this and that, trying to make him balance a glass on the top of his head and do different kinds of dances. So we went and had a lot of fun. Everybody was loose and laughing, and that's what helped to make it work.

But way before that I did a lot of homework. I weeded out a whole lot of songs. There were a lot of songs I didn't record on that album that I *wanted* to record, because I've been looking for good songs. You know who I've been listening to a lot? Tom T. Hall. Tom T. Hall has got to be the greatest country songwriter alive. I went to the K-Mart to buy a Tom T. Hall album the other day, just to hear some more of his songs. So I've got some of his songs laid back that I want to do—things he did on albums and didn't release as singles. But he's got so much great stuff.

It's not only him, either. There's other people like Rodney Crowell. Rodney has some good songs, and I'm holding some of his. I wanted to do some more of his on the album, but I didn't have room for them. So I'm looking forward to my next album, and I'm going to do my homework before I go in. And if everybody's not enjoying themselves and having fun when we get in the studio, then we'll just go home.

Carr: *Cancel the session?*

Cash: Right. After all these years, I realize that it's not especially the quality of the studio, who's got the best equipment, who's got the best sound. Jack Clement's studio happens to have a *great* sound and *great* equipment, which is why I picked that studio at that time, but I may do another session at the old Quonset Hut, Columbia Studio B, where I recorded so many times. I think I may do my next album there, because it'd be like memory time for me. Back in the Sixties I was there so many times with the Statler Brothers and the Carter Family and my group, back in times when I was having my own particular kind of fun and everyone else was sitting around waiting for old Johnny Cash to get ready to record—but now I think we could go back in there and have a good time. We may go back there, and we may go back to Jack Clement's studio, but either way . . .

Carr: *The key to it all is atmosphere, right?*

Cash: Exactly. Well, first of all, there's the songs. So I'm going to do my homework. Do a lot of listening to Tom T. Hall and Rodney Crowell and some other people.

Carr: *What other people?*

Cash: Well I really like John Prine and Steve Goodman. I got two of their songs I'm going to try, see if the feeling's right. I've got several songs myself. I've been writing like crazy. I've got enough for an album of my own things that I've written since we did the **Gone Girl** album.

Carr: *Things sound good. Sounds like you're really cooking these days.*

Cash: Well, you know I've sold my recording studio 'cause I never was interested in it in the first place. I don't know why I ever wanted one out here. I guess I do, too: because I could get Charlie Bragg to run it, and I believed in him as an engineer. But now we've gotten rid of that studio, which became kind of a burden, and Charlie's got a good job somewhere else, and the girls downstairs are turning it into a museum—which leaves me free. I guess that's it. That's another word that is important in this, too, Patrick. I feel free, you know. If I want to go to California and record, I'll do it. I'm not saying I will, but I might.

Carr: *It's getting some of that big Cash load off your back, all those responsibilities. . . .*

Cash: That's right. They're usually the ones I want to bear anyway, but things like that studio you look back on and say, "Hey, that was a status symbol, an ego trip. What'd I do that for? That was stupid, don't do that no more." But I'm free, you see. I'm free to go where I want to and record with whoever I want to.

Carr: *That seems to be the direction you've been heading in for the last three years or so.*

Cash: Yes. Freedom is the word. Not only that kind of freedom we were talking about, but freeing yourself from ideas and preconceived notions about what is expected of you. I forgot all of that crap. Forget about that I don't think about what is expected of me anymore. I'm doing what I *feel* is right for me.

For instance, I have people who say to me, "I want you to sound like you did in 1955 on Sun." I can't sing that way anymore, and people don't record that way anymore. Well, there's one cut on the **Gone Girl** album, *I Will Rock & Roll With You*, where I asked them to put that old Sun slapback on, and it's pretty much got that old Sun sound. So we'll give them a little bit of that if they ask for it, if people want to hear it. I mean, I can do that electronically. But honesty in performance and freedom of delivery, that's where it's at. I feel free in the studio now. I wish I could go back and do the **Gone Girl** album over again, and if I did, do you know what I'd do? I'd do it *exactly* the way I did.

Carr: *Has Jack Clement had much to do with this kind of spirit in you?*

Cash: Well, I haven't seen him in about two months, but I'm going to call him and pick his brains and see what kind of songs he's got. Jack has got so many great songs that he's forgotten about, you know, and I have to sit down with him and swap songs. "Hey, here's one I wrote that I forgot about!" he'll say, and he'll sing this song that you know should have been a hit when he wrote it. So I'm going to sit down with Jack and see if he's got anything else I might record, and then I'm probably going to ask him to come play rhythm with me again, 'cause I like to work with him. As a matter of fact, Jack Clement asked me to produce his next album.

Carr: *Really? That's a switch, isn't it?*

Cash: Yeah, that scared me so bad I haven't even answered him yet. I said, "What do you mean, produce you?" He said, "Oh, come down and sit and play rhythm with me and tell me when I'm doing something wrong." I said, "Man, you sure are giving me too much credit here. I'm not a producer. I don't want to be a producer." He said, "Well, just come on down and sit in with me and play rhythm with me." I said, "All right, I'll do that."

Carr: *John, how did all this freedom business start? I mean, you really weren't like this a few years ago.*

Cash: You know what? It's just going back to the basics of what it was like back before all the big years of success and all that stuff. It was freedom, and I'm just looking for that freedom again. I've seen that in people like Waylon. Waylon is more free inside, and free from the business world of the music business, than anybody I know. He demands his privacy, demands exclusiveness to be not involved in everything going around. I guess maybe that my late association with people like Waylon—like, I learned a lot from Waylon. I mean, I can handle people. I like people, and I can handle them by the dozen—you know, when they come to the shows, I can handle them backstage and all that—but Waylon handles them with so much patience because he knows that tomorrow, ain't nobody in the *world* gonna be able to find him because he's going to be hiding out resting somewhere. Tomorrow, everybody in the world will know where Johnny Cash is, 'cause I'll have a commitment somewhere. That's the way it's been, but I've become a little harder to get to. Maybe I'm going through the change of life or something, but I want more time for myself, and I want more freedom from worry and work and the hassle that goes on in the offices and the recording studios.

Carr: *It's showing in the music, you know.*

Cash: Well, I hope it'll show more the next time around. Like I said, if the feeling's not there, we won't record. We won't do it until the feeling *is* there.

Carr: *What about working with Waylon? Are you still getting him in the studio with you?*

Cash: Well, he and I have done two more songs, but the record companies are having a hassle over who's going to release it. We just did a duet that RCA Victor gave CBS permission to release, but I don't know about Waylon's status with his record company, so I don't know if that song's going to be released or not. So we got two things we're holding, and we don't have any plans to record anything more right now. We have talked about sometime doing an album if we can get enough songs that feel right, but we don't have enough songs yet. I don't talk to Waylon very often, really, 'cause he travels like I do.

Carr: *What do you think about what Carl Perkins is doing these days, John?*

Cash: I think it's great. He's really hot again in England. **Ol' Blue Suede Shoes Is Back**, that's a great album. Carl Perkins is better than he's ever been. He was always great, but now he's better than he's ever been, 'cause he's free too, you know? For a long time he was the opener for the Johnny Cash Show, and I never did feel right about it. I never did feel right about having an artist of his stature in that position. But that's what he wanted, and it worked for a long time. When he went off on his own is when he really came *into* his own, though. He's terrific. He's got it all together, in his head and his heart.

Carr: *He's sort of like you seem to be right now—he's got his family and his music, and he's doing what he wants to do. He's free to play.*

Cash: Yes, sir. He's the best there is, in his field.

Carr: *You think things are loosening up in the country music business in general, John? Last time I asked you that, about two years ago, you said basically that maybe they were, but you weren't too sure.*

Cash: I don't know. I don't read the trades. I look at the charts every week if *Cashbox* or *Billboard* or *Record World* happens to be on my desk, but I don't really know what direction country music is going in. I'm really concerned with which direction *I'm* going in.

Carr: *Maybe you're pulling back from your role as figurehead of the country music business?*

Cash: I didn't know that's what I was. I don't know what that means, really.

Carr: *Yes. No good asking you that these days, is it?*

Cash: They keep asking me every year to host the annual CMA Awards Show, and I kind of hope they don't ask me any more. I get a little embarrassed. Really, I keep thinking some of my peers are going to say, "Hey, what? We got to have him again?" But the network keeps asking for me. I enjoy doing it, but there's that other world of country music out there that is as important to the people as that CMA world. It's a weird thing for someone like me to say, but I know that there's two worlds of country music out there now. There's that CMA world and there's that other world.

Carr: *What's the other world?*

Cash: Well, there's Waylon and Willie and all the guys that you don't see on the CMA—great artists like Marty Robbins, Webb Pierce, Carl Smith, Ferlin Husky, Faron Young, Ernest Tubb, Hank Snow. All these are great, great country artists, and you don't see them on the CMA show. You don't see them as a guest or a presenter, even. The network is looking for names, for ratings, and they don't realize how important some of these names really are. But there's no greater country singer than Marty Robbins, and I've asked the last two years to get Marty Robbins on the show, and I get some kind of runaround. And I'm not really all that happy to be the host of the show for that reason. Tom T. Hall—have you ever seen Tom T. Hall on that show? That's what bugs me. That's what really gets to me, that the agent and I will talk it over, and he'll say, "Well, what do you recommend I do?" and he'll say, "Well, you're the only one that means anything to them, ratings-wise." I say, "Well, I don't *believe* that." Then we'll talk about the people that are going to be on it. I'll say, "Are they going to have any of the people on it that they've neglected in the past?" He'll say, "I don't have anything to do with that." Then I'll finally get around to talking to the producer. "Oh the talent's already set for the show." That's about as far as I get. I guess it's about time that I did let them know that I'm really galled that they don't have great people like Tom T. Hall and Marty Robbins and Ferlin Husky on there. I mean, Ferlin Husky's an entertainer. He's one of the greatest the business ever had. And just 'cause he doesn't have a hot record right now doesn't mean he's not important There's a lot of them out there that are important.

Then there's the other world of country music like Waylon and Willie or Charlie Daniels—oh, Charlie was on there this year—and the other guys who couldn't care less about the CMA or anything else that goes on, only with what they're doing and the way they want to do it, like I am right now. The way I feel about the **Gone Girl** album is I guess the way these guys feel about most everything in the business—"If it don't feel right, I ain't going to get in it." I get into a lot of things in the music business that don't feel right but I get involved in them because of who I am. Whatever that means.

Carr: *How do you feel about Jimmy Carter these days, John?*

Cash: I'm not going to talk to you about politics.

Carr: *Can I press you on one point? When we last talked, you said that you hoped Jimmy Carter might just bring back a sense of honesty and Christian values to this country. Do you think that has happened, if only a little?*

Cash: Well, it's happened to me personally, and it's happened to a lot of people around me. Jimmy Carter's been up and down in the polls, but I think he's been as good a President as a President can be. I can't imagine any man even being able to handle the job in the first place. Any man that can bear it and keep grinning like he does has to be quite a man. But I don't believe that he's directly responsible for any great Christian revival—no. There's been a lot written about his being born again, and it's become a joke in a lot of areas—even though it's not a joke, it's a spiritual truth—but no, no great spiritual revival has taken place in this country that I can see. As a matter of fact, I've seen more decadence in the last couple of years than I've ever seen before in my whole life, I believe.

But the churches are full. But you know what, Patrick? I read a book recently called *In His Steps*. It was written in 1896, and in this book the man talks about the Church and how it separates itself from the very ones who need it most—the poor, the needy—and this preacher challenges his congregation in this book to go out next week and do it as Jesus would do it. Whatever you do, whatever you say, you ask yourself, "Is this the way Jesus would do it?" and see what comes out. So there was a lot of people in the congregation took the challenge, and started going out among the poor people and giving them food packages. They started putting their Christianity into action. Stopped separating themselves in their beautiful white sepulcher of a church from the poor people, the hungry people in the slums and the ghettos. Like I say, the churches are full, but the slums and the ghettos are still full, and for the most part, the churches and the needy haven't quite gotten together yet. And until more people in the Church realize the real needs of the people, and go out rather than going in . . . I mean, to go into church is great, but to go out and put it all into action, that's where it's all at. And I haven't seen a lot of action.

Carr: *One of the things I've always liked about you is that you are a committed Christian, and yet you still work and hang around with people who might be considered backsliders or might have supposedly non-Christian habits. Funky musicians, you know? And you seem to be able to inhabit both worlds.*

Cash: Well, it's not like going both ways. I don't compromise. I don't compromise my religion. If I'm with someone who doesn't want to talk about it, I don't talk about it. I don't impose myself on anybody in *any* way, including religion. When you're imposing, you're offending, I feel. Although I *am* evangelical and I'll give the message to anyone that wants to hear it, or anybody that is willing to listen. But if they let me know that they don't want to hear it, they ain't ever going to hear it from me. If I *think* they don't want to hear it, then I will not bring it up.

It's something Waylon and I have never discussed, and we're the best of friends. We've got into some deep subjects, like—well, we got into religion a little bit; not much, but we got into some deep stuff. I never got into it with Kristofferson, really. Even when I was doing Gospel Road and he was around, we really didn't talk about it much 'cause, you know, some people are uncomfortable talking about it. But back to how Jesus did it, He was that way, and I'm just trying to be like him.

Carr: *John, is there anything you'd like to say about Mother Maybelle?*

Cash: Mother Maybelle Carter. I still get choked up. She was my fishing buddy. That was my relationship with her. I've just lost an old buddy. That's it, and I don't have too much to say. She was the greatest. She was the first and the greatest, and the music world will slowly but surely be paying its tributes to her by people recording everything she ever wrote and recorded.

Carr: *I was talking to Carl Perkins the day after she died, and he said much the same thing. He said that when he was on the road with you, he and Mother Maybelle used to sit up at night playing cards, and that's how he'd always think of her.*

Cash: I did a lot of that. We'd play poker. We'd sit up all night playing poker with Mother Maybelle.

Carr: *What about Elvis, John? Any last words on Elvis?*

Cash: Well, what has not been said? Elvis was the greatest in *his* field, of course. I'd always admired him. Every show before I went in, I'd always watch every minute of his show from the side. But I didn't see Elvis for the last eighteen years of his life, so I don't know him that well.

Carr: *What did the commercialization after his death do to you?*

Cash: Well, I didn't go out and buy a bunch of posters and junk they were selling, but it's something I expected. I'll tell you what it's done, though—it's got him a whole new world of fans. Little kids. Every little kid loves Elvis Presley. Kids John Carter's age, eight years old. I take him to school, he's singing *All Shook Up* or *Jailhouse Rock* or something, every day. Every little kid knows Elvis.

Carr: Sounds sort of like 1953 all over again.

Cash: No, I'm talking about little bitty kids, you know?

Carr: *Well, it makes a change from John Travolta, eh?*

Cash: Right.

MONROE COUNTY FAIR INTERVIEW

Don Gonyea | August 8, 1981 | Interview Transcript

"It was a really great experience, an important moment in my life," says National Public Radio's Don Gonyea of interviewing Johnny Cash at the Monroe County Fair in 1981. "I think it's fair to say that it was something I drew on in the decades and decades that followed. I took a chance, and I pressed my case, and I came away with this amazing experience, which even exceeds the content of the interview."

It was Gonyea's first interview with a celebrity—his first interview, period. "I wasn't even a journalist yet," he says. Gonyea was a DJ on Monroe, Michigan's country station WVMO, his first job out of college. He was—and remains—a huge Johnny Cash fan. When he heard Cash was appearing at the county fair, he reached out to Cash's people twice for an interview, to no response. Someone who worked at the fair told him to stand beside the tour bus and try his luck. He did—and came away with a life-changing experience.

Cash disembarked the bus, heading for the stage, but stopped to give much more than Gonyea expected. "I didn't have a big list of questions ready," Gonyea says. "He kept talking and he kept standing there, even though I expected him to walk away. There was just no reason for him to be nice to me. And to be so generous. Except I think he had some core decency. And there I was, with my sideburns and my plaid Wrangler shirt and my navy blue corduroy vest and little cassette tape recorder and microphone. For whatever reason I seemed like somebody he was OK with stopping and talking to that day. It's still pretty astounding to me, because there've been people I've interviewed who were heroes of mine and I did not come away with such a positive experience."

Over the ensuing forty years, Gonyea would make his way from commercial to public radio, rising through the ranks at NPR—from anchoring the Detroit bureau, to covering the Bush White House, to becoming national political correspondent. He has filed stories from

Moscow, Beijing, London, Islamabad, Budapest, Seoul, San Salvador, Slovenia, and Hanoi. Portions of the Cash interview that started it all were used as part of "The Man in Black Goes to the County Fair" on NPR's *Morning Edition*, February 23, 2013.

These days, he says, "I specialize in voter interviews. Getting people to open up to me who didn't wake up thinking they would be interviewed on the radio that day. Whereas somebody like Colin Powell, or a President, or a Senator, they're always in that mode because they go through their lives as a public figure. But that guy who showed up at the Top Notch Diner in Warren, Ohio, didn't know I was going to approach him and have a long conversation that becomes the thesis, or the lead scene, in a piece on NPR. This person might not even know what NPR is, as is very often the case."

Gonyea asked Cash about Bob Dylan, whose 1969 duet with Cash, "Girl from the North Country," is one of his favorite recordings: "When I asked him about recording with Dylan, he gave me a look that conveyed, 'I didn't think I'd be asked about *that* today, next to the grandstand at the Monroe County Fair.' And he gave me a nice long paragraph or two about he and Bob being part of this mutual admiration society."

Gonyea's encounter with Johnny Cash—it would be their only meeting—resonated down the decades. Especially when Gonyea eventually realized that 1981 was a difficult time for the Man in Black. Cash was competing with the *Urban Cowboy* fad of glittery, overproduced pop-country crossovers and the likes of John Travolta in a cowboy hat. Although the title track from 1981's slick, Billy Sherrill-produced *The Baron* had hit number ten—Cash's last Top 10 hit of his career—the album hadn't fared well commercially or critically. Like the one before it, and the one before that. His record label, Columbia, was spending very little to promote his work, and the relationship would soon sour. The road was the focal point of his life, and this would take a toll on him, as it had in the 1960s.

Yet, outside his tour bus on the evening of August 8, 1981, with the demolition derby ring nearby, Cash was warm and funny with rookie Don Gonyea.

"There wasn't any expectation at the station that I was going to land an interview with Johnny Cash and bring it back," Gonyea says. "It was all just me thinking this would be a cool thing to do. If it all fell apart, nobody was going to be disappointed. I'm sure I would've thought, *Oh well what do you expect, it's Johnny Cash, why's he going to stop and talk to me?* Except that he did. But I did do everything possible to make it happen. And everything had to work out just right . . . Everything had to fall in place, and it did.

"I still use that to this day. You're always reliant on luck. I walk up to people cold on the street, to do my NPR voter interviews, and I know ninety percent are gonna tell me no, but you just kinda bake that in, and you just always have to put yourself in a position to succeed, should you get lucky. And you get lucky a lot, right? This one was really spectacularly lucky." —Ed.

Don Gonyea: And here is Johnny.

Johnny Cash: Hello . . .

Gonyea: How you doing, Johnny?

Cash: Hi, how you doing?

Gonyea: Welcome to Monroe.

Cash: Thank you.

Gonyea: I'm from WVMO, the radio station here in town. Glad to have you here.

Cash: Thank you, nice to be here.

Gonyea: Do you tour as much as you used to these days? Do you still get the thrill of being on the road as when you were younger?

Cash: Yeah, I still travel as much I ever did. We're doing about a hundred and twenty concerts this year.

Gonyea: How about . . . can you tell us a little bit about the new album, *The Baron*? Is it traditional Johnny Cash or are you breaking any new ground there?

Cash: A big part of it is traditional. Of course, the title song was the reason for the album—"The Baron"—which was a fairly big seller for us, not a number-one record, but Rosanne Cash wouldn't let me in the number-one spot. But, uh, a big part of it is traditional, yeah. Songs I . . . I always try to sing the songs I'm comfortable singing. Because if I don't, the people know it.

Gonyea: You mentioned Rosanne, you pretty pleased with the way things are going for her these days?

Cash: I'm very pleased with her. I'm very happy for her.

Gonyea: Can we expect to see a Johnny Cash/Rosanne Cash duet up in the number-one spot pretty quick?

Cash: We haven't talked about that.

Gonyea: No plans yet?

Cash: No, we haven't talked about that. The song would have to come along, you know? We'd have to have the right song. It's not something we would do just for the sake of doing it. Her first duet was with Bobby Bare, which really surprised me. I didn't know until the record came out that she was going to record with Bobby. But, maybe somewhere down the line I could do that.

Gonyea: On the new album, you didn't write any of the songs. Do you prefer to write your own material? Or is it that a good song is a good song? Or . . .

Cash: A good song is a good song. I had several songs that I wrote and sang for the producer. And we recorded two or three of them, but as it turned out, they weren't used in the album. When we got down to picking songs for the album, out of sixteen we picked the ten that are there and mine weren't in it.

Gonyea: How'd you get to be the Man in Black? Can you tell our people? Is there a story behind that?

Cash: Not really. I wrote a song called "Man in Black" about 1970. Um, I've always worn black. I've always felt comfortable in it, while performing. I felt it had a kind of a distinctive look and, for one reason, it's a little more slimming. And, I don't know, in the song, if you see the lyrics of the song "Man in Black," you see where I pointed out some of the problems and the ills that we have in this country. But I point to myself as being one of those people responsible for correcting some of those problems and unfortunate things that happen to people here.

Gonyea: These days, a lot of country stars are starting to cross over into the national charts and have national hits. You did that ten years ago with "A Boy Named Sue." Is it that you were way ahead of everybody else and it's taken them a while to catch up?

Cash: It's really nothing new. I did that twenty-four years ago with "I Walk the Line." Sonny James did it with a song called "Young Love," and Jimmy Newman did it with "Falling Star," Ferlin Husky did it . . . with another big song ["Wings of a Dove," 1960]. As you say, it seems as if the record companies are trying for a crossover, quote, hit. That's not what country music is all about to me. Generally, when I'm in charge of the production of my records, I try to record the best Johnny Cash song I can find and do it in a way that's comfortable for me. And hopefully the people will like it. Usually, they're unadorned and not overproduced as in the case of "A Boy Named Sue" and "Folsom Prison Blues."

Other voice: What do you think about the trend in country music today, now, towards the *Urban Cowboy* type. A lot of Texas-type songs.

Cash: Well, I think it's healthy. People are having a lot of fun with country music, you know. And there's always been fun songs and novelty songs in country but the trends will come and go, but when this trend goes I think it will leave more solid country fans to add to the number of country fans that were already there. I think country music will always be a reckoning force in the music business.

Gonyea: Now, you went to London about a year ago to record a song, too. Why record country music in London? What's the story? Is it "Without Love," is that the song?

Cash: We were at Nick Lowe's and Carlene's house, and he had the studio in his basement and I loved the song and we were on vacation. So we called over Dave Edmunds and the other guys in Rockpile and we recorded "Without Love" in a very simple and comfortable way, like rockabilly, you know?

Gonyea: I guess it was about 1970, one of my favorite points on any album that I own, you recorded a song with Bob Dylan called "Girl from the North Country" when he was in Nashville. How'd you guys come to get together, and what's the story behind that song?

Cash: I've known Bob since 1962 or '63 when he was on the Newport Folk Festival. We were corresponding before that even, I think, it was kind of this mutual admiration thing before that. And we were writing letters to each other about our music and about what we thought about it, and then at the folk festival we really had an all-night session of singing. And then we got to be friends and visited each other and so forth. Well, I asked him to come to Nashville and record an album. He was recording here and there and everywhere and had tried a little of everything. And I thought country music was going to really be a big form of music, you know? For the whole country, for everybody, for the masses. Which, finally it has. And Bob came to Nashville and did a lot of country stuff—some other stuff, but we had a lot of fun doing it and he asked me to sing on "Girl from the North Country." Which I had a hard time doing because it was not really my thing, you know?

Gonyea: Yeah.

Other voice: Bob claimed to be born again. And I know you claimed to be a born-again entertainer. What do you believe about the second coming of Jesus Christ, John?

Cash: Well, I believe there will be a second coming of Jesus Christ, but I don't think any of us know when. As a matter of fact, Matthew 24 says we don't know when. But Bob, I believe, is a born-again Christian. The *born-again* phrase has been kicked around and thrown around until it's watered down, and in places it's become a laughing stock thing. People make jokes about it, but this is something that happened to me when I was twelve years old. I just came back to the faith twelve years ago.

Gonyea: Now, you've been an inspiration to countless aspiring young musicians. When the shoe was on the other foot, when you were learning how to play guitar—just starting out—who did you listen to? Who did you look up to?

Cash: I listened to whoever was popular at the time. Eddy Arnold, George Morgan, Ernest Tubb, Hank Snow, Carter Family, Jimmie Rodgers . . . whoever was popular. I liked a big part of country music. Some I didn't, and like you, or anybody else, you have your songs that you don't like. So I had mine that I didn't like, but the ones I did like were the ones I named.

Gonyea: Do you have a favorite song that you've recorded?

Cash: "I Walk the Line."

Gonyea: Great.

County fair official: One more question, folks. We have to get ready for the show.

Other voice: Whatever happened to the Tennessee Three? I noticed you had a different backup group?

Cash: Well, I recorded an album called *Rockabilly Blues*, which called for a more stretched-out musical arrangement on some songs. And the big thing in country music these days is five, six, seven pieces. So I have seven pieces in my band. I like to hear all those sounds in some of those songs where they belong. That's why I have seven.

Other voice: Are they still around, the Tennessee Three?

Cash: Well, they're scattered here and there. I have one of them with me on the show—W. S. Holland is still with me after 24 years. And Bob Wootton is still with me—the original guitar player with the Tennessee Three was Luther Perkins. He's dead now.

[*Someone signals to Cash.*]

Cash: [*Waving that he's done*] I'm on stage. . . .

Gonyea: Could I get you to sign this?

County fair official: Johnny, while you're signing that, one of our caretakers who's been with us for twenty-four years, his wife is a fan and also a miniature maker. She asked me to give this to you. It's a mini cash register with cash.

NORRKÖPING, SWEDEN, PRESS CONFERENCE

November 3, 1983 | Original Transcript

In the early 1980s, Johnny Cash's albums were not faring well, but his performer status remained solid, particularly overseas. Across the Atlantic, fans greeted him with intense ardor and no indication they considered him "part of country music's past." Even as he was battling depression and relapsing into pills and alcohol abuse around the time of this press conference, Johnny Cash plowed on. His struggles are not apparent here, but by the end of 1983—weeks after this press conference—he would once again hit bottom and, after an intervention, check into the new Betty Ford Clinic.

Sweden has the distinction of being the only country besides the United States where Cash recorded and released a live "prison album": *Johnny Cash på Österåker* (*Johnny Cash at Osteraker*), recorded at Österåker prison, 30 kilometers north of Stockholm, and released in early 1973 (re-released in 2007). By 1983, Cash and his manager, Lou Robin, had expanded his itinerary to include the industrial port town of Norrköping, in northeastern Sweden, on the Baltic Sea.

As often happened with their hosts, Johnny and June befriended local promoter and Cash superfan Lars Lindfors, who'd been instrumental in securing the Norrköping date for which this press conference was arranged. Lindfors claims to have attended every single concert Cash ever played in his country.

Although not in top form, Cash was touring behind his best album in years: *Johnny 99*. Producer Brian Ahern had helmed big successes by Emmylou Harris (Ahern's wife), Rosanne Cash, Rodney Crowell, and Anne Murray, to name a few, and had masterminded Cash's 1979 album *Silver*, which, while not a big seller as an LP, included the hit single "Ghost Riders in the Sky."

Johnny 99 contained no original Cash songs. But it sounded great, at times presaging the spare Rick Rubin material that was to come a decade hence. As part of the deal to produce, Ahern had insisted on relocating Cash from Nashville to Los Angeles, using mostly his own stable of ace musicians and choosing the material. In hopes of attracting the much-coveted younger demographic, and in an effort to pair Cash with material up to the standards of his own excellent past output, Ahern and Cash recorded two recent Bruce Springsteen songs for *Johnny 99*—the title track and "Highway Patrolman," both from Springsteen's critically lauded 1982 *Nebraska* album.

Despite all the above, however, *Johnny 99* did not sell. Cash's decades-long tenure at Columbia was almost over. —Ed.

June Carter Cash: By the way, this is Johnny Cash.

[*Laughter.*]

Johnny Cash: Hello, I'm Johnny Cash. Good morning, afternoon. It's nice to see ya, and it's good to be here. I'm glad we could finally make it to this city for a concert. Sweden's fourth largest city, is that right? It's good to be here. We've been to Malmö, Gothenburg, and Stockholm, and it's past time we got to come here. It's a pleasure to see ya, and to be with ya. If I can answer any questions, I'd be glad to try.

Reporter: Can you tell me something about your movie plans? You would think this [*indicating album cover photo for* Johnny 99] is from a movie.

Cash: Yes. In September of 1982, we did a movie in Georgia called *Murder in Coweta County* in which I played Sheriff Lamar Potts. It's a true story that happened in 1948, and that's why the 1948-style hat and coat I have on in that picture. Then I recorded these songs about the same time or soon after, and the record company seemed to feel that some of these songs had this midwestern/southern flavor, and the picture looked right for the songs, so that's why that picture on that album cover. *Johnny 99* is the name of the album.

Reporter: It's sort of a new direction with this album. It's not just the boom-chicka-boom sound. It's different. Is this what we can look forward to? Johnny Cash singing this type of music?

Cash: Well, I don't think . . . no, I'm not making a real departure in style of music with this album. It is, probably, I think one of the best albums I've had in a long time. But the reason for the difference in the sound was that I didn't have all of my own band there. But I went to California and recorded it in, with Brian Ahern, a producer, at his studio. And I had some very fine musicians like [guitarist] James Burton, in addition to [guitarists] Bob Wootton and Marty Stuart from my own group, who performed on the album. James Burton, and Hal Blaine on drums, and Jerry Scheff on bass. They play a little different style of music, yet having these musicians, having played so many concerts over the years with so many different artists, they had no trouble, we had no trouble working together. We did that album in a week. One week.

Reporter: Are you still writing songs? [Johnny 99 *contains no Cash original songs. —Ed.*]

Cash: Oh, I'm still writing songs. But it just so happened the producer had picked these ten songs. We had decided on these ten songs before we even looked at mine. So none of my songs are on this album, but probably my next album, half of the songs on the album will be mine. Because I'm still writing.

Reporter: How did you get to hear Bruce Springsteen songs?

Cash: Springsteen . . . Those songs come from an album of Bruce Springsteen's called *Nebraska*. We . . . John Carter heard it. Our son. June heard it. I listened to it and it sounded like those songs were just written for me. The kind of thing I'd been doing for years. Like "Highway Patrolman," the story song, y'know? And "Johnny 99," a song that's not too far removed from the style of "Folsom Prison Blues." Same kind of feeling. So I immediately identified with Bruce Springsteen's songs, especially those two.

We've got a friend who is rebuilding the boardwalk and restoring the buildings in Asbury Park, New Jersey. We're getting an apartment there. [*Laughs.*] We'll have an apartment in Bruce Springsteen's hometown. Quite by accident. But I never met Bruce, but I heard the *Nebraska* album and I listened to all of it, all the way through. And I didn't want to overdo it. There were other Springsteen songs that I like. There was "State Trooper" that I like very much in this album, that I almost recorded. But the producer finally said, "Let's select two. Let's don't overdo Springsteen." I said, "Well, I don't think you can overdo him, 'cause he's great." But we selected two out of the *Nebraska* album. Since then I've listened to more of his earlier albums. As you know, he's very heavy rock and a little out of my . . . street, y'know. But "Johnny 99" and "Highway Patrolman" were just exactly . . .

Carter Cash: Someone said he wrote that for you.

Cash: Yeah. Someone told me he wrote that for me, but I'm not sure.

Carter Cash: We heard that. We mean to ask him if we ever meet him.

Cash: I haven't talked to him.

Carter Cash: Well that's the word we got. He did write those two for him . . .

Cash: But I admire him as a writer, and I certainly admire his record as a performer and as man who has big, big box office business.

Reporter: What about your most famous collaboration with Bob Dylan? Did he have an influence on your career?

Cash: I think so. I think country music had more of an influence on Bob Dylan than Bob Dylan did on country music. [*Laughs.*] When we first heard Bob Dylan singing—what was the name of the album? First album.

Carter Cash: Where he's walkin' with a girl on the street.

Reporter: *Freewheelin' Bob Dylan.*

Cash: Yeah. *Freewheelin' Bob Dylan.* I thought boy, there's a great country singer. Because he was singing as country as anybody'd ever heard.

Reporter (to June): I have a question for you. What do you think of country music today? Is it losing its identity? So much of country music today is pop music.

Carter Cash: Well, with my background, country music to me has always been kind of a folk kind of music, I guess what you might classify as folk, I mean as folk music like the Carter Family's music, which more or less told stories in song about love or war or sickness and death and health or whatever. There is an aspect of country music today that is very commercial. It seems to be appealing to a lot of people. Country music is a very easy way of saying things. I think almost anybody can sing country music. Even *I* sing country music. You don't have to have a fine, fine voice to always be able to sell records in country music. It has a universal appeal. I still like the old folk kind of music. I prefer that. Other than some of the more commercial kinds of . . . so to speak beer-drinking café kind of country music. I prefer the other. But I love country music and I think it does have a universal appeal. I don't think it's lost. I think it's finding its way.

Reporter: Who is with you onstage tonight?

Cash: Onstage tonight is June Carter Cash, the star of the show. [*Laughter.*] And she's gonna let me do a few songs. Our guests are my twenty-two-year-old daughter, Tara Cash, is here for the first time. T-A-R-A like in *Gone with the Wind*. Tara. And John Carter is thirteen and he's doing his homework right now. So he'll be able to perform tonight. John Carter is growing up so fast, he's going to do a country song called "Swingin'" but he's also going to do a Bob Seger song called "[I Love That] Old Time Rock & Roll." He's going to be performing that with the band tonight. But you'll be hearing a lot of traditional country music from June and from myself. I'll be doing a lot of songs that have been requested that we do, like "I Walk the Line," "Ring of Fire," "Folsom Prison Blues," "Sunday Morning Coming Down." The most requested songs wherever we go.

Reporter: Who are the musicians?

Cash: My musicians, my own band. Seven very fine musicians. W. S. Holland on drums, Bob Wootton on lead guitar, Marty Stuart on guitar, Jimmy Tittle on bass, Earl Ball on piano, Jack Hale Jr. and Bob Lewin playing trumpets and French horns.

Carter Cash: And trombones and anything that blows.

Reporter: Are any of your kids into music?

Cash: Several of them are. Yes, John Carter is. Rosanne Cash is. Carlene Carter is. Carlene will be here next week. Next Monday night.

Carter Cash: Carlene Carter is playing Stockholm, I think, Sunday night. She's slightly rock and roll. [*Laughs.*] She lives in England now.

Cash: Yes, we have four daughters . . . four out of the six that definitely have music aspirations. Have a daughter named Cindy who sings with the show occasionally. Like I say, Tara is going to sing tonight, the youngest. There's Rosanne. And Rosie Carter, June's youngest, has a new recording contract with Atlantic Records.

Reporter: How about Rosanne? You've been quiet about her. She's been away from recording . . .

Cash: She had a baby. She has a record, then she has a baby, then she has a record, then a baby. [*Laughter.*] No, she's recording her new album right now. And she wrote all the songs on the album.

Reporter: What about you doing something with Nick Lowe?

Cash: Those plans have not been ruled out. As a matter of fact, though, at the end of this tour, June is going to stay in London and probably do a session with Nick Lowe, and then we're coming back to spend the whole summer in England next summer. And at that time, I'll probably do something. But at this time, I won't have time because John Carter has to get back to school, and June's gonna stay over a couple days and visit Carlene and probably do a couple songs with Nick Lowe in the studio while she's there.

Carter Cash: I intend for him to sing, and Carlene to sing, and me to hum . . . low. Then maybe I'll get a good record. [*Laughter.*]

Reporter: Do you still sing in prisons?

Cash: Occasionally. Only when I have to. [*Laughs.*] No, I get a lot of requests to. Do you know, the album that we . . . we recorded an album at Österåker prison [*På Österåker*] that was released in Europe but has never been released in the United States. We've asked CBS to please release that album in the United States. Our last prison concert was at Angola State Prison in Louisiana not too long ago. But I have a request to come to several prisons at this time. But actually we're making more appearances for policeman's benevolent funds than we are prisons right now. We're doing more concerts for retarded children, orphanages, to raise money for schools, than we are at prisons. We haven't neglected or forsaken prisons.

I have a small presentation I'd like to make, if I may. In appreciation to Lars Lindfors for his support all these years, and for his work toward bringing June and all of us back to this city in Sweden . . . In 1969, we were on ABC television every week. And during the rehearsals of all the shows, on a segment called *Ride This Train*, I wore a pair of black Levi's. Black denim pants. I want to give you those. [*Laughter.*] They are from 1969. I was a little smaller then.

Lars Lindfors: Oh! Thank you.

Carter Cash: Roll 'em up at the knees, Lars.

Lindfors: I like them very much. What size?

Cash: 36.

Lindfors: That's my size. [*Laughter.*]

Cash: I know. That's what I was in 1969. I'm 38 now. But those are 36.

Lindfors: On *Ride This Train*? Have you used them since then?

Cash: Couple times.

Carter Cash: You can push 'em down in your boots, like he does. Push 'em down in your boots.

Lindfors: In my boots? I'll try.

Carter Cash: That's why he wears his pants down in his boots. His legs are so long, none of his pants are long enough.

Lindfors: OK. I appreciate it very much.

Cash: You're welcome. Thanks for having us back.

Lindfors: Love ya.

Cash: They were black, y'know.

Carter Cash: Now they are light black.

Reporter: I asked why don't you use steel guitar in your music?

Cash: I started out on Sun Records in 1955. Sam Phillips had recorded two or three artists using a steel guitar, and he sold no records. In Nashville it was the popular thing that every country song had a steel guitar and a fiddle in it. Sam Phillips, and Jack Clement who came to work for him about '56, thought that country music had to make a change in order to be an important force in the music world. Of course, his first big discovery was Elvis Presley. And Elvis opened the door for a lot of us, like Carl Perkins, Jerry Lee Lewis, Warren Smith, and Roy Orbison. They came in and recorded, and nobody used a steel guitar and fiddle like they did in Nashville. Sam Phillips was responsible for a new form of country music taking shape out of Memphis. And it shook Nashville up. There are still country songs being recorded, of course, with a steel guitar and a fiddle—always will be. But since 1956 it's not been the same. I don't use a steel guitar because . . . it hurts my ears. [*Laughs.*] I think that's what Sam Phillips said to me when I mentioned it the first time. The steel guitar hurts his ears.

INTERVIEW

Glenn Jorgenson | 1983 | *It's Great to Be Alive*

"In all my years as president of River Park," Glenn Jorgenson wrote to his wife, Phyllis, "this is probably the most compelling interview I've done."

South Dakota Hall of Fame inductee Glenn Jorgenson was referring to his 1983 interview with Johnny Cash on Jorgenson's groundbreaking television series *It's Great to Be Alive*. The show was an offshoot of River Park, South Dakota's first nonprofit, privately funded treatment center for addiction. The Jorgensons founded River Park on the principles of Alcoholics Anonymous, approaching addiction as a disease, as opposed to a character flaw.

It's Great to Be Alive followed a talk-show format, with Jorgenson and an impressive roster of guests conversing specifically and candidly about addiction and recovery. In addition to Cash, interviewees included Betty Ford, Senator George McGovern, Dick Van Dyke, Fran Tarkenton, Brooke Shields, Native American operatic tenor White Eagle, Larry Gatlin, and Rosey Grier. Produced in South Dakota, *It's Great to Be Alive* was distributed nationwide for twenty years.

Jorgenson had been a successful businessman when he fell into alcohol and painkiller addiction in the late 1960s. He entered recovery in 1970 and soon after used a state grant to transform a Pierre, South Dakota, halfway house into an addiction treatment center. He created homey, inviting spaces, serving patients homemade pies, approaching each situation with compassion. His wife, Phyllis, was integral in creating treatments that would include families of addicts. The Jorgensons worked tirelessly to erase the stigmas around addiction, seeking to educate the public and remove shame from the equation. In the ensuing decades, River Park facilities expanded from Pierre to Rapid City and Sioux Falls, with outreach offices across the state.

In 2016, the Jorgensons and journalist Terry Woster published a book version of *It's Great to Be Alive*, tracing the development of River Park treatment programs through the eyes of Glenn and Phyllis. Weaving into the narrative compelling stories of addiction and recovery, the book details the challenges faced by addicts—celebrity and otherwise—and helps expand understanding of addictions, their effects on families and communities, and options for treatment.

In 1983, sitting down with Johnny Cash was a high point of *It's Great to Be Alive*. Jorgenson wrote to Phyllis: "I wish you could have been there as Johnny Cash spoke frankly to me of his life-threatening, years-long friendship with alcohol and other drugs. And how that friendship turned into a battle for his life, his Armageddon, and how he survived it all because of the love and understanding that someone offered. Love and understanding—the two main ingredients of treatment at River Park, right? I can see this interview with John as being one of River Park's finest television specials. He really makes a person feel that it's great to be alive." —Ed.

Glenn Jorgenson: First of all, John, I want to thank you, really, for taking the time from a very strenuous schedule to appear with us on our "It's Great to Be Alive" series. I'm just really grateful because I know someone out there is going to get some help from the program and from the comments that'll go back and forth between us, so thank you very much, John.

Johnny Cash: My pleasure. Well, the one that's probably gonna get the help is me, because I have a habit of feeding off people like you, who've got some real strength to offer people. For all of us down-and-outers, hard timers, it's still one day at a time. And every day there's an inspiration comes along like this program. Really means a lot.

Jorgenson: Well, John, we're very appreciative, and I've got to share with you that when I first met you in the early 1970s, I was early in my recovery, and you were the right person at the right time, because you gave me some early inspiration. There was an air that came from you—I really don't know how to describe it—but when I shook your hand I could feel it, a strength, a spirituality, an acceptance on your part, and I've often wondered what makes Johnny Cash a legend, an institution, an inspiration to people. With your permission, I would like to discuss some of the things that went into creating a person that has ended up being able to help so many people.

My first recollection of you when I first met you in the early '70s . . . at that time I was struck by something within you that came out in the form of a strength, an acceptance, almost like a spirituality, which was important to me, John, at that time, because I was early into my own recovery from chemical addiction. I've often wondered what it is that creates a John Cash that can have that power, and that ability to convey the message. Of course, it's in the giving away that we keep it, I know. So, I'd like to talk about some of those things.

When did you first get introduced to chemicals? What was it like in those early days?

Cash: It was beautiful. People take drugs because they make you feel good. But like I pointed out in my book [*Man in Black*], there is a demon called Deception that . . . it's like the old wino, he drinks out of the bottle so long, the bottle starts drinking out of him. Well, the pills . . . I took the pills so long. And the reversal came without me knowing it. When the pills started taking from me. I had seven years of constant habituation or addiction. It was cold, hard addiction, devotion. It was *devotion* to what I was doing. It was amphetamines, barbiturates, and alcohol, all three in a cycle for seven years. And I'm six foot two, and when I, through God, found the strength to come out of it in 1967, I weighed 152 pounds.

Jorgenson: Incredible.

Cash: . . . which is fifty pounds less than I weigh now.

You talk about you felt the spirit there. I really am glad to hear that. Because it was the spirit of the love of God that made a survivor out of me, and it's His love and care from people like yourself, and like my wife, June Carter, who, every day I feel the touch of God's love and caring that has made not only a survivor but a sustainer [out of me]. And it's not an easy road to go, and it's a very lonely fight. But it's good to turn around from your lonely struggle and find somebody there behind you that cares, and ready to help you out, or ready to inspire you, ready to give you strength and encourage you.

People on drugs, habituated to a chemical . . . if, when they decide to kick it—and only *they* can decide, nobody can decide for them—when they decide to stop it, if they have somebody who really loves them that they can cling to. You gotta shake off the old man. As [Saint] Paul says, "You gotta throw off the old life and put on the new."

I found myself having to close the door on some old friends, because they wanted to keep me down where they were. And regardless what people call me, or thought of me, I knew that God wanted me to live, so I clung to the people that I knew who cared, y'know, and had His love in their lives.

Jorgenson: I think why some of us make it back, I'm not exactly sure, except that I have to feel God sees some good in us that could be used to help other people. We who did, I think we tried just about everything. Well, I did. I tried everything there was to overcome this dependency or addiction. It was only when I gave up that I began to win. From reading your book and knowing something of your life . . . was there a point—I'm sure there was—where somehow or other you surrendered and gave up?

Cash: Yes. There was.

Jorgenson: What was the key time, or the key elements, or the key person? What was involved in your reaching what I think has got to be the miracle in our lives, when we suddenly say, "Hey, I give up."

Cash: Well, I roughly describe my condition in '67, when I came out of the addiction, if you had a picture of me at that time, you wouldn't believe it was me.

I was a spelunker. There's a cave near Chattanooga, Tennessee [Nickajack Cave], that I like to explore. There's a big room in there where Civil War soldiers stayed, and nobody really knows where all the caverns go. I'd been in there several times with my friends. Every time I would get high, I'd get in my Jeep or truck and head for Chattanooga, to the people that I thought would put up with me, y'know. I knew I'd just about worn out my welcome at everybody's house in Nashville, from keeping 'em up all night, and this and that. But finally, even my friends in Chattanooga couldn't really put up with me any much longer, and I saw it. I had turned my back on June, and on my own mother. She had given up on me and driven back to California where she lived, and had a slight heart attack on the way. At that time, that didn't bother me in the least, because there's one thing about someone addicted to pills, alcohol, as you know. They're very selfish. They don't care about anybody but themselves and the way they happen to feel *right now*. And that's all I cared about all the time: how I feel, what I want for me, y'know. And disregarded my four daughters in California, my mother.

But June Carter was a fighter. And I couldn't get over what I'd done to my mother. June found out where I was, and came to my friend's house in Chattanooga lookin' for me. I found out she was coming, so I went to the cave, twenty miles away. And I had been up two or three days and nights when she got there. So I took my beer—I was drinkin' a case of beer a day, and taking up to a hundred pills, half amphetamines and half barbiturates, keep me goin' up and down, keep the cycle goin'. I was sweatin' the beer out, so the only calories I guess was from the hops and malt, I don't know. But I remember sittin' in the mouth of that cave, crying, and then taking a little two-cell flashlight, and I started walking into that cave, and I decided I'd walk as far as I could go and lay down. And I guess I probably went a mile through one of the caverns, and my flashlight completely burned out. It was black. Black dark, so dark you could *feel* it. And I lay down flat on my back and said my goodbye prayers: "I can't handle it myself, I'm giving up, I'm going."

I must have dozed off, because I felt a *presence*. I didn't see anything, I didn't hear anything, but I felt a presence. I felt a power, and a strength, and an inner voice almost saying, "No, you don't give up. You got things to do." I mean, I'm not saying God talked to me. But I felt that power within me, come from outside of me. To make me sit up, and look around. I couldn't see any light, but . . . this is awfully corny, but an old Indian trick is to wet your finger, stick it up, see which way the wind blows. I tried everything to see, and then I finally did that. I felt cool air on one side of my finger, and I knew that . . . I kept following it. Crawling. Sometimes I'd fall twenty or thirty feet into a pit, but I'd claw my way back up. And just as I was about to give up, I saw a little fleck of light way off in the distance, and I started crawling and clawing toward that entrance. And I finally made it there, and I collapsed in the mouth of the cave.

In the mouth of this cave, when I awoke, June was there with my friends from Chattanooga. She knew it was really, really bad this time. I had a psychiatrist friend, the commissioner of mental health for Tennessee, also a country musician, and I woke up, and June was washing my face, and she said, "You're almost dead, aren't you?" and I said, "Call Nat Winston, I want to live." And she said, "Are you sure?" So I said, "Yep, I wanna go with you."

So she took me back to Nashville, and we called our friend, and he came out, looked at me [*laughs*], and he said later, "I wouldn't have given you a one-in-a-thousand chance of making it. You were so hooked and wrapped up in your own self and your own addiction." But Nat Winston asked me, "Are you deadly serious? You really mean it? You have personally decided you're gonna quit?" I said, "Yes, sir." He said, "I'll be here every day, thirty minutes after I get off work." And he was. For thirty days, he was there every day at 5:30. And knowing that Nat Winston was coming back, and June, her mother and daddy, and all my family and friends were downstairs sleeping in sleeping bags in this big house I'd bought on the lake. It kept me goin'.

About a week into breaking the addiction, they started bringing me food. The nightmares continued for about three weeks, without letup. Every time I'd lay down and close my eyes . . . the hardest thing to break was the downers. Dr. Winston told me I would crave amphetamines or want them every day for the rest of my life, and I guess he's right, because it's a one-day-at-a-time battle. But back then I was taking [anxiety medications] Equanil, meprobamate, pathibamate. I'd burned my stomach out from the beer. [*Laughs.*] I think the popular thing today, though, is Valium. I think that's the little demon called Deception today.

Jorgenson: Librium. [*Used for anxiety, alcohol withdrawal symptoms.* —*Ed.*]

Cash: Librium, yeah, I know that very well. I almost got wrapped up back in the whole cycle again because a doctor prescribed Librium for something for me that he thought I needed it for. I didn't realize what it was. But it's one of those tricky little things, makes you feel good, but then it grabs hold of ya.

Jorgenson: One of the sad parts is that people are still—we're getting better, but they have not come to understand that those so-called mild tranquilizers are very addicting. And part of the purpose of the work we're doing is trying to make people aware that it's not to be used as a way of life. It may be, under certain conditions, it's proper to use them. But to make that an ongoing thing, such as you and I did . . . that's Hell. You set out thinking you found the keys to Heaven, but find out you found the keys to Hell.

Cash: I think all those pills should be named Delilah.

Jorgenson: Delilah?

Cash: Yeah, sweet to touch, to look at, you know. It's good to window shop, but you stay with 'em very long, you get your head cut off. Not your hair, but your head.

[*Both laugh.*]

Jorgenson: So that's when you decided to quit, more or less cold turkey.

Cash: I didn't have any medication to taper off on. It was cold turkey, but like I said, the love and care of June, my mother, our families, and Dr. Winston . . .

Jorgenson: Well, I know from my profession, that what you experienced, what you survived, is a miracle. I just know that combination, that heavy, that long, could have been totally disastrous.

Cash: I know.

Jorgenson: What's life like now, then, as opposed to that?

Cash: It's still a struggle. Because the lifestyle I live is unbelievable to people. They say, "What have you been doing lately?" I say, "How lately?" Two weeks ago, I was in Budapest, Hungary. Two weeks from now, I'll be in Canada, in Saskatchewan, here or there in New York. Sometimes we eat and sleep, and sometimes we don't. There's not a day goes by that I don't want a mood elevator, or a leveler, or a sleeping pill, or an upper. Because of the erratic lifestyle I live.

I expected to have it tougher than everybody else, because in 1969 to '70, I had some fabulous success, record-wise, television-wise, and that's when I started really studying the Bible in earnest, and I realized that, and I won't quote it, I'll just paraphrase it: "He to whom much is given, much is required." And I realized that many times what the regular requirement was for the average person is gonna be required of me too, to survive. So, I made up my mind that with God's help, and the love of those who care for me, I can make it. I'll fight it. I'll whip it.

Jorgenson: And part of that, of course, is doing what you're doing here. This sharing and giving away adds to the strength. It's hard for people to understand that paradox, but we know that's how we are sustained. But I'm sure that the realization that you are making the world a better place, and you are helping some people, has to give you moments of: "It's great to be alive," or feeling "up" on life.

Cash: It does.

Jorgenson: John, if you were to change anything in the world today, what would you like to change?

Cash: Well. Life is so precious. I think grade school children should be the ones to decide on the nuclear arms balance. [*Laughter.*] For one thing, I think if we left it up to the kids, there wouldn't be one on earth. I think it's insanity that humankind exists with one nuclear warhead anywhere in the world. Well, one thing I could do to make this world a better place, there would not be one nuclear warhead in the world anywhere. Politicians can take that and go with it and work it out and get rid of 'em all, but I would also, as you just suggested, stamp out the inner holocaust that so many people are into now.

It kills me to see not just the young people and the things drugs are doing to 'em, but what alcohol is doing to people our age. Y'know, we can talk about the kids and drugs as long as we want to, but I really think the biggest drug problem we got in this country right now, or one of the biggest, is alcohol.

Jorgenson: No question about it, John. No question about it. Seven times the problem.

Cash: It's socially accepted. But in Tennessee they just passed a law that you go to jail if you're picked up and you've had two drinks within the last hour. If that was a national law, I believe people would take notice. It kills people, that's why.

Jorgenson: People forget that. Of course, that's a whole area . . . This is a death-dealing affliction. It's insane that we aren't doing more. I often say the "drug problem" is not necessarily in the streets. It's in our medicine cabinets. And we sit around discussing it with our kids with a highball in our hand. There's gotta be a change from the inside. And the people I've visited with, knowing my own experience in treating people, something has to occur within. You said in the beginning that it makes you feel good. So the reason we become addicted basically is for *comfort*. We're uncomfortable in some aspect of our life and we find that drugs, or the alcohol drug, makes us feel better. So then I guess it makes sense, doesn't it, to change that to where we feel better about ourselves inside. Maybe that's where the change has to come.

Cash: Yeah, well. A drug addict and alcoholic will argue with you all day long, as you know, that he hadn't had but about a fourth as much of what he's really had. It's back to that old demon they call Deception, there's so many things in this world that can cause the inner holocaust, that can deceive us. The medication was made for a special reason, and the doctors say they don't prescribe that because people abuse it. I don't know what people *don't* abuse in the way of medication.

I think we need a little more education on what the side effects to a lot of medications are that are going around. Personally, I have the *Physicians' Desk Reference* in my house—in three or four different rooms in my house, I have one.

Jorgenson: Where you can see the indicated counterindications.

Cash: Well my mother and father are very elderly, take a lot of medications, I got them really for their benefit. But I've learned a lot from them.

Jorgenson: John, often you've been involved in helping programs like ours, and in continuing to carry the message that there is hope and there's help, is what I hear. And I hear it in your music. Is that a proper reflection on the message that you're carrying in much of your music, kind of hope-filled?

Cash: Mm-hmm. I just finished a gospel album, and every one of these are positive, "up" songs. There's a positive force, a positive power in gospel music, as there is in the gospel. And there is hope, and there is help. I don't know anybody in this world that doesn't have somebody who loves them. If they can turn to that one person in a time of trouble, the one person they know won't fail them . . .

Jorgenson: What would you most like to be remembered for, or by?

Cash: As a good daddy and husband.

Jorgenson: That's great. That's where it begins.

SUPERSTAR CASH STILL SPEAKS FOR THE HEARTS OF AMERICANS

Robert K. Oermann | April 26, 1987 | *Nashville Tennessean*

"It was like standing in the presence of Lincoln," says longtime Nashville-based journalist and author Robert K. Oermann. "I distinctly remember when I met him, being awestruck by what a formidable presence he had, what an aura."

It was 1979, and Oermann had recently taken a job as director of technical services at the Country Music Hall of Fame. A newly installed Johnny Cash exhibit included video from a 1971 episode of *The Johnny Cash Show* entitled "Johnny Cash on Campus," filmed at Vanderbilt University. Guests included Linda Ronstadt and Neil Young. Cash performed a new, instant classic entitled "Man in Black." That segment was part of the exhibit.

An answer to countless queries about his attire, "Man in Black" was also an eloquent protest song. It called out injustices against prisoners, the poor, people of color, the "ones who are held back," and, most emphatically, those sent to fight in the Vietnam War: "I wear the black in mourning for the lives that might have been / Each week we lose a hundred fine young men."

"Man in Black" was a risky move. Up to that point, Cash's fans were predominantly blue-collar folks from rural areas, most of whom supported the Vietnam War. Cash was connecting to what he would later call "the long-haired element," whose opposition to Vietnam was only growing. Robert K. Oermann was one of those.

"'Man in Black' is a song I have always dearly loved," says Oermann. "It spoke to my generation, the Vietnam War generation. That's who I was—a longhaired hippie. I told Johnny Cash how it moved me and how I wept even all those years later when I saw the clip of him singing it before a group of students. He could not have been more gracious."

After gaining renown as a freelance music journalist, Oermann soon moved from the Country Music Hall of Fame to a staff position at the *Nashville Tennessean* newspaper and became the first country music reporter for *USA Today*. Artists, Music Row executives, and country music fans would soon come to know his work.

The 1980s were a difficult time for Johnny Cash, in almost every way. By the mid-'80s, he'd backslid into drug and alcohol abuse; his health had begun to deteriorate, with hospital stays due to pneumonia, bleeding ulcers, and a harrowing encounter with a pet ostrich, which resulted in several broken ribs and a gash—from the ostrich's talon—in Cash's stomach. His father passed away in 1985. And while he still did well as an international concert draw, Johnny Cash's records were barely selling.

Rick Blackburn was head of Columbia/Epic/CBS Records, Cash's record label. In a 1986 conversation with Oermann, Blackburn lamented that, after a string of lackluster releases, he was going to have to drop Johnny Cash. The groundbreaking artist had not had a hit since "The Baron" in 1981. At this point, the decision to let him go was not public. Cash himself was in the dark.

Oermann decided to report this scoop. It ran on the front page of the *Nashville Tennessean*: "Man in Black" Without a Label. That headline was how Johnny Cash discovered the label he'd worked for since 1958 would no longer provide a home for his music. It was front-page news in *USA Today* as well.

Cash would later say he was not devastated, but his biographer Robert Hilburn quotes Steve Popovich, head of Nashville operations for Mercury records, and a friend of Cash's, as saying Cash "was down, almost in shock."

Public reaction was intense. Blackburn and Columbia suffered withering criticism from fans and artists. Not only for the decision to drop the man who, as enraged upstart Dwight Yoakam put it, "built the building," but also for first telling a journalist rather than Cash himself.

"Rick Blackburn played tennis with the man who owned the *Tennessean*," says Oermann. "Blackburn complained. I was suspended because [the *Tennessean* owner's] tennis buddy had been wronged. I almost lost my job over it. Everybody at the paper believed I was in the right. I did the right thing. I did my job. I reported the news. Which the publisher had drummed into all of us—that was our primary job. So I was furious. On top of it, I had to write this degrading apology to Blackburn that they published in the paper, so I was the person who'd done wrong. It was humiliating."

In the melee, Johnny Cash reached out. "During my suspension, when I was at home, I got a letter from Johnny Cash," Oermann says. "It basically read: 'I'm not mad, I'm not upset. You're a newspaperman. I understand that. You're the first thing I turn to in the newspaper every morning.' It was incredibly wonderful to get a letter from Johnny Cash on his stationery, signed by him."

In retrospect, Oermann maintains Blackburn's "letting slip" that Cash was to be dropped was no accident. Blackburn knew Oermann, and he knew the seasoned journalist would break the story. The subsequent criticism of Oermann and the *Tennessean* drew focus from Blackburn. For his part, Blackburn, who passed away in 2012, always stood by his decision. For the 2011 book *The Resurrection of Johnny Cash: Hurt, Redemption, and American Recordings*, he told author Graeme Thomson, "When you're running a business, it's about everything moving forward. It's not 'What have you done for me' but 'What are you going to do for me?'"

After the dust settled, Oermann went back to work. Within months, Mercury records signed Cash. In 1987, the label released *Johnny Cash Is Coming to Town*. The album featured songs by Elvis Costello and Guy Clark. Cash called in Waylon Jennings for a duet on "The Night Hank Williams Came to Town," which was also made into an MTV-style video.

The following promotional interview for *Johnny Cash Is Coming to Town* took place in the House of Cash, the homespun museum and former recording studio in Hendersonville, Tennessee, where Cash's mother worked the register. Johnny and June and son John Carter lived nearby. Eventually, Oermann would be invited to that house for another interview. —Ed.

They call him The Man in Black, not The Superstar in Black, for despite 30 years of international renown, Johnny Cash has remained "just a man."

He's been interviewed countless times, yet he's still disarmingly candid. His life has been marked by tribulation, but he retains a wacky absurdist sense of humor. He has ascended to the loftiest heights of celebritydom, but has the warmth of an eager unknown.

"I'm aware of who I am and where I am and what I am," says Cash, seated in the wood-paneled office above his House of Cash museum in Hendersonville. "I try to be just that. And I think a few people appreciate that."

More than "a few." Cash is arguably the biggest country star of all time. He is perhaps the one name that defines Nashville throughout the world. He is perhaps the one personality that defines what it means to be a country entertainer.

Cash's hundreds of accolades would doubtless more than fill the Dyess County, Ark., shack where he was born 55 years ago. His rise from that poverty makes him one show business legend who is truly "of the people."

He rose to fame with the rockabilly sound of Memphis in 1955, vaulted to Nashville stardom in 1958, then went down in flames as a drug dependent in the 1960s.

Phoenix-like, Cash rose from his ashes in the late 1960s and became an even bigger star than ever before. He starred in his own national network TV series in 1969-71 and during the following decade became a film star too.

"During what people call my superstar years when I had my ABC television show every week, my agent says that in 1971 I sold more records than anybody in the world.

'That's when I became aware that people might know me anywhere I go."

He took the stardom in stride, accepting it as a social responsibility. Cash became an almost heroic moral American figure during those turbulent times of political upheaval, protest and unrest.

He wore black, he said, on behalf of the poor, the downtrodden and the less fortunate.

He'd sung of their lives in hits such as *Folsom Prison Blues, I Got Stripes, Five Feet High and Rising, Dark as a Dungeon* and *The Ballad of Ira Hayes*, as well as on LPs devoted to American Indians, prisoners, and working men, some of which are now regarded as country's first concept albums.

But in the late 1960s and early 1970s he made his humanitarianism more overt, as *What Is Truth, Man in Black* and *Ragged Old Flag* made clear.

"Protest is not my main forte. I've made statements.

"I get a lot of mail, hate mail from the Ku Klux Klan. I have a letter from them with their 'KKK' signed in blood. It's a threatening thing that I'm proud of. I'm really proud that a hate group knows that I'm opposed to them.

"If the focal point of any organization or institution is hate and the destruction of other people then I'm glad that my name is against that.

"I wrote *Ragged Old Flag* to remind myself of how many and how often this country's been involved in wars. It seems to me like the politicians and the military just can't wait for another one. And that really bothers me.

"It bothers me that we're going to have 50,000 men on maneuvers off the coast of Central America in May, and at the same time the Russian submarines are off the East Coast more than ever, conducting war games.

"I mean, let's face it, there's no winner in a war.

"One reason I'm so concerned is my nephew Roy Cash, Jr., the father of Miss America Kellye Cash, is going to be commander of an aircraft carrier group in those maneuvers. And I just hate to see him go.

"And I'm really on edge about this situation because [only son] John Carter Cash will have to register for the draft within a year."

John Carter Cash is 17 and has music in his blood. His proud father reports that the teenager's hard rock group, the J.C. Cash Band, has had four promising recording sessions.

Rosanne, Cash's oldest daughter, has become a Gold-selling pop/country star. One of the most striking songs from her last LP was *My Old Man*, dedicated to him.

"The first time I heard it, I had myself a big cry. Because she said such great things about me that I really didn't deserve.

"I called her and wrote her a letter and told her how much I loved her, how proud I was of her.

"I've got a big family and I can fail to do that so easily, for so long, to so many of them, because I work so much and go so fast.

"Sunday, I had all four of my daughters at my house, and we had all eight grandchildren. June's daughters Rosie and Carlene came later in the day.

"That's never happened before. I took pictures like crazy. The girls laughed and said, 'How do you want us lined up? In proper order like our age—Rosanne, Kathy, Cindy, Tara?'"

In addition to the daughters, Cash's Nashville clan includes sisters Reba and Louise, mother Carrie and younger brother Tommy. Sister JoAnn is in North Carolina. Brother Roy, Miss America's grandfather, is in Memphis.

Daughter Cindy provides harmony vocals on Cash's new LP *Johnny Cash Is Coming to Town*, as do Kathy's husband Jimmy Tittle, daughter-in-law Carlene Carter, wife June, and sisters-in-law Helen and Anita Carter.

On his new LP Cash sings his compositions *The Ballad of Barbara* and *I'd Rather Have You* as well as the songs of Guy Clark, Elvis Costello, Merle Travis, and other celebrated songwriters.

It's his first new country collection in two years. Nevertheless, his records have continued to sell. The *Folsom Prison*, *San Quentin* and *Greatest Hits* albums were all awarded multi-Platinum status last year for sales in excess of two million apiece. They join his nine previous Gold Record awards.

His 1986 religious novel, *Man in White*, also marked a reemergence. Cash's previous book, his 1975 autobiography *Man in Black*, "has sold a million and three hundred thousand, and a quarter of a million of those were in hard cover," the star reports.

The Cash film career continues as well. This fall, he'll star in a remake of 1947's John Wayne classic *Angel and the Badman*.

"It's scheduled to start September 28th, but we're going to try and start earlier that month because I have an offer to tour Brazil and we want to do that. I'm playing the John Wayne role, the 'bad man,' and as far as I know Waylon Jennings is gonna play the sheriff. I understand John Schneider's gonna play the outlaw that's always tryin' to kill me.

"They haven't found an 'angel' in Hollywood yet for the part. They ran out of virgins three years ago, and I'm sure they're having trouble finding an angel."

Cash has starred in 10 previous films and TV movies, and his music has been featured in at least seven others.

He cites his most embarrassing screen moment in his 1961 cinematic debut, the B-movie *Door to Door Maniac*. "I had no idea what I was doing."

He received his best reviews for his 1971 performance opposite Kirk Douglas in *A Gunfight*, but says his favorite role was in the 1981 TV film *The Pride of Jesse Hallam* about the problem of illiteracy in America.

"I probably have a thousand letters of response to that movie. I played the illiterate. I felt I could identify with that part because I've known people like him, exactly like him. I tried to become that man."

The role is dear to him because of its social content.

"I haven't ever backed a cause that I've regretted, but I've backed a few fruitless ones, like prison reform.

"Lately my energies are turning toward things like what June and I were involved with last year with Waylon and Jessi (Colter) on the Shelter for Battered Women.

"I'm donating something for their Fan Fair auction again this year."

By the time Fan Fair rolls around Cash should be "in the pink." He has had to cancel several recent appearances—including hosting this month's Dove Award gospel music ceremony—because of illness.

"I had high blood pressure and it was staying high. The doctor told me I had to rest to bring it down. I went off and stayed at Dickson Hospital for three days, then went to my farm in Hickman County for two days. It's been 10 days since I've had any blood pressure medicine, so I'm doin' all right."

He resumed his busy schedule in support of *Johnny Cash Is Coming to Town* last week.

"I have to reschedule everything I do, and the first thing I try to schedule is time with my family. But invariably, something will come along.

"People pull me from so many directions, so many different angles. Some are good, some are ridiculous, some are insulting, some take up a lot of time.

"And some of them are important, like folks that care about human rights."

"BIGGEST PARTY EVER" OPENS NEW CASH EXHIBIT

Robert K. Oermann | March 23, 1988 | *Nashville Tennessean*

When the House of Cash museum and gift shop opened in the early 1970s, the general public got its first impressions of Johnny Cash and June Carter Cash's fondness for archiving and memorializing their remarkable lives. But it housed only a fraction of their various collections, which steadily grew. The 1988 Johnny Cash Exhibit at the Country Music Hall of Fame expanded mightily on what the House of Cash had begun, bringing truckloads of carefully curated material from their Hendersonville home into the Hall for all to see. It would remain up for two years.

In a discussion with Robert K. Oermann for this *Tennessean* article, Cash good-naturedly used the term *pack rats* to describe his and June's tendency to hold on to virtually everything. Spartan they were not.

Since opening its doors in 1967, the Country Music Hall of Fame museum had not mounted anything so elaborate as the Johnny Cash Exhibit. Previous exhibits devoted to Dolly Parton and Willie Nelson did not—could not—approach its scope.

Country Music Hall of Fame director Bill Ivey announced: "This collection provides unprecedented documentation of country music's most distinguished career. It is extraordinarily rich due to Cash's unusual level of cooperation and interest, and the availability of his personal archives."

The public had never seen the vast majority of the artifacts. Displays were divided into seven sections: "Roots" encompassed Cash's Arkansas boyhood; "Rockabilly" covered his move to Memphis and work with Sam Phillips at Sun; "Stardom" gave insight into his tempestuous but fruitful 1960s life and work; "Screen" offered memorabilia from his television

141

and film work; "Legend" touched on his books; "Offstage" gave attendees a look at Cash's hobbies and family. Another gallery—the "Signature Collection"—included a Cash-guided video tour of Johnny and June's home.

To accompany the exhibit, Cash re-recorded many of his old hits for *Classic Cash: Hall of Fame Series*. As producer (a rarity on Cash material), he used modernisms like synthesizers and a synthesizer guitar. This album would see a European release, but outside of the CMHOF, it would not be marketed in the United States.

The year 1988 was a characteristically busy time for Cash, but it would end with his most serious health scare to date. Despite struggling with persistent laryngitis, after the exhibit opening gala, he toured both domestically and in Europe; he recorded the King James Version of the New Testament for a multitape release; and he starred as an elder Davy Crockett in Disney TV's *Davy Crockett: Rainbow in the Thunder*.

Cash's second album for Mercury, *Water from the Wells of Home*, would hit stores on October 10. As with *Johnny Cash Is Coming to Town*, longtime friend Jack Clement produced. Cash and Clement had decided to make a different kind of Johnny Cash album, calling in high-profile guests like Paul McCartney, the Everly Brothers, Waylon Jennings, Glen Campbell, Emmylou Harris, Tom T. Hall, John Carter Cash, and chart toppers of the day Hank Williams Jr. and Rosanne Cash. (Rosanne would ultimately score five number-one singles in the 1980s, including a 1988 re-recording of her father's own "Tennessee Flat-Top Box.")

Although the album was well reviewed and Cash's duet single with Waylon, "That Old Wheel," briefly charted, *Water from the Wells of Home* did not sell. Cash once again responded to the disappointment with work, albeit against doctor's orders. —Ed.

The grand opening of the Johnny Cash Exhibit at the Country Music Hall of Fame last night was easily the biggest party the museum has ever given.

And that was as it should be. For at the center of it all was a man whose name virtually defines country music throughout the world.

"There's a lot of memories here," mused Cash prior to the opening ceremony. "A lot of pictures and letters of loved ones.

"We came up with a lot of things. I think it's a terrific display."

Cash chatted patiently with national TV crews, magazine journalists, newspaper reporters and publicists while waiting for his big moment at the podium.

Around him swirled a shower of stars who had come to wish him well.

By turns he greeted Chet Atkins, Emmylou Harris, Johnny Rodriguez, former roommate Waylon Jennings, Jessi Colter and Bill Monroe. Studying the displays nearby were Mel McDaniel, Lynn Anderson, Jimmy Tittle, Earl Scruggs, Mercury Records vice president Steve Popovich, legendary Sun Records founder Sam Phillips, famed Nashville lawyer James Neal and Governor Ned McWherther.

Even British pop hit-maker and Fox television star Tracey Ullman turned up to honor Cash.

And of course there was a full complement of relatives, representing all the branches of the complex Carter/Cash kin network. Wife June Carter Cash, sister Reba Hancock, sister-in-law Anita Carter and son John Carter Cash gabbed with John's daughters as the festivities began.

Tara, Cindy, Kathy, Rosie, and Rosanne Cash were all there. Cindy brought daughter Jessica. Rosanne pointed out displayed artifacts to daughters Hannah, Chelsea and Caitlin. June's daughter Carlene introduced her daughter Tiffany to one and all.

The place was so packed you could hardly see the exhibit.

"I really haven't seen it yet, myself," The Man in Black said. "I hope to.

"June and I are kind of pack rats. We've always kept everything. The best of it is here.

"I let them [the Country Music Foundation staff] look through my house and my museum and let them choose.

"Looking back over some of the things here I see a lot of little things that people have given me through the years.

"I wanted to make it a little more personal than the average museum display. So I took pen and paper and wrote down my thoughts.

"It's got some of my favorite artifacts. We're very proud of it."

Cash cited a Frederick Remington bronze, a Helen Keller book, his antique Colt pistols, Kris Kristofferson's song lyrics, Mother Maybelle Carter's guitar and his old video clips as among his favorite collectibles.

He spoke briefly about his upcoming LP which will feature him singing duets with top stars.

"I don't know if this'll be my last album or not. But it's time I got all my old friends into the studio to sing with me. Just in case."

Popovich believes the LP will become one of the outstanding achievements in Cash's already legendary 30-year country career. That career is amply documented in the new exhibit, which opens officially today.

It is arranged in seven sections, each representing a historical or personal phase of Cash's life.

Said Cash, "I understand it is the largest exhibit the Country Music Hall of Fame has ever put on display."

Budgeted at $700,000 it is, indeed, the most ambitious one the facility has ever mounted. It is being sponsored by Holiday Inns.

To promote it, Country Music Foundation executives Bill Ivey and Diana Johnson will take videos of the display and clips of Cash's early career to TV talk shows in 10 cities—Dallas, Atlanta, Philadelphia, Detroit, Milwaukee, Indianapolis, Houston, St. Louis, Nashville and Chicago.

Holiday Inns is also helping with the CMF's ad campaign for the coming tourist season. All Hall of Fame billboards and print ads will feature the new Cash exhibit.

Congratulations flew left and right last night amid the hubbub of hundreds in attendance. Virtually everyone there could tell a Johnny Cash story.

But it was The Man in Black himself, who had the last word at the gala event. After remarks and reminiscences on stage he concluded, "I'd like to thank God, who is the source of all music. And to ask his forgiveness for all the times we've screwed it up."

QUEEN ELIZABETH THEATRE INTERVIEW

Red Robinson | July 9, 1988 | Interview Transcript

When Red Robinson interviewed Johnny Cash in July of 1988, neither man knew how pivotal the next few months would be for Cash.

Robinson began by asking Cash about the 1986 album *Class of '55: Memphis Rock & Roll Homecoming*. This Polygram release had featured Cash and fellow former Sun recording artists Roy Orbison, Jerry Lee Lewis, and Carl Perkins. Legendary producer and songwriter Chips Moman ("Do Right Woman," "Dark End of the Street") had produced it at Sun. Guests included John Fogerty, the Judds, Dave Edmunds, Ricky Nelson, Sam Phillips, and June Carter Cash. Fogerty contributed album highlight "Big Train (From Memphis)." Expectations had been high, with Dick Clark and a film crew documenting everything. But after hitting number fifteen on the Top Country Albums chart, *Class of '55* had sunk.

Today, Red Robinson says, "The album didn't sell dick, but it was good. The timing was bad. If they'd done it five years earlier, it would've sold well. Timing is everything in show business. Everything."

Robinson and Cash also discussed the massive Johnny Cash Exhibit at the Country Music Hall of Fame and commiserated on being collectors.

Cash's schedule was hectic as ever, mostly with a tour that had brought him to Vancouver. Come December, Cash's body would finally give out, if only temporarily. The fifty-six-year-old Man in Black would visit fifty-one-year-old Waylon Jennings at Nashville's Baptist Hospital, where Waylon was recuperating from triple bypass heart surgery. From there, Cash would head to a checkup, whereupon his doctor will inform him that he, too, needs to go under the knife, immediately.

Within a day of visiting Waylon, Cash was on the operating table, where doctors performed a double bypass on his heart. He and Waylon would recuperate in the hospital together.

In a July 30, 1989, interview conducted during press for June Carter Cash's *Mother Maybelle's Cookbook: A Kitchen Visit with America's First Family of Country Song*, a lively Cash said of his bypass surgery, "It's a shock to find out you're not indestructible."

He told his interviewer his heart had stopped for forty minutes, and that he'd glimpsed the other side and had been angry and sad to be brought back.

"I cried a lot," he said. "And I watched a lot of ball games. I see other people differently [now]. I've always loved my family, but I want to gather them around me more than ever."

In this interview, almost exactly a year before, under very different circumstances, at the Queen Elizabeth Theatre in Vancouver, Cash and Red Robinson enjoyed the usual promotional tête-à-tête, almost three decades after their first meeting. Following his subsequent surgery, Cash will recuperate and, surprisingly for anyone but Cash, return to touring. But this would be his last conversation with Red. —Ed.

Red Robinson: One album that you brought up that didn't get the attention I thought it should deserve, along these lines, and it must have been an emotional experience when you and Carl [Perkins] and Roy [Orbison] and Jerry Lee [Lewis] went in and did *The Class of '55*. . . . I treasure that album because it had a lot of magic moments in it.

Johnny Cash: Yeah, it really did. I enjoyed doing that. That was a "going home" kind of an album. Carl and Jerry and Roy and I really loved doing that album, although as you say, it wasn't all that big of an album, but I think it was an important album. It's like, thirty years later, here we are back doing what we do and feeling better about it than ever.

Robinson: You've got new things happening all the time. You amaze me with the fact that you'll take chances with music, and you always have an ear for what's happening new. Does it come from you? Where's that spring from—wanting to do new things?

Cash: I just keep my ears open. Y'know, I never have worried about competition, but I'm always aware of who is *good*, and who's out there.

I'm a big music *fan*. I listen to a lot of music. I listen to a lot of country, and because of John Carter, in recent years I listen to a lot of rock.

Robinson: You must be proud of him, too. Let's not skate by having a son that's a performer, too. How do you feel about that, John?

Cash: I don't think he ever thought about being anything else. Just like me, y'know? He's never seriously considered that he wanted to do anything else with his life except perform. And he is really a good performer and songwriter and musician.

Robinson: Tell me, because I've been following it in the trade magazines and of course in *USA Today* and *People* magazine, your wonderful display of memorabilia going on in Nashville. Really, it's "the Johnny Cash Story." And I didn't know this about you, and I've known you all these years, that you *save* things. You're like I am. Do you ever throw anything out? I don't.

Cash: No. We don't throw anything away. We've got everything. We've got a house and an office building completely full, every corner stacked full of things we've collected over the years, and we've collected a lot, we've been a lot of places, had a lot of things given to us, bought a lot of things, and we have it all. And this display at the Country Music Hall of Fame is my special Hall of Fame exhibit that is sponsored by Holiday Inn for two years. And it's the biggest exhibit they've ever had. It's like the one they had for Dolly, one they had for Willie, except mine runs two years and it is the biggest one they've had. It's got a collection, or it's got pieces from different collections of things—we have furniture, some of June's silver, ancient Roman coins that I collect, Roman and Greek coins, an autographed book or two from my autographed book collection. I got an autographed book—*My Life Story* by Helen Keller, which is my favorite autographed book that I've got. It's got pictures and artifacts up through the years through the last thirty-two years, highlighting different phases and times in my career.

ROCK & ROLL HALL OF FAME INDUCTION

Lyle Lovett | January 15, 1992 | Original Transcript

For Johnny Cash, the third time was the charm with the Rock & Roll Hall of Fame. He'd been on the ballot twice before and did not make the cut. But in 1991, voters acknowledged his contributions, innovations, and legacy, and voted him in. At this writing, he is one of eleven to be inducted into both the Country Music Hall of Fame and the Rock & Roll Hall of Fame, alongside Hank Williams, the Everly Brothers, Sam Phillips, Brenda Lee, Floyd Cramer, Bob Wills, Bill Monroe, Chet Atkins, Jimmie Rodgers, and Elvis Presley.

In a heartfelt, personal speech, transcribed here, singer-songwriter Lyle Lovett officially inducted Johnny Cash into the Hall on January 15, 1992.

In the ensuing decades, the night of "the Class of '92" would be regarded as one for the books. Other inductees: the Yardbirds, inducted by U2's The Edge; Sam and Dave, inducted by Billy Joel; Booker T and the MG's, inducted by Stax Records cofounder Jim Stewart; the Isley Brothers, inducted by Little Richard; the Jimi Hendrix Experience, inducted by Neil Young; and Bobbie Blue Bland, inducted by B. B. King; nonperformers: guitar designer Leo Fender, inducted by Keith Richards; songwriter Doc Pomus, inducted by Phil Spector; and promoter Bill Graham, inducted by Carlos Santana.

The seventh annual Rock & Roll Hall of Fame induction ceremony took place in a ballroom at New York City's Waldorf-Astoria Hotel. In those days, the event was much smaller than today. It was not filmed for television, and no tickets were sold to the public. The I. M. Pei–designed Rock Hall itself was under construction in Cleveland and would finally open in 1995. Without TV cameras and the eyes of an audience, these occasions were raucous, unpredictable, messy, and long, with often-unwieldy jam sessions capping off the night. Rock stars, movie stars, and celebrities donned evening wear, dinner was served, and all manner of spirits flowed.

Although in hindsight it seems strange, in *Cash: The Life*, biographer Robert Hilburn notes that at the Waldorf, Johnny Cash wasn't initially excited, but rather "was on edge. He had never considered himself a true rock 'n' roller, and he worried that performers who were closer to the rock tradition would resent his inclusion. Indeed, there was some questioning of Cash's credentials . . ."

The names of whoever did that questioning are lost to time. But the disparagement was enough to merit an impassioned defense in the *New York Times* from Karen Schoemer: "At the Rock & Roll Hall of Fame dinner in January, there was some grumbling behind the scenes that Johnny Cash, an inductee this year, didn't really deserve to be included. Mr. Cash was a country singer; what was he doing in the Rock & Roll Hall of Fame?"

Schoemer averred that yes, when Cash was called upon to join an epic jam session at the end of the night, he did not know the chords to "Purple Haze," but nevertheless, "Mr. Cash, now at 60 years old, has a strong rock-and-roll pedigree. He got his start in Memphis at Sun Records, the label that launched Elvis Presley, Carl Perkins, Jerry Lee Lewis and a host of other rockabilly singers; he patented, if not invented, a rollicking boom-chicka-boom rhythm that has become an integral part of the rock vernacular."

Johnny Cash's worry over whether he belonged wasn't the only thing eating at him; 1991 had been a rough year. His much-beloved mother, Carrie Rivers Cash, had passed away from cancer in May; a plan to cut back on touring and open a theater in Branson, Missouri, had fallen through; he'd undergone several failed surgeries to repair his many-times-broken jaw, with doctors finally grafting a titanium plate in to keep the bone together. He was in almost constant pain. But through the grief, hurt, and disappointment, he'd stayed on the road.

At the induction ceremony, however, everything ultimately worked out fine. Even though parts of Cash's off-the-cuff acceptance speech could be construed as a little defensive, with citations of his credibility and shoutouts to Memphis R&B stations, he would soon feel the embrace of the fellow icons on hand, and all would be well. He told *Rolling Stone*'s Steve Pond of his encounter with one such icon in the men's room: "I was standing at the urinal and Keith Richards walked in and stood behind me and started singing 'Loading Coal' from the *Ride This Train* album. And then he said, 'Look at this. I'm takin' a piss with Johnny Cash. We need a picture of this.' I said 'No, Keith, we *don't* need a picture of this.'"

Cash told Robert Hilburn that "Loading Coal" "was one of the most obscure songs I ever recorded, and I wondered who in the world could be singing that song, and when I looked around, I saw Keith, and he had a big smile on his face. So I turned around and we sang the chorus together. That's when I guess I knew everything was going to be okay."

Within the year, Cash would take a meeting with famed hip-hop and metal producer Rick Rubin. Soon after that, no one would be questioning his rock 'n' roll bona fides. The notion that anyone ever did would be rendered ridiculous. —Ed.

Lyle Lovett: "I Walk the Line" was the first song of his I ever heard. My aunt and uncle owned the record, and my cousin Wanda and I would wait until her mother went out of the house, and then we'd play it really loud.

But I can't remember the very first time I heard "I Walk the Line." To me, it was simply a part of the world as I knew it. Like a part of nature. More like air and like water than like a song that someone, some man, sat down and actually wrote and sang. "I Walk the Line" was a hit in November of 1956. That's about a year before I was born, so it really is a part of the world that I know. But that's the way it seems with great songs and with great artists. Their impact on people is such that you can't imagine what the world would be like, or sound like, without them.

He was born in rural Arkansas in 1932. He moved to Detroit in his late teens. He joined the Air Force, where he became a radio operator. After the Air Force, he moved to Memphis, where he made his first recordings for Sam Phillips and for Sun Records in 1955. It was there and then when the world of music began to feel his impact, as he wrote and recorded songs like "Cry! Cry! Cry!" "Hey Porter," and "I Walk the Line." He helped show the world what happens when rural sensibilities and values mix with an urban environment. Over the years he's demonstrated a broad musical perspective, never being afraid to record songs of social commentary, and always being eager to seek out new songs by talented young songwriters such as Bob Dylan, Kris Kristofferson, and Bruce Springsteen. He's had 48 songs in the pop charts, 135 on the country charts, and he's sold more than 50 million records.

His music, his artistry, his point of view helped form and define what we know as rock and roll. This is the biggest deal of my life. It's a great honor for me to present to you and to the Rock & Roll Hall of Fame: Johnny Cash.

Johnny Cash: Thank you very much. Hello Phil [Spector], I'm Johnny Cash. I would like to thank Sam Phillips, and I'd like to thank Jack Clement, who steered the career and directed recording activities of myself for Sam, as well as recording activities of a lot of other people, including Elvis, Carl Perkins, Jerry Lee Lewis, and my dearest buddy Roy Orbison. By the way, I'd like to make one correction if you don't mind. The name of the store on Beale Street was *Lansky* Brothers, not Lasky Brothers. That's where we hung out, bought those shining lamé clothes. In the mid-fifties. Just down the street was Home of the Blues record shop, where I spent all my money. I realized some of my first dreams, which was actually owning recordings of some of my heroes, people that'd influenced me and made an impression on my life. Of course there was the Hanks—Hank Williams, Hank Snow. The Carter Family. Country, folk from the hill country, they called 'em back then. But there were also other stations that I listened to in Memphis. I lived near Memphis in northeast Arkansas and I listened to WHBQ, and they had a program on there called "Red Hot & Blue" late at night, where they played back then what they called "race music." There I heard some of my earliest heroes. It was at the Home of the Blues record shop where I bought my first recording of Sister Rosetta Tharpe singing those great gospel songs. I can still see Sister Rosetta playing that Stella guitar. Sorry Mr. Fender, it was a Stella that Sister Rosetta was playing.

I bought some of the recordings by Alan Lomax. He did some field recordings back in the thirties and forties—he took his wire recorder into the alleys and honky-tonks in Mississippi and South Carolina and Louisiana. And I listened to those by the hour and by the day, by the week and the month, and they influenced a lot of my writing. Songs like "Big River" and "Get Rhythm"—some of the earlier songs that I wrote were influenced by people like Sister Rosetta Tharpe, and by Pink Anderson, and Blind Lemon Jefferson, and some of the Carolina street singers.

So I don't know, maybe I was trying to make sure that I belong here tonight, and make you see I might possibly actually belong in the Rock

& Roll Hall of Fame. I'm extremely proud of it, and whether I belong or not, I'm gonna take it home and show it off at home . . . take it home with June, who's here with me tonight, my wife, June.

Always had a big family that I've been proud of. While we're at it, my daughter Rosanne Cash is here, my daughter Carlene Carter, and my son, who is ready, Phil [Spector], John Carter Cash is here tonight.

I'm taking too much time. I want to thank you very much. As Little Richard said at the beginning of this program, he and I were talking. He said, "God is watching over things tonight." And I feel that, Richard. I thank you for reminding me of that. I asked June, "What do I say when I get up there?" She said, "Just ask God to guide you, and it'll be all right." I found that works, not only tonight, but every day of my life. Thank you very much. God bless you all.

JOHNNY CASH AND JUNE CARTER CASH INTERVIEW

Robert K. Oermann | March 1995 | Interview Transcript

All told, 1995 was a good year for Johnny Cash. His eighty-first album, *American Recordings*, out since April of 1994, was the career-defining hit for which he'd long hoped, a genuine return-to-form. It would sell more copies than any Johnny Cash album since 1971's *Man in Black* and inspire critics to write effusive reviews. Most important, and most pleasurable to Cash, however, was how the album captivated a new, younger audience. They flocked in droves to see him perform, cheered thunderously, and bought the CD.

Produced by hip-hop and heavy metal producer Rick Rubin, and released on Rubin's label of the same name, *American Recordings* would usher in a remarkable surprise fourth act for Cash. And while Cash's physical health was not great—he was still in almost constant pain from his repaired jaw and a facial nerve damaged by surgery—it was not yet in precipitous decline.

Writer and journalist Robert K. Oermann couldn't have been happier about *American Recordings*. "I took great pleasure in the fact that Johnny Cash's victory lap did not belong to CBS," he says. "It belonged to Universal, *American Recordings*' distributor."

CBS/Columbia had infamously put Johnny Cash out to pasture in 1986. He'd been on the label almost three decades, netting them untold cachet and money. Oermann had broken the story, resulting in much public outcry.

"Music Row doesn't give a shit about the past," Oermann says. "They just care where their next hit is coming from. They had already written off Johnny Cash. It was irrelevant to them who he was working with. Nobody cared. It was like: go ahead do whatever you want. In the business, he was totally irrelevant. Fans cared. I cared. Those of us who loved him and his music, we cared. Then, when [*American Recordings*] became successful, Music Row was like: 'We love him, he's one of us.' *Then* they were interested."

Rubin had approached Cash in 1993, shortly after Cash accepted U2's invitation to perform a guest vocal on "The Wanderer," from their soon-to-be-multi-platinum album *Zooropa*. Although it was sonically unlike anything he'd ever done, the synthesizer-driven track, with postapocalyptic lyrics inspired by the book of Ecclesiastes, was bespoke for Cash, and he delivered. Critics often cited "The Wanderer" as a bracing highlight of *Zooropa*. It augured what was to come.

Yet, Cash was still unsure. Although emboldened by his experience with the biggest band on the planet, he still smarted from past wounds, and pondered his place as an artist in the modern world. He strongly considered retiring. Rubin soon convinced him he was far from done, and they got to work.

American Recordings would be unlike any album—country or otherwise—of the era. It was dark yet vulnerable, deeply spiritual and uncompromising—the stripped-down, solo acoustic work Cash had wanted to release for years. It contained originals he'd held onto rather than put them out on an album no one would hear—"Drive On" and "Let the Train Blow the Whistle"—as well as versions of songs by Leonard Cohen, Glen Danzig, Tom Waits, Kris Kristofferson, and Nick Lowe. Cash wanted to call it *Late and Alone* but deferred to Rubin's choice of *American Recordings*.

After sonically capturing Cash solo acoustic in his living room, in Cash's Hendersonville cabin, and before a famously hip audience (Johnny Depp, Sean Penn, the Red Hot Chili Peppers) at the intimate Viper Room club in West Hollywood, Rubin had been instrumental in promoting and marketing *American Recordings*. He'd arranged a controversial black-and-white video of murder ballad and album opener "Delia's Gone," shot by noted rock photographer and filmmaker Anton Corbijn. In it, Cash shovels dirt onto the beautiful dead face of Delia. Cash gave the keynote speech at the 1994 South by Southwest festival in Austin and performed a set before a much younger crowd than usual, a far cry from the disinterested attendees at his dismal 1994 performances at the Wayne Newton Theatre in Branson, Missouri. He'd also wowed a tastemaker crowd at New York City's tiny Fez Café on April 13. On June 26, he gave a barnstorming performance before fifty thousand on the main stage at the Glastonbury Festival. On September 14, he'd sold out Carnegie Hall again, then headed to San Francisco to play a packed Fillmore.

All of this activity spilled into 1995, when Cash and Rubin began work on what would become 1996's *American II: Unchained*. While those wheels were turning, this interview, conducted at Johnny and June's Hendersonville home, coincided with *American Recordings* receiving the Best Contemporary Folk Grammy on March 1, 1995.

"Cash came downstairs in his jammies," Oermann says. Oermann had been talking to June in the kitchen, and who should bound in but Johnny Cash in his sleep attire. The interview commenced without June, but she soon joined in for a recounting of the couple's entwined histories as musicians and members of an esteemed group of artists creating work they hoped would outlive them. In the case of both Johnny and June, it would. —Ed.

Robert K. Oermann: I remember the first time I heard "Man in Black," and it made me cry. I still cry when I listen to it today. It moved me so deeply because it spoke to me . . . it said something for me. Can you tell me how you came to write it?

Johnny Cash: A lot of people asked me for years why I wore black. I had my own reasons, but I never really had said anything. But then we were well into the Vietnam War and the loss of American lives was, at that particular time I wrote the song, a hundred a week. And I wrote it for the Vietnam veterans. I started—that's the verse I started: "Each week we lose a hundred fine young men." I wrote it for a special show [an episode of *The Johnny Cash Show*] called "Johnny Cash on Campus." We did it at Vanderbilt University, in the auditorium there. But then I got to thinking about the questions about why I wore black, and I answered a lot of other questions about why I was wearin' black at the time I wrote "Man in Black." But it was really for Vietnam, for the boys and girls that were our troops in Vietnam at the time. And for the ones that we were losin'.

Oermann: They do think of you as deeply compassionate. And this is something that seemed to have been going out of American society—compassion toward the powerless and the homeless and the disenfranchised, the prisoners, the American Indians, and people who have no voice in the system. What was it about your upbringing that made you that way?

Cash: Well that's what folk, or country, music is all about—givin' a voice to the people who have no voice. Anybody can sing these songs, y'know.

And sometimes I would write a song from the standpoint of my father, or write a song about a town bum named Abner Brown, which is one of my favorite songs I wrote. I also wrote a song about someone committed to an institution called "Committed to Parkview." Sometimes I wrote songs and put 'em in the second person, or write 'em about myself, but they're actually about another situation that I know about, y'know? But as far as prisons are concerned, Merle Haggard said one time, 'Johnny Cash understands what it's like to be in prison, but he doesn't *know*.' I thank God I don't know. But I do understand, havin' been four years in the Air Force away from home in a foreign land, where I didn't really want to be for three [of those years]. The songs of prison really came out of that loneliness and isolation, which I'm sure any convict will tell you is not the same thing. But when I started going into prisons to do concerts, then I wrote more and more from conversations I had with 'em. They seemed to just flow out of me. The things that were pumped into me, I poured 'em back out.

Oermann: What was it that made so many incredibly gifted people who changed the face of American music concentrate in Memphis, Tennessee, in the mid '50s? Was that just some happy accident? Was there really a creative cauldron going on? Why did you go?

Cash: I went to Memphis to record 'cause I lived there. Elvis and Carl and Jerry Lee, all of us had roughly the same background, y'know? We lived within a hundred miles of the Memphis radio stations. Grew up within a hundred miles of the Mississippi or the Memphis radio stations. And there was programs on the air like Dewey Phillips' *Red Hot & Blue*. Which they called race music at the time. There was also black gospel programs featuring artists like Sister Rosetta Tharpe. There were also live country folk jamboree shows, like the Light Crust Dough Boys, that I listened to faithfully, or Smilin' Eddie Hill and the Louvin Brothers. All of these people, some stations program 'em all. Some stations like WHBQ had what was called race music.

I listened to all those stations. And so did Elvis, and so did Carl, and we grew up on that kind of music. Elvis of course was the one that opened the door for all of us. Singin' that kind of music, but singin' the old country songs with a black feel. Like "Blue Moon of Kentucky," "That's All Right." He was very bold for a Southerner of his time. But his boldness certainly paid off and opened the door for a lot of others. I came along lovin' Hank Snow, and a lot of gospel. And I managed to finally record a lot of that. Carl was cut from the same cloth. He was very country, but he had a feel for the rhythm and blues. And then Jerry Lee, the biggest soul man of all, from Faraday, Louisiana, came in one day. At a Carl Perkins session we asked him to set down at the piano and sing one for us and well . . . I knew Sam [Phillips] had found another one, you know? That's a unique one there as well.

Oermann: I hear you loud and clear about Hank Snow. I got Hank Snow's new box set. I listen to it all the time.

Cash: I do, too.

Oermann: You have always had an image as an outsider in this town, in a way.

Cash: See, I would never have written a song like "Big River" if I hadn't had the black gospel and blues influence, and I've always been just a little bit outside of Nashville . . . always. When I came here to appear on the Grand Ole Opry the first time, I waited two hours out in the waiting room before the manager of the Opry finally said, "Come on in." He looked at my black clothes and long hair and sideburns and said, "What makes you think you belong on the Grand Ole Opry?" So I said, "Well, I've got a record in the Top 10 Best Sellers"—which was "Folsom Prison Blues"—I said, "I think they'd like to hear me." So he said, "You're on." But I never . . . in the '70s and, you know, I marked time there after a while, after the big time of my TV shows. I kind of marked time here and just fulfilled my contract for whatever interest there was in a Johnny Cash record in Nashville.

Oermann: Did you like what Waylon and Willie were doing? Taking control of their production and basically fighting that fight for everyone?

Cash: Yeah, I think what Willie and Waylon did in the '70s was really important for the music business. You know, if you're locked in to tryin' to get one hit record with the same general sound out of Nashville, record after record, you could get pretty locked into it. And it was good that Willie and Waylon weren't locked into anything, that their minds were still open. Like I try to keep mine open. And it's only outside of that particular kind of record machine that I've been able to do a lot of things that I'm most proud of.

[*June Carter Cash enters.*]

Oermann: John, tell me about the first time you ever heard the Carter Family.

Cash: I think the first time I heard the Carter Family was on the radio at night when I was very small. They were comin' over the airwaves from XERA, XERF, Del Rio, Texas. I scanned the radio dial when I was a little kid on the cotton farm in Arkansas. And it was the most wonderful, magical thing in the world to be able to turn that dial and hear different singers in different places.

Oermann: What was it about the songs?

Cash: Well, the simplicity of the deliverance and the emotions and the performance in those songs was like . . . like my life, y'know? Things were pretty cut and dried, black and white, straight ahead. And that's the way the Carter Family came at you. Right in the face, y'know? And it felt good.

Oermann: Do you recall the first time you ever saw June Carter?

Cash: First time I ever saw her? We took our senior trip in 1950, from Dyess High School, Dyess, Arkansas. And one of the stops was the Grand Ole Opry on Saturday night in Nashville. And I was sittin' up in the balcony of the Ryman Auditorium with my class, all in there together in two rows. And there she was down onstage.

[*June laughs.*]

Little Jimmie Dickens, June Carter. That's all I remember.

[*June laughs.*]

I said, "One of these days I'm gonna get her autograph."

[*June laughs.*]

I actually got it in 1956, first time I performed on the Grand Ole Opry. She asked me for some of my records. The next Saturday night I brought them to her and got an autographed picture from her and gave her my autographed records, two of 'em.

Oermann: [*To June*] Do you remember when the college students started liking the Carter Family music and really worshipping Mother Maybelle? Was there a specific show or a specific time?

June Carter Cash: Well, it seems to me I can't remember exactly the days on it. But they had the beginning of what they called the hootenanny days. And the first thing I knew we were playing a lot of colleges. That must have been late '50s, early '60s, somethin' kinda like that. And then they would give classes where they would talk about the music of the Carter Family. And then so many of the young people started to try to play guitar or autoharp. And they thought a lot of my mother. And we played a lot of those hootenanny shows and there was a show called *Hootenanny Hoot.*

Cash: Uh huh. That was a movie I was in [1963].

Carter Cash: Yeah that was your movie. That's right. But we used to do a lot of these shindig shows. They called 'em shindigs. And we would meet two or three other groups sometimes. Or sometimes it was just us and we played a lot of the colleges. We played all over.

Oermann: A lot of the Nashville acts at that time did not want to get involved with the folkies.

Carter Cash: Well, we were right at home. We felt we were. We were just kind of like "Carter Family Music." I don't know if you would say we were more in the folk field and some of them were real country entertainers, like Webb [Pierce] and Faron [Young] and Ferlin [Husky] and Carl [Smith]. All of them were singing hardcore country. But we were kind of in the folk field, my mother and sisters and I. But we were country as well, so I don't know where we belonged. We were just in both places, runnin' both directions as hard as we could go.

Cash: There were TV shows like *Hootenanny* and *Shindig.* I did both of those shows. What was happenin' in the late '50s was the music fans were discoverin' the real thing, like the Carter Family. You know there was a folk song revival—that was big then. But they started discoverin' the real thing, like the roots of folk music. Or the best in folk music. Carter Family were of that ilk. I loved that kind of music all my life, but I took it into the studio and electrified some of it, too. But then I did some of it acoustic-style back in the '50s as well. But that kind of music has always been my cup of tea. But when they discovered the real thing, they discovered the Carter Family.

Oermann: Was it just a happy accident that you were doing what they liked?

Cash: No, I don't think so. I was just writing things that I knew about, which is, I think, a pretty good order of the day for a writer, y'know. Write what you know. I was writing things like "Pickin' Time," about working on a cotton farm, "Five Feet High and Rising" about the flood. "Big River," about the Mississippi, y'know, which held me in awe. I lived close to it. We respected it, we were afraid of it, y'know, because it would flood you and run you out of your home. The cotton—all the cotton songs I wrote. The railroad songs, from stories that my father told me. And things I'd seen myself from riding the train through the flooded cotton lands tryin' to get to the hills before they rose over the train itself. Songs about things like these that I wrote that I'm sure would be called folk songs, or should be called folk songs because they were songs about life of the people, of the common people, of the poor people, told in lyric and melody.

Oermann: Can you tell me about "If I Were a Carpenter"?

Cash: I remember hearin' it first from Jack Elliott, right, June?

Carter Cash: Yes, he would start playin' it on the guitar and he would never quit playin' it on the guitar.

Cash: Yeah, yeah.

Carter Cash: He would play it for about two hours. So we got to hear it a lot of the time when we were visitin' with Bob Dylan and Ramblin' Jack.

Cash: Ramblin' Jack had a very unique performance. He liked to take his guitar in the cafés and walk right up to your table and play it in your face, you know? And it was pretty impressive, pretty bold stroke to come up to your table and play his guitar in your face, and sing "If I Were a Carpenter."

Carter Cash: For two hours.

Cash: Yeah. And he sang it on and on and on, and you know the song just never ended. And June and I were in the car with him goin' to Bob Dylan's house in Woodstock in '64 . . .

Carter Cash: It was Al Grossman's house, but we were meeting Bob was what it was.

Cash: Al Grossman's house, yeah. And Jack was singin' "If I Were a Carpenter" I think all the way.

Oermann: I tried to get Kris Kristofferson to tell me the helicopter story, but he wouldn't do it. He said, "You have to ask Johnny to tell it." And I said, "Why? Does he tell it better than you?" And he said, "Yes, he does."

Cash: He says I tell it different than he does. Well, people remember things different ways, y'know? Like time has a way of changin' things, your perspective, or the way you think you saw things. I don't know, I've heard so many stories comin' from so many different directions, y'know. And you get right down to the nucleus, the truth of the thing, and it's pretty simple. But actually, Kristofferson was a janitor at Columbia Records when he first came to town. Tryin' to get, he wanted to get his songs heard, but he wanted to eat, too. And so he got a job as a janitor, and I was always comin' in to record and June and I were always at the studio seemed like a lot when Kris was first come to town. And he was writin' all these songs, and rather than take a chance on gettin' fired by bringin' the songs directly to me—which they told him they'd do if he bothered me, I didn't know that—but he would slip the songs to her and she'd put 'em in her purse.

[June laughs.]

And, uh, after, after on the way home or after we'd get home, she would hand 'em to me. And usually I wouldn't listen to 'em, y'know. I was gettin' a lot of songs. I just wasn't listenin'.

Carter Cash: I have about fifty copies of something called "The Golden Idol."

Cash: Yeah, "The Golden Idol." Never did record it. But Kris was determined that I was gonna listen to his songs. So one Sunday afternoon during the middle of that, he landed a helicopter in our yard. And I was asleep and she came in and woke me up, says, "Some fool has landed a helicopter . . . "—I mean they were comin' by road and water, now they're comin' by air—"has landed a helicopter in your yard." And I went out and it was Kris. And he fell out of the helicopter with a tape in one hand and a beer in the other. And I said, "I'm gonna listen to your song, you know." Anybody that got this far. I did. I listened to it.

Oermann: What song was it?

Cash: It was "Sunday Morning Coming Down." Kris said it was somethin' else. You can cut that right there where I said Kris said it was somethin' else.

[*Laughter.*]

Oermann: How did your friendship with Dylan come about? At a festival?

Cash: You know on airplanes, those air sickness bags you get out of the back of the seat in front of you? I'd heard Bob Dylan, and I took one of those bags and wrote him a letter and wrapped it up and put a stamp on that air sickness bag and mailed it to him. Told him I liked his singin', liked his records. Didn't say I liked his singin', I said, "I like your recordings." I got a letter right back from him and talkin' about the—

Carter Cash: He was still in the cold water flat then.

Cash: Yeah. Yeah he was. He was just, you know, just barely started. And he was—

Carter Cash: I gave you his first record, remember?

Cash: . . . of Bob Dylan, yeah. Right. And June and I wore them out in Las Vegas. We were playin' The Mint. Backstage, and in the hotel room, we had Bob Dylan playin' all the time. So we started the correspondence that led up to our meeting in Newport. And that's where we met Bob and Joan and the whole bunch.

I'd love to hear an album today of the recordings, some of the recordings in our living room, our lakeside room, where we passed around the guitar. We had a guitar pull. This was '68, '69, '70. One night there was—at our house—Kris Kristofferson singin' "Me and Bobby McGee," Bob Dylan was there, sang "Lay, Lady, Lay," Joni Mitchell sang "Both Sides Now," Graham Nash sang "Marrakesh Express," and Shel Silverstein sang "A Boy Named Sue." That was the first time anybody heard any of those songs—they were sung that night at our lakeside room, here at Hendersonville. And it was such a high time that, you know, there was no alcohol, there was just the music and just all of us gettin' together . . . That was so exciting that Joni went upstairs to lie down. Said she couldn't stand all the excitement, you know. She had to take a break from it, then came back down and joined us again and we went on and on and into the night swappin' songs after that. And everybody sang. Mickey Newbury was there, sang "San Francisco Joy." Who else, June?

Carter Cash: Oh gosh. They came at different times, but that night, I don't know, there was about fifty of us.

Cash: Roy Orbison was there, sang a new song. I don't remember what it was right now, but—

Carter Cash: Roy was there a lot of times. We used to just invite friends and then sometime if we knew a new songwriter or somebody who was just tryin' to get started, we would—

Cash: Vince Matthews.

Carter Cash: We would bring them to the house and have them sing. And then sometimes that person went on to make it a few times. We made Larry Gatlin sing. We made Kris sing. We made a lot of 'em sing. It was a lot of fun.

Oermann: Tell me about the TV show. Did you run into resistance from the network [ABC]? I mean there you were booking people who were not that big at the time.

Cash: Well, I think Bill Carruthers came to us first with the idea of the network show.

Carter Cash: That was when we first went on.

Cash: That was '68, yeah. With six shows at first, I believe it was. And then the network was interested in picking us up for a full season. And they had all these rules, I guess. I heard they did, but I had my own. I said, if I host a show where I introduce new singer-songwriters that I like and appreciate, I want some real American artists on there. Some people with some backbone, with some grit, that really mean something as far as the songs of this country—of our country—are concerned. And I pointed out: I like the Weavers songs, so I'd like to have Pete Seeger. Well, they made a big deal out of that for a while, but they finally said OK. And they came to realize that Pete Seeger was just what I said he was, a great musician and singer. And I said Bob Dylan. I would like to ask for Bob Dylan to be on the first show. And of course they agreed to that. But there were so many other people that—

Carter Cash: Neil Diamond.

Cash: Neil Diamond. Mahalia Jackson. There was the Who, Kenny Rogers and the First Edition.

Carter Cash: And Creedence Clearwater Revival.

Cash: Yeah, and Linda Ronstadt was on it, on our show four times. Her first appearances.

Carter Cash: And then of course we had country acts on there too, but we were trying to pull in some people that we liked that were still a part of what we felt like we were. I mean we didn't know which foot we were on.

Cash: And also there were people that we wanted on. Like Irvin and Gordon Rouse, the Rouse Brothers who wrote "Orange Blossom Special." Had them come on, the producer did, from Florida, videotaped 'em doing three or four songs and then didn't put 'em on the show. Which was a great disappointment to me. They didn't really understand their style of performance, I suppose. They were popular in the '30s.

Carter Cash: Very pure.

Cash: Yeah, very, very pure. Ethnic. And I did a segment called "Ride This Train," and it called for a lot of dialogue as well as songs. Stories as you take an imaginary train trip to the West, or the coal mines, or to the prisons. Tell stories and sing songs, and I asked if they would hire Merle Travis to be one of the writers for that, to give it a touch of authenticity that I wanted. That I wanted it to sound real and look real and so they finally did, which is—

Carter Cash: And we hired Kris Kristofferson, too.

Cash: Yeah, and [writer] Larry Murray, that wrote part of "Ride This Train." It was things I asked for that the network didn't give a hoot about, y'know, as far as their ratings are concerned, which is what they were concerned about. But I did because I wanted to, I wanted to do something credible on that show.

Oermann: So many young people are coming into country music now.

Cash: Boy, y'know, if the young people that are comin' into country music don't know a little about their tradition and their own heritage in the music they love, they really are missin' it. And I really hate to see it. I don't expect country radio to give me a lot of airplay . . . an artist my age, they just don't do it. But that's just fine. But just some, say, so that the young fans can get tradition and to know what their inheritance and their heritage is in our music that we love so much. And I thank God that some stations are now having special days of the week or special hours of the day that they're programmin' country classics . . . goin' all the way back to the '30s. And I think that's so important. It is to me. I love to hear the new stuff, some of it. But I love to hear some of the old stuff too, like Gene Autry as well as the Carter Family. I was talkin' to Gene Autry not long ago in California and we were reminiscing about the old songs. And he was saying the same thing about how he loved the old songs and he loved to hear them. So Willie and Kristofferson and Waylon and I and June were sittin' around singin' old songs from Gene Autry's days. And it was one of the greatest times of our lives, and it would be wonderful if country fans could do that today. Sit around and swap those old songs. But first they gotta hear 'em.

Oermann: June, can you recall for me Elvis Presley?

Carter Cash: Well, sometimes it was a little scary. I mean it was somethin' to see how the people reacted, how the young women reacted. He had this charisma about him that was really . . . it was somethin' to see. Got a little . . . I think the word was *scary* at times. But he really was a talented man. He could sing so well. And he had this . . . there was this sexual side to him that he managed to hook the whole audience with in a way. And he was truly a very charismatic man.

Oermann: Can you explain for me the charisma of Johnny Cash? What is it about John?

Carter Cash: Well, I don't know. John is one of those people who is . . . I don't know what happens. I've seen two or three of these people in my lifetime. Elvis was one of them. But John has always maybe had more . . . I say the word might be *presence*, charisma, whatever you wanna call it. Uncle A. P. Carter could do it. When he walks into a room, the whole atmosphere changes. They become as big as the room. They became bigger than life. And so people are, well, they pick up on that and whatever that is that they have. Where, I don't know. There is a depth to John. I mean there was a sexual kind of thing with Elvis that had to do, and I don't mean with me. I mean with crowds. I mean with the people who heard him sing. But there is a depth to John that is spiritual as well. And—

Cash: —as well as sexual.

Carter Cash: [*Laughing.*] As well as sexual. [*Cash laughs.*] Absolutely right.

1-800-TRY-CASH

Rosanne Cash | December 1996 | *Interview*

"It's not something I normally would have done," Rosanne Cash says of this published conversation with her dad from the winter of 1996. "But I liked *Interview*."

It was a pivotal time for both father and daughter. Rosanne Cash's *10 Song Demo*—her first album for Capitol Records, and the most stripped-down effort of her career—had been released the previous spring. It included "The Western Wall," which Linda Ronstadt and Emmylou Harris would cover on their album *Western Wall: The Tucson Sessions*. Hyperion Books had recently published her well-received short-story collection *Bodies of Water*, her first foray as an author.

The occasion for this *Interview* piece was sixty-four-year-old Johnny Cash's Rick Rubin–produced 1996 album *American II: Unchained*, the second in the acclaimed Rubin-helmed American Recordings series. Although most listeners would eventually regard the pairing of Cash-Rubin as one of the most productive of Cash's long career, initial news of the collaboration didn't sit well with his protective eldest child.

"Before he worked with Rick, Dad and I had a conversation," Rosanne says. "I was really nervous about it. I knew Rick as a hip-hop guy. And Dad had made some bad decisions during the Mercury years. He'd recently been asked to do Lollapalooza, and he was feeling really ungrounded, and searching. It was like a classic midlife crisis, but a lot bigger because he was a great artist. He was having a crisis about himself, and his place in the world, and his work, and everything. So I said, 'Please don't do Lollapalooza. Please. You won't get the respect you deserve. You'll have a bunch of fourteen-year-olds who don't know who you are, and it'll be awful.' So he didn't do it.

"I felt a little of the same way when he said he was going to work with Rick. I was like, 'Are you sure about that? He's a hip-hop guy.' But he said, 'I feel really good about it.'"

The first Rubin-produced work Rosanne would subsequently hear was her father's performance of the 1959 Jimmy Driftwood chestnut "Tennessee Stud," recorded live at West Hollywood club the Viper Room, and "Delia's Gone," a Cash-altered public domain murder ballad rendered in Rubin's home studio. Both are solo acoustic—stark and powerful in their restraint, more akin to field recordings than anything one would hear in the mid-1990s.

Like Cash's 1969 Shel Silverstein–penned hit "A Boy Named Sue" and the entirety of his breakthrough 1968 *At Folsom Prison* album, "Tennessee Stud" features the raw sound of an enthralled audience—many, if not all, new to the song—hanging on every word. They react with whoops, cheers, and wild applause. The first-person narrative includes gunplay, murder, Cash's home state of Arkansas, and a love for both a woman and a special horse. Propelling it all is Cash's distinctively primitive rhythmic acoustic strumming, the pulse of his classic recordings—long missing from his recorded output.

Similarly, as with Cash's 1955 breakthrough "Folsom Prison Blues," *American Recordings* opener "Delia's Gone" is a first-person account of a murderer, haunted and penitent, suffering from a jail cell. Cash once again effortlessly captures a particular darkness of the soul with authenticity and, crucially, compassion.

Upon hearing these recordings, Rosanne Cash's worries evaporated.

"It became clear that Rick *saw* him," she says. "He knew the essence of my dad and respected that, and wanted that. He wanted to peel away all these other layers, this kind of empire Dad had built around himself musically, out on the road.

"Rick was so refreshing. Dad had really felt the burden of having all these expectations piled on him, all of these extraneous people, and what it created. Rick goes, 'Let's just get rid of that. Who you are is enough.'

"It was such a relief. Such an unburdening. Such a joy for him. We owe Rick a great debt. That recognition gave Dad back his vitality, his life force."

American Recordings was both a critical and commercial success, netting Cash a Best Contemporary Folk Album Grammy. It set in motion an unexpected burst of activity that would continue even as Cash's health declined.

Fast-forward to 1996. *American II: Unchained* was a riskier and ultimately even more successful affair. Rubin culled a wider variety of songs—drawing from Beck ("Rowboat"), Tom Petty ("Southern Accents"), Josh Haden ("Spiritual"), and even Dean Martin ("Memories Are Made of This"—penned in 1955 by Terry Gilkyson, Richard Dehr, and Frank Miller). He broadened the sonic palette with studio guests Tom Petty and the Heartbreakers, Nashville veteran (and erstwhile Johnny Cash band member) Marty Stuart, Red Hot Chili Peppers bassist Flea, and Fleetwood Mac's Lindsey Buckingham and Mick Fleetwood.

Rubin ingeniously rearranged Soundgarden's caterwauling "Rusty Cage" to suit Cash's burnished voice and presence. This would become the most popular *Unchained* selection, garnering Cash a Best Country Vocal Performance Grammy. *Unchained* would win the Grammy for Best Country Album.

In the preceding three decades, the press had claimed repeatedly: "Cash is back!" This time it was true.

As the public was processing it all, Rosanne and her father checked in with each other for Andy Warhol-founded *Interview* magazine. While father and daughter lightheartedly touched on some aforementioned elements, they spent as much time chatting about fashion, gardening, and traveling. Rosanne was curious about where her father stood on certain moral and political issues, like Planned Parenthood, and whether the country, then at the end of Bill Clinton's first term, was ready for a president who was not a white man.

Johnny Cash, invigorated by his work and the presence of his beaming eldest child, was hardy, ready for action, and prescient. —Ed.

ROSANNE CASH: Hi, Dad.

JOHNNY CASH: How are you, honey?

RC: Good. So tell me, if you were to step back and take an overview of your new record, what would you say?

JC: Well, I would say it's probably the most comprehensive thing I have ever done in terms of stretching out and covering a broad spectrum of what I like in music. I've chosen songs from real '40s country, '50s rockabilly, '60s stuff, and more recent things as well. And not just country, songs from rock 'n' roll too.

RC: At a time when most people are stultifying and getting rigid in their sense of themselves, you've got this rebirth going on. How did that happen?

JC: Well, I got a producer [Rick Rubin] who was really interested in me and my work, and not in trying to [make me] sound like everybody else in town. He said, "Let's sit down with the guitar, and you sing to me for a few days the things you want to record." It was the most freedom I've had since I started on Sun Records [in 1955].

RC: Do you think music has the power to heal?

JC: Oh yeah, that more than anything else. I can be in pain, go onstage, my pain disappears.

RC: Why do you think that happens?

JC: Doctors have said it's because of adrenaline. As far as I'm concerned, it's a power that comes to you from God.

RC: Here's a question that my friends and I discuss: Which do you think we'll have first—a black male president or a female president?

JC: [*clears throat*] The way things are going right now, I'd say it's pretty even. But if I had my bets, I would say that a black man will be first and then a woman, because this country is, I think, more prejudiced against women than black men.

RC: I would agree.

JC: A lot of black people wouldn't agree with that, but in the South, where I live, you know how it is. The girl is graduating from high school, if they don't have a connection somewhere, then they got to go down and try to get a job that pays minimum wage sacking groceries. Then there's the question of teenage pregnancy. You know, the boy gets the girl pregnant and skips out 90 percent of the time. He leaves her to fend for herself, and then what's the government gonna do for her?

RC: Are you a supporter of Planned Parenthood and sex education in schools?

JC: Yes I am. That education is a part of life, and a part of the love thing that you need to know about.

RC: Dad, what did your mom teach you about women, either spoken or unspoken?

JC: I grew up in the '40s, in the country, in a Southern Baptist family. I think I was taught that there are good women and bad women. I also found out that sometimes bad women are good women, and good women can be bad, just like men. I learned that at an early age.

RC: How important is fashion to you?

JC: It's not really important.

RC: **What's your feeling about clothing in general? I mean, do you *have* any feelings about it?**

JC: I don't know. I put on the same black business shirt this morning when I got ready to go. I'm sitting there with that on and black socks. And I don't wear underwear, so all I got on is black.

RC: **[*laughs*] So we can safely say that your sense of fashion has not changed.**

JC: Rosanne, you know, you open my closet, it's *dark* in there.

RC: **Do you remember a time before you wanted to be a musician?**

JC: I can't. Before I ever started school, I would sit with my mother and she'd teach me to sing along with her. That's what she called "seconding" to her. My voice was high until I was eighteen, so I could do that. And I remember singing as I walked across the fields carrying water to the workers. When I'd get to them, they'd kid me about it. They'd say, "We heard you singing all the way from the spring."

RC: **Were you melancholy as a young man?**

JC: Yeah, I was very shy.

RC: **Do you think you kept the work ethic you learned growing up working in the fields?**

JC: Maybe. But on the other hand, I really hated that work.

RC: **So you don't feel guilty when you take a vacation?**

JC: [*laughs*] No, I don't. When I do take one, I deserve it. [I'll say] "Why isn't there a Ritz-Carlton in that town?"

RC: **What do you like most about traveling?**

JC: The performances. But also, every new motel is an adventure. And, of course, you check and see if you got all the conveniences, like a hair dryer—

RC: **Right, you love those amenities.**

JC: Oh, yes, I love a piece of chocolate on my pillow.

RC: Turndown service is the height of civilization.

JC: I love that. And I love big, thick feather pillows.

RC: Are you a collector by nature?

JC: I used to be. I have a collection of Roman coins. I like touching something that Jesus Christ or Caesar might have touched.

RC: Did you plant a garden this year?

JC: I'm working in my little vineyard. Remember the arbor that your Grandpa and Gramma Cash had in California?

RC: I sure do.

JC: I took cuttings from that, and brought them back to Tennessee in a suitcase and stuck 'em out. This year I had about a half a bushel of grapes. I'm thrilled to death with my little grape arbor.

RC: [*with admiration*] Oh, Dad! That's great! Well, we better stop.

JC: O.K. I really enjoyed this talk with you.

RC: I've enjoyed it, too. I love you, Dad.

JC: I love you. Bye-bye.

INTERVIEW

Terry Gross | November 4, 1997 | *Fresh Air*

Just prior to Johnny Cash's November 4, 1997, *Fresh Air* interview with Terry Gross, he'd struggled through an October 25 performance in Flint, Michigan, almost falling down when he bent to retrieve a dropped guitar pick. He announced to a stunned audience he was suffering from Parkinson's disease, which ran in his family. He wasn't. This was the first of several misdiagnoses. The only certainty was his days on the road had finally come to an end.

On October 7, HarperCollins had published *Cash*, Johnny Cash's second autobiography, which Cash had undertaken with his frequent interlocutor Patrick Carr. Due to his worsening physical condition, the book tour would be canceled. This *Fresh Air* interview was one of the few promotional duties Cash kept. In his conversation with Gross, he did not mention illness.

Within weeks, doctors would give Cash perhaps eighteen months to live due to Shy-Drager syndrome, a debilitating disorder of the central and sympathetic nervous systems. This was also wrong. He would enter Baptist Hospital again, suffering from pneumonia. Doctors would place him on a ventilator and induce a coma, with June initiating the first of many online prayer vigils.

Not long after that, Cash would be home, recuperating, planning what would become *American III: Solitary Man* with Rick Rubin.

Cash and Patrick Carr had begun *Cash* in 1995.

"I decided I wanted to do a Cash bio," Carr says. "I sent him a letter: 'What would be your position on that? Would you help, would you oppose it, what would be your attitude?' Next thing I knew the phone rang. He said, 'No I don't want you to do a bio. I want you to do my autobiography with me.'

"It turned out [Johnny Cash's longtime manager] Lou Robin had been receiving offers from publishers. There was money on the table. Then this letter arrives, and June says, 'Whoa, it's kismet.'

"The whole thing took the better part of a year, in fits and starts. We began in Jamaica, where he and June had a wonderful place—Cinnamon Hill, near Montego Bay. He invited me and my wife to spend Christmas with them there. That's how we kicked it off. I went to Houston. Got on his bus with him. Went off into Arizona, couple other places for a few days. I went to his house Bon Aqua, a little farmhouse west of Nashville. To a house in Newport Richey, Florida, that had been Mother Maybelle's. She lived there seasonally for a good part of her life. They had a whole routine of shifting from place to place. And then of course I went to his house on the lake in Nashville. Took a road trip to Portland. We went all the way down the West Coast to San Francisco for a gig at the Fillmore.

"The publishers had given us an insane deadline, like three months. I said there's no way this can be done. And [manager] Lou Robin said, 'Never mind, we'll sign this contract and we'll deal with it. When they explode, we'll deal with it. Don't worry. I'll take care of it.'

"I told them there's just no way it can be done in that amount of time. They exploded. The editor calls Lou, Lou calls the lawyers, and they all get together, had this confab; they decide it's Patrick's fault. Let's just fire Patrick, and the publisher has a sportswriter, and he delivers. Patrick will give him all the tapes, tell him who's who, and we'll give Patrick a consultant fee. And we'll get it done in a month and that'll be good.

"I'm not sure what exactly Cash said at that point. But anyway, it ended up they got this guy and he produced a chapter, and it was erroneous trash. No way could that see the light of day. It was just a disaster. They said, 'What do we need to do?' I said, we need to kidnap me and stick me someplace, any place not near my wife and children, and I will do what I have to do, and you will tell Mr. Cash he has to deliver on his end.

"And that's how we did it. They kidnapped me, took me to San Francisco, and stuck me in this condo with a computer and a transcription service and bike messenger. It was fucking nuts.

"Cash and I sit down, we turn on the tape recorder, and we talk about whatever it is we're gonna talk about it.

"Cash talked in prose. What I mean by that is how he talked with an ear and a mind towards how this was going to look on a page. I knew he was doing that. We never mentioned it. But he talked very carefully, and very clearly. Which was terrifically unusual among the usual celebrity interviews. That's not what happens. But Cash was almost *reciting* this stuff. That was because he was so damned intelligent, and so good with the language, and so clear about what he wanted to say. I didn't have to edit pretty much anything. I would clean little things up here and there, but they were little things. I did not have to write new stuff in order for this to look good. It was all there in what Cash actually said." —Ed.

Terry Gross: Your career has in many ways been about both the sacred and the profane. You've always been Christian and have always sung hymns. And, on the other hand, there were times in your life, as you write in your book, when you've been in and out of jails, hospitals, car wrecks, when you were a walking vision of death, and that's exactly how you felt, you say in your book.

Johnny Cash: Mm-hmm.

Gross: Have you always been aware of that contradiction, you know, of the sacred and the profane running through your life?

Cash: Mm-hmm. Yeah. Kristofferson wrote a song, and in that song was a line that says—he wrote the song about me—"He's a walking contradiction, partly truth and partly fiction" ["The Pilgrim, Chapter 33"]. And I've always explored the various areas of society and the lovely young people, and I had an empathy for prisoners and did concerts for them, back when I thought that it would make a difference, you know, that they really were there to be rehabilitated.

Gross: You grew up during the Depression. What are some of the things that your father did to make a living while you were a boy?

Cash: My father was a cotton farmer first, but he didn't have any land, or what land he had he lost it in the Depression. So he worked as a woodsman and cut pulpwood for the paper mills. He rode the rails in boxcars going from one harvest to another to try to make a little money picking fruit or vegetables. Did every kind of work imaginable, from painting to shoveling to herding cattle. And he's always been such an inspiration to me because of the varied kinds of things that he did and the kind of life he lived. He inspired me so, all the things he did so far from being a soldier in World War I to being an old man in his patio sitting on the porch watching the dogs, you know? I think about his life, and it would inspire me to go my own other direction, and I just like to explore minds and the desires of people out there.

Gross: You know, it's interesting that you say your father inspired you so much. I'm sure you wouldn't have wanted to lead his life picking cotton.

Cash: I did, until I was eighteen years old, that is. Then I picked the guitar and I've been picking it since.

Gross: Right. [*Laughs.*] Did you have a plan to get out? Did you very much want to get out of the town where you were brought up and get out of picking cotton?

Cash: Yeah. I knew that when I left there at the age of eighteen, I wouldn't be back. And it was common knowledge among all the people there that when you graduate from high school here, you go to college or go get a job or something and do it on your own. And having been familiar with hard work, it was no problem for me. At first, I hitchhiked to Pontiac, Michigan, and got a job working in Fisher Body making those 1951 Pontiacs. I worked there three weeks, got really sick of it, went back home and joined the Air Force.

Gross: You have such a wonderful deep voice. Did you start singing before your voice changed?

Cash: Oh, yeah. I got no teeth. Plus, today, I've got a cold. But when I was so young, I had a high tenor voice. I used to sing Bill Monroe songs, and I'd sing Dennis Day songs . . .

Gross: Oh, no.

Cash: Yeah, songs that they'd sing on "The Jack Benny Show."

Gross: Wow.

Cash: Every week he sang an old Irish folk song, and next day in the fields, I'd be singing that song if I was working in the fields. And I always loved those songs, and with my high tenor, I thought I was pretty good, you know, almost as good as Dennis Day, but when I was sixteen, my father and I cut wood all day long, swinging that crosscut saw and hauling wood. And when I walked in the back door late that afternoon, I was singing, "Everybody gonna have religion and glory, everybody gonna be singin' the story." I'd sing those old gospel songs for my mother, and she said, "Is that you?" And I said, "Yes, ma'am." And she came over and put her arms around me and said, "God's got his hands on you." I still think of that, you know?

Gross: She realized you had a gift.

Cash: That's what she said, yeah. She called it "the gift."

Gross: How did you feel about your voice changing? It must have stunned you, if you were singing like Dennis Day and then suddenly you're singing like Johnny Cash.

Cash: . . . I don't know. I guess when I was a tenor, I just—and when it changed, I thought, *Well, it goes right along with these hormones and everything's working out really good, you know?* I felt like my voice was becoming a man's voice.

Gross: Right. Right. So did you start singing different songs as your voice got deeper?

Cash: Mm-hmm. "Lucky Old Sun," "Memories Are Made of This," "Sixteen Tons." I developed a pretty unusual style, I think. If I'm anything, I'm not a singer, but I'm a song stylist.

Gross: What's the difference?

Cash: Well, I say I'm not a singer, so that means I can't sing, but— doesn't it?

Gross: Well—but, I mean, that's not true. I understand you're making a distinction, but you certainly can sing. Yeah.

Cash: Thank you.

Gross: Go ahead.

Cash: Well, a song stylist just likes to take an old folk song like "Delia's Gone" and do a modern white man's version of it. A lot of those I did that way, you know? I would take songs that I'd loved as a child and redo them in my mind for the new voice I had, the low voice.

Gross: I know that you briefly took singing lessons, and you say in your new book that your singing teacher told you, you know, "Don't let

anybody change your voice. Don't even bother with the singing lessons."
How did you end up taking lessons in the first place?

Cash: My mother did that, and she was determined that I was going to
leave the farm and do well in life. And she thought with the gift I might
be able to do that. So she took in washing. She got a washing machine
in 1942 as soon as we got electricity, and she took in washing. She'd
wash the schoolteacher's clothes and anybody she could and sent me
for singing lessons for three dollars per lesson, and that's how she made
the money to send me.

Gross: What was your reaction when the teacher told you, "Don't let
anybody change what you're doing," you know, "I'm not going to teach
you anymore"?

Cash: I was pretty happy about that. I didn't really want to change, you
know? I felt good about my voice.

Gross: You left home when you were about eighteen. And then how old
were you when you actually went to Memphis?

Cash: Well, I went to Memphis after I finished the Air Force in 1954.
I lived on that farm until I went to the Air Force. I was in there four
years, and when I came back, I got married and moved to Memphis, got
an apartment, started trying to sell appliances at a place called Home
Equipment Company. But I couldn't sell anything. I didn't really want to.
All I wanted was the music then. If somebody in the house was playing
music when I would come, I would stop and sing with them. Like one
time, Gus Cannon, the man who wrote, "Walk Right In," which was a
hit for the Rooftop Singers—and I sat on the front porch with him day
after day, when I found him, and sang those songs.

Gross: When you got to Memphis, Elvis Presley had already recorded
"That's All Right." Sam Phillips had produced him for his label Sun
Records. You called Sam Phillips and asked for an audition. Did it take
a lot of nerve to make that phone call?

Cash: No. It just took the right time. I was fully confident that I was
going to see Sam Phillips and to record for him, but when I called him,
I thought, "I'm going to get on Sun Records." So I called him and he

turned me down flat. Then two weeks later, I called him, turned down again. He told me over the phone that he couldn't sell gospel music because it was independent and not a lot of money, you know? So I didn't press that issue. But one day I just decided I'm ready to go, so I went down with my guitar and sat on the front steps of his recording studio. I met him when he came in, and I said, "I'm John Cash. I'm the one who's been calling. And if you'd listen to me, I believe you'll be glad you did." And he said, "Come on in." That was a good lesson for me, you know, to believe in myself.

Gross: What was the audition like?

Cash: It was about three hours of singing with just my guitar, songs, a lot of them, like the songs that are in my first *American Recordings* album.

Gross: So what did Phillips actually respond to most of the songs that you played him?

Cash: He responded most to a song of mine called "Hey Porter," which was on the first record. But he asked me to go write a love song or maybe a bitter weeper. So I wrote a song called "Cry! Cry! Cry!," went back in, and recorded that for the other side of the record.

Gross: Now you say in your book you had to do thirty-five takes of "Cry! Cry! Cry!" Why did it take so many takes?

Cash: It was too simple. We were trying to make something complicated out of it, and it was the simplest song in the world ever written. And invariably, at some time during a take, the guitar player would mess up or the bass player, or I would mess up and we'd have to do it over. It's not unusual, though, to do a song thirty-five times.

Gross: So, this record was the beginning of your recording career. What was it like when you started to go on tour? You know, after coming from the cotton fields—it's true, I mean, you'd been in the Army [Air Force] and you'd been abroad, you know, with the Army [Air Force]. But what was it like for you in the early days of getting recognized, you know, traveling around the country?

Cash: Well, when I started playing concerts, I went out from Memphis to Arkansas, Louisiana, and Tennessee, played the little towns there. But I would go out myself in my car and set up the show or get the show booked in those theaters. And then along about three months later, Elvis Presley asked me to sing with him at the Overton Park Shell in Memphis. And I sang "Cry! Cry! Cry!" and "Hey Porter." And from that time on, I was on my way, and I knew it, I felt it, and I loved it. So Elvis asked me to go on tour with him, and I did. I worked with Elvis four or five tours in the next year or so. And I was always intrigued by his charisma. You know, I just—you can't be in a building with Elvis without looking at him, you know, and he inspired me so with his fire and energy that I guess that inspiration from him really helped me to go.

Gross: It's funny, I think of your charisma and his charisma as being very different forms of charisma because, I mean, he would move around so much on stage, and I think of your charisma as being a very kind of still, stoic kind of charisma.

Cash: Mm-hmm. Mm-hmm. Well, I'm an old man to him. I'm four years older than he was. [*Laughs.*] So I was twenty-three when I started recording and Elvis was nineteen. And I was married, he wasn't. So we didn't have a lot in common, common family life. But we liked each other and appreciated each other, so he asked me to tour with him.

Gross: Did you want that kind of adulation that he was getting from girls who would come see him?

Cash: I don't remember if I wanted it, but I loved it.

Gross: Mm-hmm. Mm-hmm.

Cash: Yeah, I did. But I only got it to a very small degree compared to Elvis.

Gross: Right. What were the temptations like for a young married man like yourself on the road, you know, slowly becoming a star?

Cash: Fame was pretty hard to handle, actually. The country boy in me tried to break loose and take me back to the country, but the music was stronger. The urge to go out and do the gift was a lot stronger. And the temptations were women, girls, which I loved, and then amphetamines, not very much later, running all night, you know, in their cars on tour. And the doctors got these nice pills that give us energy and keep us awake. So I started taking those, and I liked them so much I got addicted to them. And then I started taking downers or sleeping pills to come down and rest after two or three days. So it became a cycle. I was taking the pills for a while and then the pills started taking me.

Gross: I want to play what I think was your first big hit, "I Walk the Line."

Cash: Mm-hmm. That was my third record.

Gross: And you wrote this song. Tell me the story of how you wrote it and what you were thinking about at the time.

Cash: In the Air Force, I had an old Wilcox-Gay recorder and used to hear guitar runs on that recorder going "doon, doon, doon, doon," like the chords on "I Walk the Line." And I always wanted to write a love song using that theme, you know, that tune. And so I started to write the song. And I was in Gladewater, Texas, one night with Carl Perkins, and I said, "I've got a good idea for a song." And I sang him the first verse that I had written, and I said, "It's called 'Because You're Mine.'" And he says, "'I Walk the Line' is a better title." And so I changed it to "I Walk the Line."

Gross: No reading of your own life when you wrote that?

Cash: Mm-hmm. It was kind of a prodding to myself to play it straight, Johnny.

Gross: And was this—I think I read that this was supposed to be a ballad. I mean, it was supposed to be slow when you first wrote it.

Cash: That's the way I sing it, yeah, at first. But Sam wanted it, you know, up-tempo, and I put paper in the strings of my guitar to get that *oom chi, oom chi chi, oom chi* sound, and with a bass and a lead guitar, there it was, bare and stark, that song was, when it was released. And I heard it on the radio and I really didn't like it, and I called Sam Phillips and asked him to please not send out any more records of that song.

Gross: Why?

Cash: He laughed at me. I just didn't like the way it sounded to me. I didn't know I sounded that way, and I didn't like it; I don't know. But he said, "Let's give it a chance." And it was just a few days until—that's all it took to take off.

Gross: That's funny. I mean, you'd heard your voice before, hadn't you?

Cash: Mm-hmm.

Gross: But—so it was something in your own singing you weren't liking when you heard it?

Cash: Well, the music and my voice together, I just felt like it was really weird, but I got used to it very quickly. I don't know that—I didn't hate it, but I just didn't like it. I thought I could do better.

Gross: I think it was in the late 1950s that you started doing prison concerts, which you eventually became very famous for.

Cash: Mm-hmm.

Gross: What got you started performing in prison?

Cash: Well, I had a song called "Folsom Prison Blues" that was a hit just before "I Walk the Line." And people in Texas heard about it at the state prison and got to writing me letters asking me to come down there. So I responded, and then the warden called me and asked if I would come down and do a show for the prisoners in Texas. And so I went down, and there's a rodeo at all these shows that the prisoners have there, and in between the rodeo things, they asked me to set up and do two or three songs. So that was what I did. I did "Folsom Prison Blues," which they thought was their song, you know; and "I Walk the Line," "Ring of Fire," "Hey Porter," "Cry! Cry! Cry!"

And then the word got around on the grapevine that Johnny Cash was all right and that you ought to see him, so the requests started coming in from other prisons all over the United States. And then the word got around. So I always wanted to record that, you know, to record a show. Because of the reaction I got, it was far and above anything I had ever had in my life, the complete explosion of noise and reaction that they gave me with every song. So then I came back the next year and played the prison again, the New Year's Day show; came back again a third year and did the show. And then I kept talking to my producers at Columbia about recording one of those shows. "It's so exciting," I said, "that the people out there ought to share that, you know, and feel that excitement, too." So a preacher friend of mine named Floyd Gressett set it up for us, and Lou Robin and a lot of other people involved at Folsom Prison. So we went into Folsom on February 11, 1968, and recorded a show live.

Gross: Before we hear one of the tracks from that live album, tell me what kind of reaction surprised you the most when you were performing for prisoners.

Cash: Well, what really surprised me was any kind of prison song I could do no wrong, you know. Whatever, "The Prisoner's Song" or "San Quentin" song of mine. But they felt like they could identify with me, I suppose. I came from—I sing songs like "Dark as a Dungeon" or "Bottom of a Mountain," songs about the working man and the hard life. And, of course, they'd been through the hard life, all of them, or they wouldn't be there, so they kind of related to all that, I guess, the songs that I chose. Very little of love songs, very few; mostly, you know, songs about the down-and-outer. And so then requests started coming in for me to go to other prisons, and it got overwhelming. So I decided I would do two or three and I wouldn't do any more because, for one thing, my wife was scared to death, and the other women on the show were, too, so I decided not to. It was still a great experience to get on stage and perform for those people.

Gross: I guess Merle Haggard was in the audience for one of your San Quentin concerts.

Cash: Mm-hmm.

Gross: It must have been pretty exciting to find that out. That was before he had recorded, I think, that he was in there.

Cash: Yeah. Yeah, '68 and '69, right on the front row was Merle Haggard.

Gross: Yeah, and who knew?

Cash: I didn't know. I didn't know that until about 1963, '62 [*1972–73 —Ed.*]. He told me all about it. He saw every show that I did there, and, of course, the rest is history for Merle. He came out and immediately had success himself.

Gross: You know, it's interesting; you've always or almost always worn black during your career. And I was interested in reading that your mother hated it, too.

Cash: Yeah. Yeah, she did.

Gross: So we have something in common. Mothers don't like black.

Cash: Yeah. I love it.

Gross: Me, too. But you gave in for a while. She started making you bright, flashy outfits, even a nice white suit.

Cash: Yes. Mm-hmm.

Gross: What did it feel like for you to be on stage in bright colors or all in white?

Cash: Well, that was 1956 and I hadn't been wearing the black for very long. Color's OK. I would wear anything my mother made me, you know. I just couldn't afford to turn her down. But before long, I decided to start with the black and stick with it because it felt good to me on stage that—a figure there in black and everything coming out his face; that's the way I wanted to do it.

Gross: What was it like traveling with a family instead of being on your own, being on your own leaving the family behind?

Cash: I really don't like to do an appearance without June Carter. And what it would be like being alone, it would be awfully lonely, to me. I'm very comfortable with, you know, how we do it, my wife and my son on the show and a daughter or two. And it feels so good. I would hate to think to have to do it all alone.

Gross: Did it change your life to have a family that really understood the performing life because it was their life, too?

Cash: Very much so, yeah. Right.

Gross: What was the difference? I mean, why was that so important?

Cash: Well, there's something about families singing together that is just better than any other groups you can pick up or make, you know. If it's family, there's blood on blood, and it's going to be better. The voices singing their parts are going to be tighter and they're going to be more on pitch because, as I say, it's bloodline on bloodline. And it's always really comfortable and easy for me to sing with June or any of those girls.

Gross: A few years ago, you started making records with Rick Rubin. Tell me how you and he first met up. It seemed initially like a very improbable match. He had produced a lot of rap records and produced the Beastie Boys and the Red Hot Chili Peppers. You know, it would seem like a surprising match. It ended up being a fantastic match. How did he approach you?

Cash: Well, my contract with Mercury/Polygram in Nashville was about to expire, and I never had really been happy. The record company just didn't put any promotion behind me. I think one album, maybe the last one I did, they had pressed five hundred copies. And I was just disgusted with it. So I decided I'll just do my thing, I'll do my tours and writing and that's all I need. So that's what I was trying to do. But I got hungry to be back in the studio, to be creative and put something down, you know, for the fans to hear. And about that time that I got to feeling that way, Lou Robin, my manager, came to me and talked to me about a man called Rick Rubin that he had been talking to that wanted me to sign with his record company; it was American Recordings. I said, "I like the name. Maybe it'll be OK." So, I said, "I'd like to meet the guy. I'd like for him to tell me what he can do with me that they're not doing now."

So he came to my concert in Orange County, California—I believe this was, like, '83 [*1993* —*Ed.*] when he first came—and listened to the show, and then afterwards, I went in the dressing room and sat and talked to him. And, you know, he had his hair—I don't think it's ever been cut, and very—dresses like a hobo, usually. Clean, but [*Laughs.*]—well, it's the kind of guy I really felt comfortable with, actually. I think I was more comfortable with him than I would have been with a producer with a suit on. But I said, "What are you going to do with me that nobody else has been able to do, to sell records with me?" And he said, "Well, I don't know that we will sell records." He says, "I would like you to go with me and sit in my living room with a guitar and two microphones and just sing to your heart's content everything you ever wanted to record." I said, "That sounds good to me."

So I did that. And day after day, three weeks, I sang for him. And when I finally stopped, he had been saying—like the last day or so, he'd been saying, "Now I think we should put this one in your album." So without him saying, "I want to record you and release an album," he started saying, "Let's put this one in the album." So the album, this big question, you know, began to take form, take shape. And Rick and I would weed out the songs. There were songs that didn't feel good to us that we would say, "Let's don't consider that one." And then we'd focus on the ones that we did like, that felt right and sounded right. And if I didn't like the performance on that song, I would keep trying it and do take after take until it felt comfortable with me and felt that it was coming out of me and my guitar and my voice as one, that it was right from my soul. That's how I felt about, you know, all those things in that first album, and I got really excited about it.

But then we went into the studio and tried to record some with different musicians, and it didn't sound good; it didn't work. So we put together the album with just the guitar and myself.

Gross: Now aren't you really glad you did it that way? There's something just so naked about it. There's something so . . .

Cash: Mm-hmm.

Gross: . . . just so emotionally naked . . . and there's so much emotion in your voice. And it just all, you know, comes across really clearly.

Cash: Thank you.

Gross: I think these records and the touring that you've done with them has helped introduce you to a younger audience that wasn't around during your earlier hits and maybe knew your reputation but didn't really know your music very well. And I'm wondering what that experience has been like for you to play to younger audiences who are first getting acquainted with your music.

Cash: Oh, it feels like 1955 all over again. It really does. It really does. And the ones who've been into my new recordings are becoming familiar with some of the old stuff like "Folsom" and "I Walk the Line" and "Ring of Fire," and those songs now just really get a reaction like I did on my songs back in the '50s. But it feels so good with those young people, and the adulation, I just love it. I've always been a big ham; I just eat it up. No, I'm very appreciative to them.

Gross: I want to play something from your first collaboration with Rick Rubin, which came out, I guess, a couple of years ago. And this is your reworking of the old song "Delia's Gone."

Cash: Mm-hmm.

Gross: And you made this the story of a murderer, and it's a very chilling song with the lyric that you've written and the way that you sing it. Tell me why you wanted to rewrite the song and how you first knew the song.

Cash: Well, there were bits in the lyrics of the old song of a good story. I mean, he thinks about the woman, he kills the woman and buries her. And then he hears her footprints in the night around his cell. But the song is an old "levee camp holler" that was sung by the people who were building the levees back in the teens and in the '20s. And I always loved the song, but when I recorded it the first time in the early '60s, I changed some of the lyrics and added some. And then when I recorded the song this time, I wrote a couple of new verses and changed some of the other words. So the song, it seems to me, is still part of me in my soul, on my mind, and that's why I worked it over and added something to it.

Gross: Why don't we hear "Delia's Gone" from Johnny Cash's *American Recordings* CD? And, Johnny Cash, I want to thank you so much for talking with us.

Cash: I want to say you're really good at what you do, and I appreciate you. Thank you.

INTERVIEW

Anthony DeCurtis | October 2000 and February 2002 | Interview Transcript

"Everybody talks about denial as a bad thing, and it obviously is, but I think it helped John. He refused to accept the fact he couldn't do certain things. He would *make* himself do them. It was powerful and inspiring. But there's only so long he was able to do that."

Grammy-winning writer, former VH1 correspondent, and longtime *Rolling Stone* contributing editor Anthony DeCurtis is talking about witnessing Johnny Cash perform several times in "the American Recordings years"—1994 until 2003. These stage appearances occurred between some of the most fruitful studio sessions of Cash's life. Starting around 1997, when Cash's physical health rapidly deteriorated, the performances became ever more brief but were still moving.

"That's the way they would do things once he got sick," DeCurtis says. "He would reserve his strength and then come out and do two or three songs. I saw him do that at [New York City club] the Bottom Line. He did it at a TV special I wrote devoted to him [*An All-Star Tribute to Johnny Cash*, 1999]. He came out at the end. He wasn't in peak form, but everybody was thrilled to see him up there."

Rather than tour, in the American Recordings years Cash and producer Rick Rubin focused their combined energies on creating music heralded as some of Cash's best, a dramatic renaissance. Their work included *American Recordings* (1994), *American II: Unchained* (1996), *American III: Solitary Man* (2000), *American IV: The Man Comes Around* (2002), and the posthumous *Unearthed* (2003), *American V: A Hundred Highways* (2006), and *American VI: Ain't No Grave* (2010).

"All of it is very good," DeCurtis says. "Even the stuff at the end, when John's mortality is apparent. It's still very, very strong. I still listen to it with a lot of pleasure. They found a groove for him. He just took big swings. It really shows how one decision can open up a whole realm of creativity: the right collaborator."

Like most people, DeCurtis was initially struck by the incongruity of the Cash-Rubin pairing. "I'm not sure John spent much time listening to [Rick Rubin productions] LL Cool J or Slayer. But he had good instincts. And he trusted Rick, who found him good material. It was a genuine partnership. Rick was largely dealing in John's wheelhouse, but pushed him a little bit. They found a way to render those songs very beautifully. They had quite a run."

The most obvious examples of Rubin-curated songs beyond Cash's comfort zone— Soundgarden's "Rusty Cage" (1996) and Nine Inch Nails' "Hurt" (2002)—are also the most popular singles from the American Recordings series. The latter, written by NIN front man Trent Reznor, is far and away the most streamed Johnny Cash song on Spotify (at this writing: 446 million streams) and the most viewed Johnny Cash video (139 million views). While both selections feature full-band arrangements, the majority of American Recordings songs are spare, often just guitar and voice.

DeCurtis says, "I always think about how Rick credited himself on those early rap records [Run-DMC, Beastie Boys, Hollis Crew]: 'Reduced by Rick Rubin.' There was this element of getting artists to their essence. And I think that's what he did with John. John had wanted to do it for a long time."

The success of this collaboration, DeCurtis explains, came down to Rubin recognizing Cash's intellect. "Rick found something that was very true about John but was not necessarily apparent: how smart and open-minded he was.

"Those early rock n' roll guys are always seen as all instinct, whereas with John, there was also a level of intelligence . . . he was just so thoughtful and *smart*, and Rick assumed that. That appealed to John. Rick certainly didn't feel like he had to direct John's career. He thought: 'there's a really smart guy. I'm going to put some interesting stuff in front of him and see what he does.' It's so simple.

"I always thought it must be amazing to have somebody you're working with so closely, someone you genuinely feel absolutely understands you, and has your best interests at heart, and can guide you over a long period of time. Theirs was a genuine collaboration. It's amazing it doesn't happen more often. But it takes two very particular people to achieve it. And they did."

These comprehensive interviews with Anthony DeCurtis, portions of which appeared in *Rolling Stone* and DeCurtis's own book *In Other Words: Artists Talk About Life and Work*, offer a window into Johnny Cash's remarkably fertile last years, during which seismic events—Columbine, 9/11—were transpiring in the background. Despite these tragedies, and his failing physical health, Cash's creative energy was flowing strong.

The first conversation was on the eve of the release of *American III: Solitary Man* (2000), as well as the simultaneous release of the acclaimed box set *Love, God, Murder*; the second interview was in the wake of *American IV: The Man Comes Around* (2002), the last of the series to be released in Cash's lifetime. In 2003, Cash's health would fall apart quickly.

At the time of these interviews, however, Cash's industriousness was contagious. In 2000, June Carter Cash's recently released, John Carter Cash-produced album *Press On*—only her second solo album—had won a Grammy, and she was enjoying the spotlight. Talking to DeCurtis, Cash revisited the story of her willpower helping to save his life in the 1960s.

The year 2002 saw a dizzying amount of Johnny Cash material on the market. DeCurtis and Cash covered the upcoming (then-untitled) *American III: Solitary Man* and the rerelease of some classic Cash albums from the 1960s. Columbia and Cash had parted ways in 1986, but in the wake of the American Recordings success, the label—now owned by Sony—was repackaging and, under the Legacy imprint, rereleasing the Cash-June Carter duets album *Carryin' On with Johnny Cash & June Carter*, as well as Cash's *Orange Blossom Special*, *The Fabulous Johnny Cash*, *Hymns by Johnny Cash*, and the groundbreaking concept album *Ride This Train*, which Cash cited as his all-time favorite work. —Ed.

October 4, 2000

Anthony DeCurtis: In your career there has been the Outlaw image for you, and a really deep spiritual experience that you've always had. Your younger audience in particular seems drawn to the Outlaw side of things. Do you feel funny about that, or are you OK with it?

Johnny Cash: I'm OK with it. They're just as spiritual as we are or anybody else. I find they're very spiritual people. This younger generation—I find they're very spiritual people. I do spirituals in my albums—I don't know of an album that I've released that I haven't had one or two. Matter of fact, the last one for American had a song called "Spiritual," which I thought was a fabulous song. The young people loved it. It's another side that I think they believe me. I think they think . . . I believe what

I say, but that don't necessarily make me right. I think my daughter Rosanne said that—"My dad believes what he says he believes, but that don't make him right." But that's OK too. I respect anybody's right to believe or not believe.

DeCurtis: I think you were suggesting that one side of it lends credibility to another side of it. It's not as if you're standing there putting yourself forward as some perfect specimen.

Cash: There's nothing hypocritical about it. I confess right up front that I'm the biggest sinner of 'em all. There is a spiritual side that goes real deep, that's really personal. There's no reason to talk about it with people who are not into that, who don't want to talk about that. That's just fine with me too. I'll talk about ancient Roman history if you want to.

DeCurtis: In light of the murders of those kids at Columbine High School, and a lot of concern about young people, and people trying to say that it's in part about the music they listen to or the movies they watch, and obviously you're the guy who wrote "I shot a man in Reno just to watch him die . . ." Do you feel like this stuff does have an effect on people negatively? Make them do the things that people are singing about?

Cash: Nope. I don't think the music and the movies does it. I think it's in the person. There's a certain madness in mobs. They get together where one guy wouldn't do that, they get together and say let's do this, and the more they say let's do this, they will do it.

I'm an entertainer. "I shot a man in Reno just to watch him die" is a fantasy thing. I didn't shoot anybody in Reno. I didn't kill Delia. It's fun to sing about it and my music—country music—goes way back. The murder ballads go way back in country. Even the Carter Family—they got some really bloody records. You know "The Banks of the Ohio"—"Stuck a knife in her breast and watched her as she went down under the water and the bubbles came up out of her mouth and the water turned red," and all that . . . Jimmie Rodgers: "I'm gonna buy me a shotgun just as long as I am tall/ I'm gonna shoot poor Thelma just to see her jump and fall." That's right up there with "shot a man in Reno" . . . .

These songs are for singin'. We always knew that, the singers did. I'm not suggesting to *anybody* that they even own a gun. I'm not suggesting that they even consider learning how to shoot one. Although I do. I used to collect antique Colt pistols, but they weren't for shooting, they were for collecting. Like ancient coins. I collect ancient coins too. But the coins aren't for spending and the guns aren't for shooting. It's a complicated thing. There's so many people that are saying the music and the movies are causing it. I don't believe that. It's in the people. It's a spiritual hunger in the people for goodness, for righteousness, or it's an emptiness. There's something missing there that they're trying to fill. I don't know why they go about it the way they do. But I don't think music and movies have got a lot to do with it.

DeCurtis: These are questions that go back to Cain and Abel. I wanted to ask you one of the things that's been really powerful about June's shows is when she discusses writing "Ring of Fire" and her feeling about you at the time. What's your recollection of that? What's your memory of that period and that song and her bringing it to you?

Cash: When she had the first of the lyrics—and she was writing those songs with Merle Kilgore—she had some words that rhyme . . . she had a line that called her "the Fire Ring Woman" and then she changed that and I said, "You got it right when you called yourself a Fire Ring Woman, because that's exactly where I am." We hadn't really pledged our love, so to speak. We hadn't said, "I love you." It was a long time after that before we actually ever said it. We were both afraid to say it because we knew what was gonna happen—that we eventually both were gonna be divorced and we were gonna go through hell, which we did. But "Ring of Fire" was not the hell. That was kind of a sweet fire. That was the redemptive fire. The ring of fire that I found myself in with June Carter was the fire of redemption. It cleansed. It made me believe everything was all right because it felt so good.

DeCurtis: I remember you saying she saved your life.

Cash: Yes, she did that. When we fell in love, she took it upon herself to be responsible for me staying alive because she wanted me to live. I didn't think I was killing myself, but I was, I was close to it. She saw that I was. She took it upon herself to try to fight me to make me stop the drugs. She would get them and dispose of them, and then we'd have a big fight over that and I'd get some more and she'd do the same thing again. I'd make her promise not to do it anymore, but she would. She fought me with everything she had. She would lie to me about it, she'd do anything. She'd hide my money so I couldn't buy any. And she really fought hard, and I'm sure there are a few times that just the fact that a simple little thing like hiding my money might've saved my life because I couldn't buy any. Or flushing 'em down the commode might've saved my life because they weren't handy. But I never seriously tried to take my life. Never thought about suicide. Even though you're on the suicide track when you're doing what I was doing—amphetamines and alcohol. Make you crazy. Boy.

DeCurtis: You came up at a time when that interplay between country and rock and roll and rockabilly was such an outburst of energy and creativity and wildness. As you were doing it, did you have a sense of the kind of impact that all of this stuff was gonna make?

Cash: No. I really didn't. The songs that I put the most into were songs that I never even thought about selling any records on. The songs that I liked especially, like "The Legend of John Henry's Hammer" or "Mr. Garfield" or "Hardin Wouldn't Run" or "You Wild Colorado." Some of these songs that weren't in any way meant to be commercial . . . I told June a couple of times: "I like this one so much I'm not gonna let anybody hear it. This song is just for me and you." Said that about a lot of songs I wrote.

DeCurtis: Did you feel like there was a difference between that sort of stuff and who Johnny Cash was or had become? Did you feel a remove from the public figure you had become?

Cash: Yeah. Maybe I was trying to. I didn't like that public figure business, that American Statesman stuff, that Great Spiritual Leader stuff. . . . I was a very private person about a lot of that stuff. So many times I said. . . . all this stuff would come up and there'd be something I'd have to do that I really didn't have my heart in doing. I'd say, "All I ever wanted to do was play my guitar and sing a simple song." That's all I ever wanted to do. And that's still all I ever want to do.

DeCurtis: One of the things you did in terms of breaking down barriers was when you were hosting your own television program and exposing people to a lot of kinds of music. Just the other day I was talking to Eric Andersen, who was talking about being on your show . . . You had Bob Dylan and all these other people that you brought to a public that wasn't used to seeing folks like that on mainstream television. For a private person, here you are hosting your TV show. What was that like?

Cash: They kept bugging me to do a TV show, and I did six. I did a summer replacement show for somebody and I did six, and I had people like Steve Martin on there. Then they came to me with a series—to do an ABC weekly series of twenty-six shows, a whole season. I said, "I don't want to do that, it's too confining, it's awful hard." You gotta give your life to that camera.

So they kept after me. They kept begging, calling meetings, and they would come down here from New York and I would have meetings with them, and finally I said, "June and I have been talking about it and we'll give it a try if we can have the guests that we want on the show." They said, "Anybody, anything you want." And at that particular time Pete Seeger was in the news again, he'd appeared before the House subcommittee on Communist leanings [the House Un-American Activities Committee] or whatever, and I said, "First of all, I want Pete Seeger on," and they all looked at each other and kind of nodded their heads, and I said, "But the musical guest I want on the first show is Bob Dylan," and they looked at each other again and said, "Bob Dylan?" I said, "Yeah. If I can't have him, I don't want to do a show." So they said, "OK we'll try to get him . . ." I said, "No, you don't have to. I'll ask him myself." I was trying to keep him from going through that hassle, with the agents and the deals and all that. They did get involved, of course, but I asked him myself first. He said he didn't do TV, but he'd do it for me. He asked me if I could help protect him from people that come backstage—the press and all that. And I said, "I'll do my best. I don't know what I can do, but I'll do my best."

So they had all kinds of security, every exit blocked and nobody could see Bob—that was the word that went out. Nobody—that means you— you don't see Bob Dylan, you don't talk to him, you leave him alone. So they did. But the third day—we started Monday, Tuesday, Wednesday, we taped on Thursday. So on Wednesday a reporter from the *Nashville Banner*—Red O'Donnell—called me up at home and said, "You have to get me in to see Bob Dylan." I said, "No, I promised him I wouldn't," he said, "We go way back, Johnny." I said, "I can't help that, I can't do it, I promised him I wouldn't do it." And he said, "Will you ask him?" and I said, "No, he's already said he won't talk to press . . ." and he said, "Just ask him for me," and I said, "I'll mention to him that you called."

So at rehearsal on Wednesday I asked Bob, "Red O'Donnell is the number-one man in the music column in town on the newspaper, you want to talk to him?" and he said, "No." So I called Red back and I said, "Bob don't want to talk to you . . ." So he said, "Ask him if I can give him ten written questions . . ." and I said, "No, this is too much. I don't wanna do that." So he said, "Ask him if I can give him three written questions . . ." So I went back to Bob: "He wants to know if he can write down three questions and you give him an answer," and Bob said, "Oh. . . . no, I don't think so." I said, "Good. OK." So I told Red and he says, "Ask him if I can write down one question." I said, "What's the question?" He said, "I don't know, but just ask him." I said, "You're wearing me out, Red." So I went to Bob and said, "Will you answer one question that this reporter wants to ask you?" He said, "What's the question?" I said, "I don't know." He said, "Ask him what the question is . . ." So Red had his foot in the door. We were at rehearsal and suddenly into Bob's room walks Red O'Donnell, and he had on sunglasses. I said, "Bob, this is Red O'Donnell," and Bob looked at me like, "How did he get in here?" I didn't have a clue and I knew that Bob was upset. So I don't know what the question was, this will be an eternal mystery. I honestly don't remember what the question was. It wasn't important. But Bob would not answer it. The one question. And he kept following him around this little room. Bob would move around to one corner, Red would move in on him, he'd come out, walk to the other corner, and this went on and on and on and Red kept asking the same question over and over and

Bob would not open his mouth, wouldn't say a word. And finally Red shook hands with me and said, "I'll see ya later Johnny." And I started laughing. I couldn't help it. But Bob wasn't laughing, he wasn't happy. I said, "I'm sorry about that—I had nothing to do with him getting in here. I don't know how he did it." And Bob said, "I would've talked to him except for one thing." I said, "What's that?" He said, "He wouldn't take off his sunglasses." I said, "I don't blame you." [*Laughs.*]

DeCurtis: At that tribute show recently [*An All-Star Tribute to Johnny Cash* on the TNT Network], Dylan made such a nice statement at the beginning about how you were a big supporter of his early on. What was it that you heard in Bob Dylan's songs? And what was it about him as a person that made you such a supporter?

Cash: The first time I heard him—I don't know where it was, I believe in Las Vegas—I thought it was an old country singer. And then I realized somebody told me who he was—and I said, this is really unbelievable that he could get airplay singing that kind of music. Then I bought his records. I bought *Freewheelin'* and the *Bob Dylan* album, then I wrote him a letter and he wrote back, and we wrote each other back and forth for weeks, months. I just heard a fresh approach to some old themes, but really done well with an insight that had never been put on record. I just loved his work, loved him. Always have. Still do. I just think he's still the best thing out there.

DeCurtis: A lot of the figures that came up at the same time as you—Jerry Lee Lewis, Elvis. . . . are you in touch with Jerry Lee or any of the others? Still feel a connection to some of those guys from back in the day?

Cash: Yeah, well most of 'em are dead. Carl Perkins and his brothers are all dead. Bill Black, Elvis, Roy Orbison—who was not only my best friend but my next-door neighbor for twenty years. Marshall Grant, who played bass for me for so long—he and I are friends, we talk a lot. The ones that are still left, I talk to them. Jack Clement, I probably talk to Jack more than any of 'em. Still really good friends, really close. We don't really do a lot of Good Old Days sessions. We don't talk a lot about it. But when something comes up, we'll argue about who's right about this or that, y'know. I don't see many of them. I don't see many people at all, since I got sick.

DeCurtis: Now you're working on a new record. What's the stuff you're working on now? Have you gotten far along on another record with Rick?

Cash: Yeah, we've recorded fifteen or sixteen songs already, and we're gonna do that many more. I don't know what the theme of it is. There's only one guitar, two at the most, on the record so far. We may do some overdubbing, we may not. There's no theme so far. It's just that all these good songs that I've wanted to record the last time, we're recording those but also some that have come in or been written since then. And some really good ones that I'm really proud of. There's some real old stuff . . . one of 'em is a Stephen Foster song called "Hard Times Come Again No More." Written in 1859. [*This would appear on the posthumous* Unearthed. —*Ed.*] Really a good song, wonderful song. Then there's a Burt Williams song written about 1890 called "Nobody." [*Sings*] *I ain't never done nothin' to nobody / I ain't never got nothin' from nobody no time / And until I get something from somebody sometime / I don't intend to do nothin' for nobody no time. . . . When the winter's blowin' down a street / I got no shoes upon my feet / Who says "Here's a dollar, go and eat?" / Nobody.* It's a great old song. Dean Martin had a record on it. I don't know who else. Then there's some really good new songs that I'm recording. "The Mercy Seat," it's a Nick Cave song.

DeCurtis: Have you done much writing yourself for this record?

Cash: Yeah, I'm writing three or four songs. I'm writing three or four at the same time. First time I've ever had 'em bombard my brain. When I started recording, I started writing. I hadn't written since I got sick. Over a year. But when I started recording, the ideas started coming. I've got all these pads laying around everywhere with four or five lines, two verses or a verse and a chorus. One of 'em's finished. But I'll finish 'em as we work. That's when I write the best—when I'm working. Then I go home and go to bed, then I have to get up and write something down.

DeCurtis: What are the plans for release? You have a schedule in mind?

Cash: Nope. Just whenever it's ready. We're gonna try and finish it this summer.

DeCurtis: Other plans? Other projects you're working on? Or are you gonna take it easy this summer apart from the record?

Cash: I just recorded a daily devotional for Franklin Electronics—a Bible. Like 365 verses. You punch in your birthday, see what your verse is. I recorded them in Jamaica, and I recorded the old King James Version of the Bible and the New International Version. The New International Version is much easier to understand for someone who hasn't read the Bible a lot. It's like a little computer. You put it in your pocket. Then you punch in the verse and Johnny speaks to you. It'll be for sale at Radio Shack.

DeCurtis: Lou [*Robin, Cash's manager —Ed.*] had mentioned that you were doing a project of lesser-known songs from your catalog. Time-Life is gonna put it out?

Cash: *Reader's Digest.* [*Sony Legacy, actually. —Ed.*] It's out, I think. I think Sony's releasing three albums from their Legacy Series. They're releasing an album called *Murder* . . . murder ballads, and one called *Love Songs* and *Gospel*. Three-CD box set. That's ready to go. [*Box set actually entitled* Love, God, Murder. *—Ed.*]

DeCurtis: As you look ahead, what is it now that you're interested in? You've built this tremendous body of work, you've had some struggles in recent years . . . what is your frame of mind at this point, what is it that drives you?

Cash: There's always another song to sing, they're always there. And I've got songs laying all over my desk and bookcases here and I'm always planning a new one, maybe an old one, but it's a new one. Like the Stephen Foster song—it's just as country and as real as anything I've ever done.

DeCurtis: I was reading an interview with Dylan and he was saying, "People don't learn the old songs now, everybody has to write all their own stuff . . ." and the guy that was doing the interview said, "Well that's kind of your fault." [*Johnny laughs.*] That idea that it's new when you sing it—you make it your own.

Cash: I can't help it, I find these old songs and I've gotta record 'em. I love 'em. These songs that I'm doing, this album. Some of 'em I really love.

DeCurtis: You have a title yet?

Cash: Nope. Haven't even discussed it.

DeCurtis: You're recording in Nashville?

Cash: We're recording in a log house in the woods right straight across the road from my house. It's a log house I built in '78 and it's one room, it's got a kitchen, a bathroom off the back, and state-of-the-art equipment. And we're surrounded by goats and deer and peacocks and crows. We have to stop tape sometime because the goats get on the porch and tromp around.

DeCurtis: Sounds like an environment in which Mr. Rubin would be very comfortable.

Cash: He loves it. We all do.

DeCurtis: Your relationship with him continues to be as fertile and alive as . . .

Cash: Yeah, we get along really good.

DeCurtis: When did you feel like you were done [*with* American II: Unchained]?

Cash: I don't think I ever felt like I was done. But these are the tracks because it was so painful sometimes to not include some songs that you really loved. I worked on this record so long—like up to three years. A lot of the songs that I like the most are not on there because they didn't really—in the final picture they didn't shape up to what we were expecting. Every song in there I love very much. I spent a lot of time on all of them, as did all of the people that I worked with. The overall picture: I see a lot of outtakes laying there. [*Laughs.*]

DeCurtis: Some for next time. Talk a little bit about recording "One." That was obviously a great U2 single. What drew you to that track?

Cash: I heard the song when it first came out by U2 and never thought about recording it until Rick Rubin suggested it would be a good one for me. So I said at that time, I was in Tennessee and he was in California, and I had been doing some recording in what we call the Cash Cabin Studio there near my house and he had been back there working with me in the studio, so he sent a guitar track for me to listen to—an acoustic, scaled-down version. And I listened to it, and I thought this might be the right approach to this song. I certainly won't go big sound or anything like that, but I love the song so much and I love what the song said that I felt like I had to record it. So Rick made it very comfortable for me to do that. And with his expertise and the musicians that worked on it, it came out really good, I think.

DeCurtis: Yeah, it's great. So spare and clear. Like a cry from the heart. Talk about some of the new songs you came up with. Obviously you've been writing. "Field of Diamonds . . ."

Cash: That's a song Jack Routh—who was my son-in-law at the time—he and I wrote that . . . that's one of those things that just flowed, it came from out of the sky. We were lying on our backs in Jamaica in the yard—the family—looking at the stars. They're so bright there. I just started singing "Field of diamonds in the sky . . ." the song just flowed until he and I together had finished it. Another song I wrote called "Before My Time" came about what with working on all these really old songs . . . actually the one that inspired it is not on the album, but if I ever do an album of outtakes it'll be on there. It's a song of Stephen Foster's called "Hard Times." I was recording "Hard Times" and I got to thinking about things that songwriters said 100, 150, 200 years ago, and I was thinking about the fact that we say the same thing but we say it different ways. And that's what "Before My Time" is about—love is universal and it doesn't change in a century or two.

DeCurtis: A couple of lighter hearted things on the record—"I'm Leaving Now," "Country Trash."

Cash: Merle Haggard and I did "I'm Leaving Now." That's the one and only full take we did on that song. He came back to the cabin studio in Tennessee and did that song with me. It's a song I wrote about fifteen years ago. As with "Country Trash," that's kind of a fun song that I wrote. I used to write them for myself to amuse myself and they wind up on my records.

DeCurtis: Did Merle happen to come by?

Cash: No, no. It was planned. I planned to have him come out the next time he was in Tennessee and he did. It was scheduled about two months in advance. I knew he was coming.

DeCurtis: Tom Petty turned up again. Talk about working with him and that song in particular.

Cash: Working with Tom was a joy. He and all the Heartbreakers were with me on the *Unchained* album. There's always a song or two on a session, when I'm doing an album, where I say I may not get this on this album but it'll be on the next one, that's for sure. And I felt that way about "I Won't Back Down." I mentioned that to Rick and he got the song for me, and I learned it and we did some of the recording in Tennessee, some in California. It gets kinda fuzzy to me. It was all the same, really. The same spirit, the same feel, no matter where we were. The song "I Won't Back Down" says a lot of things that I wanted to say. It probably means different things to me than it did to Tom, who wrote it, which is great, that's the way it ought to be. I like the line in there that says, "I know what's right / I have just one life / So I stand my ground and I won't back down." To me that means I'll stand up to adversity and disease, to illness, I stand up on my faith in God that there is my power and I won't back down from that. But then there's the line "Hey Baby, there ain't no easy way out." [*Laughs.*] I get to trying to analyze a song and then there'll be a line like that that'll screw up everything I'm trying to say.

DeCurtis: The liner notes that you wrote for the record are so inspirational.

Cash: Thank you.

DeCurtis: That sense, when you're talking about that song, confronting illness and that sort of thing . . . now you've been in this situation . . . my understanding is that you're feeling better these days.

Cash: I feel great.

DeCurtis: And there's some question about whether the original diagnosis was correct.

Cash: It was a misdiagnosis. I don't have any kind of old nasty disease with an ugly name. It was diagnosed three years ago as Shy-Drager syndrome, but then it was a misdiagnosis . . . my doctors decided a year or so ago that I didn't have that or I'd be dead, and I wasn't dead at the time. [*Laughs.*]

DeCurtis: What is the situation now? Do they have a sense of what you're struggling with?

Cash: No. I'm fine. I don't have anything. I don't have any disease. I'm in New York enjoying myself. We're going to a Broadway show tonight, going to buy some new shoes after I finish talking to you. I'm enjoying myself. I'm not sick.

DeCurtis: Wow. That's incredible. Are you going to be performing at all with this record?

Cash: I don't have any plans to right now. I just want to see what happens. It's been awhile. It's been three years. I'm not gonna say never again, but I don't have any plans to go out.

DeCurtis: It must've been an amazing thing to be relieved of that burden.

Cash: I lived through all that and I've found that life is better and richer than it ever was, and I'm just enjoying living with my family and my home and going to movies and watching videos, this and that. Taking it easy.

DeCurtis: Some of the songs on the album seem to address coming up against the idea of mortality . . . "I See a Darkness," "The Mercy Seat." Talk about getting that deep into. . . .

Cash: "I See a Darkness" is a nice song. I see that as a song . . . I don't know how anybody else, even the writer, saw it and he was with me on the record, he sang with me—Will Oldham. But I saw it as a song of friendship, of love, man/woman or two friends, two men being friends and bonding. Calling on each other to help each other pull through the hard times. That's the way I saw that song. And the other one, "The Mercy Seat" is a song about the electric chair by Nick Cave as I understand it. It's a scary thing, capital punishment. The whole idea of it is terrifying to me.

DeCurtis: It seems like in the country at large there seems to be a shift in thinking about it. It seemed like it was political suicide to even raise a question about it a few years back, and now people are looking at it harder.

Cash: A long time ago I stopped being scared about what I might say. If something is scary, it's scary, and that's what that is to me. Capital punishment is really a terrifying notion.

DeCurtis: You had a couple other guests—Sheryl Crow, June . . . Talk about singing with them.

Cash: Sister Sheryl Crow—she is really good, I really like her. She came and sang on "Field of Diamonds" with my wife June. She and June did the backgrounds with me. It's always great to see her and work with her. I love her very much. Met her in Hollywood when I did a show there at the Pantages Theater back when I had my first record on American. She came to the show and we've been friends since then.

DeCurtis: She did that tribute show [*An All-Star Tribute to Johnny Cash*].

Cash: Yes she did. She was so good on that. She's so great. She's one of those people I really love, like Tom.

DeCurtis: I've been hearing some rumors about the possibility of a Highwaymen reunion. Is this anything?

Cash: That's the first I've heard of it. I don't think so. My energies are not going in that direction. Kristofferson is making movies, Willie's got a new album of blues—he's doing really great, and Waylon I don't see or hear from very much anymore, so I don't know. The Highwaymen thing had a ten-year run. I think that was enough. Unless something really special comes up. I never say never, but I don't think so.

DeCurtis: What things do you have in mind right now?

Cash: When I quit the road three years ago . . . I'm trying to take all that energy. . . . the most pitiful thing that happened to me in my recording career is squeezing an album in between tours and you've got no reserve. So now that I've decided that I don't have to go on the road, I take that energy and creativity and put it into the songs and into recording. I'm much happier that way. I'm enjoying my life very, very much. Up to now I'm enjoying it a whole lot more than I did when I was on the road. I don't have any plans to go back and do concerts. I want to channel that energy into writing and recording.

DeCurtis: You taking a break now, or are you gonna get back into working on a new . . .

Cash: No, I'm not taking a break, we just got started. We're talking about a CD of outtakes from the last American sessions and maybe putting all three CDs together, putting together a box set next year, I'm talking about recording a Christmas song next year, maybe even a Christmas album. I'm not sure about that. I have an album of country gospel that any time we want to release it we have it, it's there.

DeCurtis: You did that with Rick?

Cash: Yeah. We did that over the course of recording all these albums. Just my guitar and I. That may be my favorite work that I've done in a long time. We hope to put all that together in some kind of package next year. That's what I'm working toward now. All those projects, plus going fishin' . . . [*Laughs.*]

DeCurtis: You spending most of your time in Tennessee and Jamaica?

Cash: Yeah, we probably spend most of the winter in Jamaica, yeah. We'll go down there about Thanksgiving.

DeCurtis: You had your box set come out earlier this year—*Love, God, Murder*. What was it like going back through all that material and coming up with that conceptual frame to put on it?

Cash: All those old songs, every one of 'em has a memory for me, and it'd be hard to tell all those memories of all those songs on all those CDs, but the box set is called *Love, God, Murder* and it's on Sony. It's a collection of mine and the producers' or compilers' favorites along each theme. They were coming up with this idea of love songs, gospel songs, and prison songs, and I said why don't you just simplify it and call it *Love, God, Murder*, so they went for that. Along those three lines, I worked with them by telephone picking out the songs that I thought should be in there. Those are the ones that are on those three CDs.

DeCurtis: Wow. Strong stuff.

Cash: Thank you.

February 15, 2002

DeCurtis: You wanna talk about all these great records you got coming out?

Cash: Yeah, sure.

DeCurtis: Excellent. One thing that would strike anybody listening to them is the range of musical styles that you cover over a six- or seven-year period . . . it seems like you were bursting with musical ideas and a desire to move in every direction, from concept albums about America to a spirituals record to really defining the rockabilly and country and rock stuff you were doing. Do you remember that sense of ambition?

Cash: When I met with Rick Rubin at American Records ten years ago, I asked him what he would do with me that nobody else had done, and he said, "I'd like you to sit in front of a microphone with your guitar and sing everything you want to record." And I said, "Whoa—that's a tall order. There are lotta songs over the years I've always wanted to record." He said, "Those are the ones that I want to hear."

DeCurtis: And the stuff that Columbia's putting out right now?

Cash: I'm excited about these things Sony's putting out. [*Sony had purchased Columbia Records in 1988. —Ed.*] *Life Is Strange* is my favorite that I ever did, and I'm really glad to see that somebody got it on CD. *Orange Blossom Special*—I've listened to all five of them all the way through as well as *The Essential Johnny Cash*, if you can believe that. I don't like to listen to my own records, but I felt like I needed to because

I knew what they were trying to do with these. They were really trying to get me out there, and I needed to know what they were all about. I'm very well pleased with all of them. I'm pleased with the one thing that they added—bonus tracks to all these albums. That might make them worth buying, y'know?

DeCurtis: What was your impression going back and listening to them? The thing that strikes me is the level of musical ambition and energy. It seemed like you wanted to do everything. You hit it so hard. What is your recollection of your state of mind and your desire at those times?

Cash: Sounds like my hormones were really flowing! [*Laughter.*] I was hitting those bass notes really well. I'm proud of that work. I can't understand an artist who has done a great body of work that is not proud of it. If not, then why did we do it? Of course, I'm proud of it. I don't think anybody else ever did it like I do it. That wasn't the point, to try to do it like nobody else has done it. I just wanted to do it my way. I used basically the same instrumentation on all these albums and the same backup singers whenever I did use backup singers. I used the Carter Family—June and her sisters and mother. I'm very well pleased with these records. *Orange Blossom Special* and if you'll pardon the expression—*The Fabulous Johnny Cash. Ride This Train.* The duet album with June [*Carryin' on with Johnny Cash & June Carter*]—"Jackson." It's memory time for me. Old memory time. Sweet memories. Because I can listen to the duets with June and think about what was going on in our lives at that time.

DeCurtis: You defined your persona then—the austere Man in Black, she being beautiful and playful, and you guys having fun with each other on "Long Legged Guitar Man" and "Big Mouth Woman" . . . almost a theatrical element that you guys used to bring to performance.

Cash: Yeah. We did have a lot of fun with it. We had a lot of fun with each other.

DeCurtis: The *Hymns* record is obviously a significant record for you and part of the reason you went to Columbia in the first place. In many ways that spiritual aspect has been the most consistent thing running through your entire career.

Cash: I could not convince Sam Phillips how important that was to me. He knew it was important to me, but his answer when I mentioned doing an album of spirituals or gospel songs or hymns was, "I don't know how to sell hymns. I can't sell enough with this little record company to make it worth recording." I understand that. It was a very small company, even when "I Walk the Line" was released, he only had distribution in fourteen states. It was asking a lot of Sam Phillips to record and release a hymns album. But whatever the reason I wanted to do it, it was asking a lot of him to do it. But it was one of the reasons I did go to Columbia because I didn't want to be restrained, I didn't want to be held back from doing anything that I felt was important for me to do record-wise, I didn't want to be held back as a writer. If I wrote these kinds of songs, I wanted to put them on record and I didn't want anything to stop me from doing what I wanted to do record-wise.

DeCurtis: Artists and musicians often try to play up the rebellion and outrage, and here's an element where you're going into the most traditional, the deepest, an aspect that plays down rebellion and plays up submission to a higher power . . . Talk a bit about that interplay, that dynamic in you and in your listeners, in people, human beings.

Cash: My faith in God has always been a solid rock that I've stood on no matter where I was or what I was doing. I was a bad boy at times, but God was always there for me and I knew that. I guess I took advantage of that fact. It's hard to justify the two as far as you're concerned, but to me it's not. Roy Orbison wrote a song called "My Best Friend," and there's a line in there that says "A diamond is a diamond and a stone is a stone / But man is part good and part bad," and I've always believed that—that the good will ultimately prevail, but there's that bad side of us that we have to keep warring against. I do at least. A lot of people do.

DeCurtis: One of the things that struck me listening to this music now is something like *Ride This Train* and its appreciation of what America is and its fondness and affection for the way this country was built. It seems to have a special resonance in the wake of September 11th. What are your feelings about that?

Cash: September 11th broke my heart. I watched that on television. I guess I wanted to kill somebody myself.

DeCurtis: Yeah. A lot of us did.

Cash: It was a real heartbreaker for me. Because I do love this country and I saw that somebody was taking a really good shot at it, taking a good shot at trying to disrupt not only our finances, but our morale. We were hit a striking blow that really hurt. It did hurt me. But I recovered like the country's recovering. I believe ultimately that this country will prevail. In righting all these wrongs . . . these people will not go unpunished. I certainly hope they won't go unpunished. Every time somebody mentions it to me . . . I'm reminded my daughter Rosanne lives twenty blocks from the World Trade Center. She was walking her little girl to school that morning when the second plane hit the building. It was right there in their faces, and they ran home and locked the doors and stayed in for days. I'm sure a lot of people wanted to stick their head in the sand and hide and not do anything about it for fear that something worse might happen, but I think of my little granddaughter and how it affected her—that she cried when people would pull the curtains. She wanted to stay inside and not be bothered with it anymore, didn't want to hear any more about it. She would turn off the television if it came on. I think the country is recovering and Rosanne, their little girl, her husband, their little boy will be here late this afternoon on vacation to spend with us and we're looking forward to laughing and having fun. We'll get the fuzzy wuzzies in the end.

DeCurtis: I don't want to embarrass you, but in many ways the celebration of your seventieth birthday is, in a lot of people's minds, a celebration . . . that in some essential way you embody a lot of what people think are the best aspects of what America is. You've been a great artist for a long time and spoken to people in their hearts and their spirits in a lot of different ways, and I wondered if, as all of this music is being reissued and coming back, you must smile a little bit to think about what all of this has meant to people.

Cash: Yeah. [*Laughs.*] Yeah, I did. Kind of humorous to think that it means anything to anybody when in each song there's a special memory for me, with each one of 'em. I look at the titles and I'll smile and think of something that happened while recording it or when I first heard it or when I was singing it.

DeCurtis: You were a great champion of Bob Dylan. I wonder if you could say a few words about him and what his music meant to you back then and your discovery of what his music was and your desire to put it on in front of people and often in front of an audience that wouldn't typically be thought to be receptive to somebody like Bob Dylan.

Cash: There's no doubt that Bob Dylan's influence on my music and myself in general . . . On the *Orange Blossom Special* album, there are two or three Bob Dylan contributions in that album. We became friends and I'd already become a fan of Bob's and I still am. I still buy his records. I go to the record shop with every release he has and buy his new CD. His latest one, by the way, is the best one yet. It's terrific.

DeCurtis: In many ways it almost reminds me of something like *Ride This Train.* Getting back into all of the aspects of what American music has been.

Cash: Bob is timeless. Walking along in the yard the other day, I started singing "Maggie's Farm" of all things. Just comes out of the sky through my head and I start singing it. Invariably before every day ends, there will be a Bob Dylan song that'll float through me. I appreciate Bob in that he has given me music. All these people that have contributed music for me to sing and feast on—like Kris Kristofferson, for instance, over the years—I love and appreciate very much. Bob Dylan is one of those who I truly love and appreciate.

DeCurtis: On a sadder note, I wanted to ask you about Waylon Jennings. I was reading his book and he called you his soul mate. He said when he would look at you, "I felt like I was looking at myself."

Cash: We were that way. Waylon and I are soul mates. We're buddies and everything else. Speaking of sharing music, he and I shared as much music as I ever shared with anybody. Onstage as part of the Highwaymen. It was all a joy, a great joy that we had, that we shared all this music together with Kris. I was talking to Kristofferson last night, and after we cried awhile we got to talking about some funny things that happened to Waylon and I onstage as part of the Highwaymen, in-house kind of things that we kidded each other about. Waylon was as close as a brother could be. Just couldn't be any closer.

DeCurtis: Do you have a good Waylon Jennings story that gets at who he is?

Cash: Let me tell you somethin': I was booked in Toronto, a week in a theater up there. This was about ten years ago. My guitar player was ill. I found out the morning I was to leave for Toronto to work five days that he wouldn't be able to go at all. And I called Waylon, panicking, I said, "You gotta help me find a guitar player that can play my stuff that knows my records, that I can give him titles and he'll know what key they're in, everything." Waylon said, "I'll find you somebody." Well, he called me back about two hours later and said, "I found you somebody." I said, "Who's that?" He said, "Me." I said, "No, I'm not gonna ask you to do it, Waylon." He said, "You didn't ask me, I volunteered, I'm going with you tomorrow. I'm gonna play guitar for ya." Nobody could play it any better than Waylon. My old style of Luther Perkins guitar—Waylon was really good at it. I said, "I can't do this to you, you're a superstar, you can't stand out there and be my guitar player!" He said, "You just watch me . . ."

So he was on the plane with me the next day. I said, "Do me this: let me put you in the dark the first part of the show and then let the people find you, and when I see that they've found you, then let me introduce you." He said, "All right." So that's the way we played it. He was not lighted at all, but people kept looking at him. There was a certain amount of light that we couldn't kill . . .

DeCurtis: Who's that guy standing in the shadows? Who's that masked man?

Cash: And it was Waylon. He did all five days, all five shows, and not only did he play guitar for me, he wouldn't take any money for it. He said, "I won't play for a guitar player's fee." [*Laughs.*] I said, "All right, I owe you one." I never got to pay him back. I did go about five years ago to Littlefield, Texas, to the Waylon Jennings Homecoming. But how could I ever pay that back? That was really something.

DeCurtis: Could you tell me a little bit about his music? What was really distinctive about his music, what he'll be remembered for?

Cash: He'll probably be remembered for the Outlaw albums, but he'll also be remembered as one of the Highwaymen. He had a certain growl in his singing that the people will remember that says, "I love you but not all that much." [*Laughs.*] "I love you, but don't tell anybody." That kind of persona that he had that he'll be remembered for.

DeCurtis: Tell me one thing about the record you're working on with Rick . . .

Cash: Working title is *American IV*. Songs are coming from every direction. I wrote about three of them. I recorded a Sting song called "I Hung My Head." I recorded a Marty Robbins song called "Big Iron." Recording "The First Time Ever I Saw Your Face," the Roberta Flack song. And I'm recording "Hurt," a Nine Inch Nails song. When I heard that song, I thought, "That sounds like something I could've written in the '60s."

DeCurtis: A lot of people think that that's just a noisy crazy band, but Trent Reznor's a really interesting songwriter.

Cash: There's more heart and soul and pain in that song than any that's come along in a long time. It's a good song. I love it. I've already got a track on it. I'm recording it.

DeCurtis: Excellent. You guys been working in Tennessee, or is he coming down to Jamaica?

Cash: We've had one session here in Jamaica. We're gonna have one more at the end of this month and then I'll go to California, and finish recording in Rick Rubin's living room.

THE MAN IN BLACK AND WHITE . . . AND EVERY SHADE IN-BETWEEN

Bill Friskics-Warren | November–December 2002 | *No Depression*

In his work for the *Los Angeles Times*, *New York Times*, *Washington Post*, *No Depression*, *Oxford American*, and multiple others, journalist and author Bill Friskics-Warren has crossed paths with many luminaries. He interviewed Johnny Cash in 1999 and 2002. That latter interview, for *No Depression*, took place on a beautiful September morning at the Carter Family ancestral home, the Carter Fold, in Maces Spring, Virginia. It is reprinted here.

"He was definitely more curious than most," Friskics-Warren says of Johnny Cash. "As with seemingly everything about the man, he sought *connection* at every turn. He wanted to *connect*. He wanted to know about your family, wanted to know what you think about something most people wouldn't consider the business of their conversation partner, especially in the formal interview setting. I found this very refreshing—his interest in what someone else thought.

"My father is ninety-four and a huge Johnny Cash fan. He bought a lot of Cash records, none canonical. He liked the ones with Billy Graham, and the favorite hymns, the train song albums. Dad didn't have any of the hit stuff. He didn't even have a solid greatest hits collection. And we watched *The Johnny Cash Show* together. That's another place Cash connected. Think about those uniting ties—guests from the Who to Louis Armstrong to Mahalia Jackson to Bob Dylan. There's a vision of a beloved community somewhere at work in that spirit."

Cash was not physically well at the Carter Fold. "He suffered neuropathy from diabetes, his eyes were cloudy," Friskics-Warren says. "He did not stand the entire time I was there. There was a great deal of vulnerability in terms of his physical health, but he had the command . . . an almost biblical prophet persona. So authoritative. It was a real contrast to have him be physically weak yet so inquisitive, possessed of strong opinions, thoroughly engaged."

Although his body was failing him, Cash was riding high artistically from his work with Rick Rubin. During the interview, a FedEx package arrived with a mockup of the cover of *American IV: The Man Comes Around* for Cash to approve. He asked Friskics-Warren what he thought. The album would be released that November and would feature the Trent Reznor / Nine Inch Nails song "Hurt," the most successful single and video of Johnny Cash's career.

On the horizon was James Mangold's *Walk the Line*, then in preproduction. Cash asked Friskics-Warren about the prospect of Nashville native Reese Witherspoon as June. Friskics-Warren made the astute observation that an accurate portrayal of Cash would include as much sunshine as darkness and encompass his activism and love of family and home as much as his drug history, heartbreak, and misadventures. Both men somehow seemed to know *Walk the Line* would not offer such a broad picture.

Although very pleased, vindicated, and satisfied with the Rubin work, Cash expressed misgivings about fans—especially new fans—seeing him as a dark figure. Says Friskics-Warren, "I really appreciated the way he was open to saying, 'I regret I didn't put my foot down or take a more active role in the shaping of my latter-day persona.' Saying in hindsight, 'I wish I'd stressed other dimensions more.' It was pretty amazing to have someone of his stature convey vulnerability and humility."

When the interview was over, Cash directed Friskics-Warren to the nearby cemetery, to look at A.P. and Sara Carter's graves. Friskics-Warren knew he wouldn't be seeing either Johnny or June again.

"I remember getting in the car and feeling very emotional, and being taken aback by it," he says. "Shedding tears. For the nobility of this couple, how they'd endured, their frailty, as well and the fact that they wouldn't be around much longer. There was a grieving quality to it. But I was very uplifted, too." —Ed.

Take I-23 north from Kingsport, Tennessee, or south from Wise, Virginia, and you'll find more or less the same mix of old and new Appalachia: roadside flea markets within sight of Wal-Mart Supercenters, generations-old strip mining operations alongside latter-day pulp mills, doublewides in hollers overlooked by McMansions on the hill.

That's not the case once you get off the interstate and the road narrows to two lanes, as it does when you cross the Tennessee-Virginia line and wind northeast on Highway 58 toward the Carter Family homestead in Scott County. It isn't that the landscape suggests a bygone era; the shady blacktop that snakes its way through this corner of southwest Virginia reveals more than its share of late-model pickups, trailers and prefab homes. It's just that, bereft of billboards and fast-food chains, its rugged recesses have yet to be inundated by the more garish trappings of modernity.

This is even more the case further up the road in blink-or-miss-it Hiltons (pop. 30), where a filling station/cafe with a rabies advisory in its window marks the turnoff to the Carter Family Fold, which lies just three miles down A.P. Carter Highway in Maces Spring.

"Fold" is the name that Joe Carter, A.P. and Sara's son, gave the barn-like amphitheater he built into the rise just to the left of his father's old grocery store (now a museum) in 1976. Invested with biblical freight, the term could hardly sound more antediluvian, conjuring either an enclosure for sheep or a congregation, a "flock" bound together by shared values or beliefs. Or, for that matter, a cloud of witnesses like the one that gathers, at the behest of Joe Carter's sister Janette, in the Fold's hodgepodge of chairs, benches and transplanted school bus seats every Saturday night to listen and dance to the old-time music that's synonymous with the Carters and the mountains of Southern Appalachia.

"Fold" has a broader connotation here, though. It's also an old English term for a small basin or drainage very much like Poor Valley, the narrow holler bisected by A.P. Carter Highway that encompasses everything from the log cabin where A.P. was born to Mt. Vernon United Methodist Church, the white clapboard chapel behind which he and Sara are buried. The brooding slabs of pink granite under which they lay are adorned with copper plaques, shaped like 78-rpm records, inscribed with the refrain "Keep On The Sunny Side."

Mother Maybelle Carter and her husband, A.P.'s brother Ezra ("Eck"), are buried just outside Nashville, but the modest white cottage with the wraparound porch they built in the early 1940s is here at the Fold as well. The house, which is lined with box elders and Canadian hemlocks and sits a couple hundred yards off the road facing south, now belongs to the couple's only surviving daughter, June Carter, and her husband, Johnny Cash.

The Cashes are there the sunny Friday morning in September I make the trip out to the Fold. The man of the house—dressed only half in black, a white work shirt being his concession to the light—is sitting in the living room where Mother Maybelle and her daughters Helen, Anita and June used to rehearse. Photos of kin, many of them taken by Johnny, including a cherubic shot of a young Rosanne, compete with space among knick-knacks and Carter-Cash memorabilia on every wall and countertop.

His feet elevated to prevent them from swelling due to water retention brought on by diabetes, Cash has been at the Fold working on June's follow-up to 1999's exquisitely unvarnished *Press On*. The album is scheduled for release on Dualtone early next year. Cash's own *The Man Comes Around*, the fourth installment in his series of recordings with producer Rick Rubin, comes out November 5 on Lost Highway.

It's been a week since the Man in Black made a surprise appearance at the Americana Music Association Awards in Nashville to receive the first-ever Spirit of Americana Free Speech Award for his lifelong commitment to voicing the struggles of those who languish on society's margins. More surprising still, especially given his retirement from public performance, was Cash's return to the stage at the AMAs to sing with his wife and several generations of Carter women. His cameo prompted June, always in fine comedic form, to dub him a "Carter brother."

"June asked me to sing a song or two on her album and I said, 'OK, I'll be first brother.' Or maybe *she* called me Carter Brother first; anyway, I got a real kick out of singing along with her," says Cash. He looks more frail than imposing, propped up in his black leather recliner. Yet at 70, and beset by asthma, diabetes and glaucoma, it's remarkable just how vital, even unassailable, Cash and his craggy baritone remain.

He and June still maintain three houses, splitting time between their place at the Fold and their homes in Hendersonville, Tennessee, and Jamaica. Cash continues to seek out and write new material to record, the most striking case of the latter being the title track of his new album, an eschatological wonder seemingly inspired by the Book of Revelations. He remains hungry and plugged in, spurred on not just by his renewed popularity among urban hipsters drawn to his dark side, but nurtured as well by the comforts afforded by faith, family and home. Tellingly, perhaps, he takes his coffee black, but with three sweeteners.

"You see, Mother Maybelle and the Carter Sisters sang all those songs all those years they were on my show," Cash goes on. "I guess it was getting me ready for this, because it came so easy, these sessions did. I'm singing songs like 'Sinking In The Lonesome Sea' and 'Keep On The Sunny Side,' all those songs that the Carter Family had. They're so comfortable, so easy for me, that I feel like a brother in there singing with all those girls."

Cash, who's been a Carter-in-law for 34 years now, more than qualifies as a member of the fold. Yet at this point, he's less a brother than the family's musical patriarch, an inheritor—and then some—of A.P. Carter's prodigious musical legacy, as well as those of Sara and Mother Maybelle.

The young John R. Cash (Sam Phillips later re-christened him "Johnny") listened often to the Carters when, growing up the son of Arkansas sharecroppers, he tuned in the group's broadcasts on Mexican border station XERA. The way that Cash, after the manner of A.P., was "bassin' in" with the Carter women at the AMAs in September suggests he was particularly attuned to the male voice in the trio.

A case can likewise be made for the influence of Mother Maybelle's driving thumb-brush rhythms on the amped-up boom-chuck that Cash—and guitarist Luther Perkins and doghouse bass player Marshall Grant—patented at Sun Records during the '50s. Cash has also devoted himself to collecting songs and tracing their genealogies, much as A.P. Carter did in his day.

"I've always been impressed with A.P.'s work in collecting and writing these songs for the Carter Family," says Cash. "His contribution was momentous. Of course, so was Maybelle's contribution, so far as writing and collecting. And Sara's.

"A.P., he went out there and was selling fruit trees sometimes, and he'd trade a fruit tree for a song. He was a prolific collector. He went all over these hills and these mountains and these valleys around here, listening to songs and collecting different verses, and different songs from different people.

"I've followed in that tradition of collecting and writing," continues Cash, who has a voluminous catalog of recordings, covers as well as originals, to show for it. "You never know where you'll find a good song, and I've always got my ears open, now more so than ever.

"Someone will say, 'I've got this old song,' and immediately I'll think, 'I bet I know every word of it.' They'll start in, maybe on a verse I'm familiar with, but then they'll go southwest, or then they'll go a different direction than I thought they would have gone. There'll be lyrics I never heard before, and I'll say, 'Where'd that come from?' Sometimes they can explain it to my satisfaction, and sometimes they can't."

The influence of the Carter Family extended not just to Cash's music, but to his moral and spiritual development as well. "June and her family have kept me steadily on course at times when the rudder was shaky," Cash told me in 1999. "Maybelle was a great friend, she and Pop Carter both. They were like parents to me.

"My parents were living in California at the time," continued Cash, referring to the mid-'60s, when he and June were first getting together. "[My parents] were happy, after they got to know a little about them, that I was spending a lot of time with the Carters, because they were people who truly cared for me, as did June. They knew she did. So it was their love and care for me, and the musical influence, and the musical sharing, eventually, with all of them, that was very binding. And we're all still kind of bound up that way."

Indeed, much as the Carters did, Cash has long been committed to preserving and nurturing the family fold. "June and I have six daughters and one son, and neither of us have ever used the term 'stepdaughter,'" he says, his tired yet searching eyes filled with pride.

"Talking about family relationships and harmony in the house, you put your arm around your stepdaughter and say, 'This is my daughter' when introducing her to somebody, and it makes her day. It makes mine too. I don't understand this 'step' junk. I know people do it, as a matter of course, but I don't. I just don't do it. I never have gotten any flack for it from anybody, not even their mothers." (Not even, one suspects, for maintaining ties to his singing ex-sons-in-law Marty Stuart, Nick Lowe and Rodney Crowell.)

"I'm a family man," Cash adds. "I'm a home man. I love my home. I love my peace and quiet more than anything in the world."

Somewhat vexing, then, is the extent to which Cash's commitment to home and kin has been eclipsed by the solitary and decidedly Gothic image he's projected since he started working on his bracing series of "American Recordings" with Rick Rubin. Then again, maybe it's less the persona that Cash has cultivated these past few years than the one the marketing and publicity departments of his record companies and the press have projected onto *him*.

First came the sepia-toned cover of his 1994 *American Recordings* album, which pictured Cash, draped in a billowing black duster and framed by a brooding sky, scowling like someone's idea of the grim reaper (and seemingly willing to oblige). Then there was [the] record's kickoff track, a remake of "Delia's Gone," the grisly murder ballad Cash first cut for Columbia in 1962.

Rock critics, of course, ate it up, as they did Cash's subsequent covers of songs by the likes of Soundgarden and Beck. The mainstream press soon began lionizing the Man in Black as an avatar of darkness—equal parts proto-punk and forerunner of the modern gangsta MC. It certainly came as no surprise when the *Murder* volume of Cash's tripartite retrospective *Love God Murder* received lots more attention in print—and outsold—the volumes in the series that spoke to the romantic and devotional sides of his persona.

None of which is to deny that Cash's dark side—his addictions, his hell-raising, his bouts of illness and emotional turbulence—defines a big part of his myth. Or, for that matter, that many people identify with the outlaw hero tradition of which that myth is an extension.

"I understand them obsessing on the dark side," Cash says. "Everybody's got a dark side. In the 19th century, the biggest ballad of all, of the whole century, was 'The Ballad Of Jesse James,' and it didn't come along until the 1880s. And that's up against Stephen Foster and the rest of them, you know? Americans have a history of upholding their outlaw heroes, of holding them up as people to be admired and emulated. Jesse James brought down the establishment, at least in his own mind he did."

Despite Cash's appreciation for—and embodiment of—the outlaw hero mystique, he also admits that he has, in some ways, contributed to this increasingly narrow perception of his image and legacy. "I pigeon-holed *myself* a lot," he says. "It's true that maybe I'm defining myself more as an artist, and maybe as a person, in these latter years. I don't know. But looking back at myself, and at what I projected out there, there seems to be a hardness and a bitterness and a coldness . . . and I'm not sure I'm too happy with that. I'm not sure that's the image I want to project, because I'm a pretty happy man."

It's almost impossible, hearing these comments at the Carter Fold, not to be reminded of the melioristic admonition of the Carters' signature song, "Keep On The Sunny Side," especially the tension between darkness and light it recognizes. Cash has struggled to embrace that dialectic at least since he cut "I Walk The Line" for Sun in '56. He's said that he wrote the song as a pledge of fidelity to his first wife Vivian Liberto, and no doubt that's the case. But over the years "I Walk The Line" took on much greater significance as Cash—the first person elected to both the country and rock 'n' roll halls of fame—emerged as one of the most iconic and complex figures of the second half of the 20th century.

A mass of contradictions, he was a doper and a lay evangelist; a protester of the Vietnam war who palled around with Richard Nixon's pet preacher Billy Graham; a singer of grim odes to murder like "Cocaine Blues" and an aficionado of clodhopper cornpone who once released an LP called *Everybody Loves A Nut*. Cash is truly one of the few who, with Walt Whitman, can say, "Do I contradict myself, very well then, I contradict myself. I am large, I contain multitudes."

Above all, this hard-won multiplicity, this struggle—not nearly as easy as "I Walk The Line" claims—to remain true to that unruly heart of his, is what makes Cash so heroic. Witness how, over the obdurate beat of the Tennessee Two, he sings of keeping the ends out for the tie that binds. Like a down-home dialectician—and in a baritone that's somehow both tender and unyielding—Cash is confessing just how desperately he wants to unite the disparate strands of his gloriously conflicted self in hopes of subduing the beast within.

The Man Comes Around, Cash's new album with Rick Rubin, reflects this dialectical sensibility better than on any of its three predecessors. This isn't to say it's a better record than, say, *American Recordings* or *Unchained* (it's not, being much too reliant on covers of overexposed rock and pop material); but it offers a more complete picture of the man—a more or less equal complement of love, God and murder.

Covers of Ewan MacColl's "The First Time Ever I Saw Your Face," the Eagles' "Desperado" and Hank Williams' "I'm So Lonesome I Could Cry" (a duet with Nick Cave) give love its due. Versions of "We'll Meet Again," "Bridge Over Troubled Water" and the apocalyptic title track (a recent Cash composition) speak to issues of transcendence, while stabs at "The Streets Of Laredo," Sting's "I Hung My Head" and Cash's own "Sam Hall" do murder proud.

The arrangements on the album are also richer and more evocative—less monochromatic—than Cash's other records with Rubin. The prevalence of piano is of particular note, as is the ambient cast of many of the album's tracks. "It's not so much production as kind of a cushioning for my ragged voice," Cash says. "I think that's why Rick added some of those things. There's much more instrumentation on this one, but it fits. It works."

Indeed, and while Cash's stentorian vocals may sound tattered, they still convey an almost Biblical authority, a reverberant mix of judgment, hope, and, above all, steadfastness.

The flood of reissues—and pair of tribute albums—that have greeted the 70th anniversary of Cash's birth have likewise done justice to the complexity of his seemingly inexhaustible persona and legacy. Long out-of-print collections of devotional, patriotic, historical, protest and humorous numbers Cash made for Columbia during the '60s and '70s have resurfaced as part of the ongoing repackaging (by the label's Legacy division) of his back catalog. Also included in this series is *Songs Of Our Soil*, a concept LP from 1959 in which Cash looks back on his hard-knock childhood in the cotton camps of the Arkansas Delta, and *The Fabulous Johnny Cash*, also from '59 and the best single album of his career.

Three concert recordings are newly available as well—not just Cash's famous dates at Folsom Prison and San Quentin, but also a previously unreleased document of a show at Madison Square Garden in December 1969. Most revealing about the last of these is the range of material and emotion it encompasses. Alongside serious signature numbers "I Walk The Line" and "I Still Miss Someone" are the seriously funny "A Boy Named Sue" and knotty political statements such as "Last Night I Had The Strangest Dream," more a dialectical than polemical number— dove with claws, indeed—about the war in Vietnam.

Nor was there a lack of gospel and sentimental fare on the program at Madison Square Garden that night. With contributions from the Carter Family, Cash's brother Tommy (their father, Ray Cash, was in the front row of the audience for the show), old pal Carl Perkins, and the Statler Brothers (whom Cash discovered), the set finds the Man in Black gathering unto himself virtually everything he holds dear. All that's really missing are the comedy sketches of his wife June, who was at home, soon to give birth to the couple's son, John Carter Cash.

Columbia's release of the Madison Square Garden concert also serves as a reminder of the pivotal variety show Cash hosted on ABC from 1969 to 1971. More than any broadcast before it, and maybe since, "The Johnny Cash Show" made hillbilly culture "cool" with mainstream and even countercultural audiences.

"A big deal was going down all right; I could tell by how the crowds were swelling and the press kept getting bigger and bigger," Cash recalls of the show, which ABC broadcast from the Ryman Auditorium, at that time still the home of the Grand Ole Opry. With guests ranging from country stalwarts Roy Acuff and Minnie Pearl to cross-cultural icons Mahalia Jackson, Louis Armstrong and the Who, "The Johnny Cash Show" offered further evidence of Cash's commitment to reaching out for the ties that bind rather than divide people.

Indicative of where Cash's head and heart were during this era was "A Boy Named Sue," a wry talking-blues that *Playboy* cartoonist Shel Silverstein wrote about the generation gap. Whereas "Okie From Muskogee," one of Merle Haggard's singles from the same year (1969), was a joke turned fightin' words, "A Boy Named Sue" was a joke that rang out like an anthem. Communication, even to the point of conflict, Cash was saying, is the best way to breed the tolerance and mutual understanding needed to bridge any gap.

Things come to a head in the song during its final scene, in which the character played by Cash, happening upon his father dealing poker in a dingy saloon, thunders across the room: "My name is Sue, how do you do?/Now you gonna die!" (And how he manages to make those lines sound scary, after all the punchlines that have preceded them, is an honest-to-goodness marvel.)

A brawl of Rabelaisian proportions ensues, the two men kicking, gouging and bloodying themselves beyond recognition as the Tennessee Three's jabbing rhythms and Carl Perkins' guitar provide rollicking ringside commentary. It's not until Cash pulls his gun that the old man finally explains why he named him Sue (although not why he ditched him and his mother in the first place).

"Son, this world is rough and if a man's gonna make it he's gotta be tough . . . And it's that name that's made you strong," his father tells him, the implication being that by giving him a name like Sue—its "sissy" connotations just the sort implied in the gibes at hippies in "Okie"—he made his son the man he had become. The kid relents after the old man says his piece, and the two reconcile, but it's not so much because the son believes his father made him who he is. No, it's that after mixing it up with him and hearing him out, he finally knows, right or wrong, where the man he now calls Pa is coming from.

Speaking not only to the silent majority who presumably tuned in country radio, but also to the longhairs who listened to rock stations, "A Boy Named Sue" nearly topped both the country (#1) and pop (#2) charts in 1969. (By contrast, "Okie" spoke only to one side of the debate, going #1 country but stalling just outside the pop Top 40.)

Nevertheless, apart from scattered singles and his prison albums, many historians and critics, particularly those of a revisionist bent, view the music Cash made after leaving Sun as less emblematic of who he is than the more elemental sessions he did with Sam Phillips and, four decades later, Rick Rubin. More expansive and often more produced records such as "Ring Of Fire" and "Sunday Mornin' Comin' Down" that

Cash made for Columbia with producers Don Law and Bob Johnston— or those he did with old Sun cohort Jack Clement later on—apparently didn't fit the picture some critics had of the "rough cut" Cash.

"Look at the years that I spent on each body of work and you'll see that I put in a lot more years on the Jack Clement and Don Law kind of productions that don't get touted as much lately by the press," says Cash, countering the prevailing rock-crit perspective. That said, Cash admits that he got "off track record-wise" as the '70s gave way to the '80s.

"I was not interested in the records I was making," he says. "I was grinding them out just because I had a record deal. And the less interest I showed in my work, the worse my records sounded, until I came to the point I was totally disinterested, and at that time [1985], CBS dropped me.

"Which was fine with me," he adds. "A lot of people really got upset over that, but I didn't, not in the least. I knew it was coming. I was kind of hoping it was coming, because I wanted out of there. I wanted an excuse to get away. I wanted to escape. Trouble was, I didn't know where I was going when I *did* get out of there. It would still be seven or eight years [after a brief, and fairly inspired, stint with Mercury] before I would have a record deal with Rick Rubin.

"It was like déjà vu with my Sun days when Rick said, 'Just come in, sit down with your guitar and sing me the songs you want to record,'" Cash remembers. "That's what Sam Phillips said. Sam Phillips said, 'Come in and play anything that you like.' So I started singing my songs, Hank Snow songs, Carter Family songs, a little bit of everything."

Cash still recalls his days at Sun with relish (a denim shirt embroidered with the Sun logo was hanging on the line to dry the day I visited the house at the Fold). "Those were very heady times," he says; "'55, I was at Sun Records and there was Elvis Presley, Carl Perkins, Jerry Lee Lewis and myself, and we went out on tour and we had a party.

"We loved what we were doing. We hoped and prayed that it would never end. Of course, when it's going like that, you don't think it ever will. But Elvis left, and then the whole bunch of us kind of fell apart at Sun Records and we all went our separate ways. That was a sad time for all of us.

"At Sun Records, Sam Phillips was always the boss," Cash continues. "He was always Mr. Phillips. We all called him Mr. Phillips. I still have a hard time calling him Sam, because we all had so much respect for him. He was a man who knew what he was about. We all believed in Sam Phillips. We always believed if Sam said it, it had to be right. Even if he told you that's all the money you made in royalties, you tried to believe him."

Even then, though, Cash was holding disparate strands in tension, playing the "devil's music" while thanking heaven for blessing him with the gifts to do so. "Sam Phillips would call me to come in and record, but there might be someone else there too recording," Cash explains. "So I would go in and I'd wait my turn, and if things were going good, he'd keep going with me. Nobody else would take over the time. I don't think I ever had anybody take my time. Elvis *could* have but he didn't; he never did come in and take over my time. Jerry Lee Lewis did once, but he didn't take it for very long. Nobody follows the Killer.

"The Killer was always the Killer," Cash adds. "Jerry Lee Lewis was always the same back then as he is today. He never has changed, and he never will. I never will forget going on tour the first time with him in a car. He'd start in preaching to us. See, he hadn't been out of seminary long. He started in preaching to us telling us we were all going to hell. And I said, 'Well, what about you?' And he said, 'Well, I'm going to hell too. We're all out here doing the devil's work.' I said, 'I'm not doing the devil's work. I'm doing it by the grace of God because it's what I want to do.'"

One of the reasons Cash left Sun in 1958 was to record what became *Hymns By Johnny Cash*, the gospel album Phillips wouldn't let him make.

This dialectical sensibility, this drive to unite putatively conflicting musical and cultural threads, is writ large in the way Cash reached out to Bob Dylan in the early '60s. The relationship the two men forged not only shaped *their* lives and music, it transformed the country and pop worlds as well—especially after Dylan recorded in Nashville, a move that anointed country music (and the laid-back, less-is-more approach to playing which defined "The Nashville Sound") as hip for the rock crowd.

Dylan, of course, was singing Cash's songs long before he left Hibbing, Minnesota, for New York in 1960. "I used to sing this before I ever *wrote* a song," Dylan says on the Cash tribute *Kindred Spirits*, by way of introducing "Train Of Love." In fact, it's arguable, at least in part, that Dylan picked up aspects of his vocal phrasing—as well as his penchant for surrealism—from the likes of "Big River."

Cash would later return the favor, recording Dylan's "Don't Think Twice, It's All Right," "Mama, You Been On My Mind" and "It Ain't Me Babe" (a top-5 country duet with June in 1964) for his *Orange Blossom Special* LP. Cash and Dylan teamed up to record "Girl From The North Country" for Dylan's 1969 album *Nashville Skyline*, which featured liner notes penned by Cash. The duo reprised "Girl From The North Country" on the premiere episode of Cash's TV show later that year. Bootlegs of the recordings they made in Nashville after the *Skyline* sessions, including versions of "Blue Yodel," "Guess Things Happen That Way," and a chugging take of "Mountain Dew" with Carl Perkins on guitar, have been circulating ever since.

Cash first sought out Dylan in Greenwich Village in late 1963 or early 1964. "I had his record called *Bob Dylan*, and then *The Freewheelin' Bob Dylan*, so I went down to the Village looking for Bob one night," recalls Cash, who has always been something of a folksinger at heart. "They said that he had been there but he had gone. So I said to myself, 'If I hang out here in the Village long enough, I'll run into him.'

"June and I were working together then, and I'd go onstage in those little places, and I'd sing my songs and call them folk songs, waiting for Bob to show up. He never did show up in the Village, but I was booked at the Newport Folk Festival in Newport, Rhode Island [in 1964], and that's where I met him. And Joan Baez too. Bob came in my room with Joan Baez and started jumping up and down on my bed and hollering 'Johnny Cash! Johnny Cash! It's really you!' He was laughing, and just acting the fool, you know? It was a lot of fun. And June was there, June, Joan and Bob."

According to Dylan biographer Robert Shelton, following Cash's performance at Newport Friday night, the four of them retreated to Baez's room at the Viking Motor Inn, where the two men committed a bunch of songs to tape. As a token of thanks, Cash gave Dylan one of his guitars.

"I always admired Bob so much for his writing," Cash says. "What I admired about him too was his delivery. I loved his singing. I thought he was the best hillbilly singer I ever heard. When I first heard him, I told June, 'That's the best hillbilly singer you've ever heard. He don't think he is, but he is. The very best.'

"Boy, and he sang those songs with conviction too. 'The Lonesome Death Of Hattie Carroll.'

"'Lone Ranger and Tonto headin' down the line,'" Cash sings, just above a whisper. "'Fixin' up everybody's trouble, everybody's but mine/ Somebody musta told 'em I was doin' fine.'"

The Newport Folk Festival also proved a crucial point of convergence for Cash and Kris Kristofferson, another Nashville outsider the Man in Black befriended. In the process, Cash helped introduce country music to a new breed of songwriter who, with the likes of Mickey Newbury and Tom T. Hall, would infuse Music Row with a plainspoken existentialism derived as much from Hank Williams as from Bob Dylan and the Beats.

"Kris was at my house for a dinner party one night," Cash says. "This was 1967. I told him, 'June and I are going to Newport to do the Folk Festival again. I'd love for you to do a song on the show if you can get up there.' He said, 'I'll be there,' and he hitchhiked up there.

"When it came time for him to go onstage, I said, 'Kris, you go out and do whatever you feel like doing, then call me back out and I'll come back on.' So it came time for him to go on and he stood there frozen. He couldn't move. I said, 'Kris, the emcee's calling you,' and he still couldn't move. He couldn't speak. He was petrified. Well, finally, June walked up to him, kicked him in the seat of the pants, and said, 'Get out there.'

"So he went out and he did 'Sunday Mornin' Comin' Down' and 'Me And Bobby McGee.' I forget what else he did, but the next day, on the front page of *The New York Times*, it said, 'Kris Kristofferson Takes Newport.' I was really proud of that for Kris. He really needed that break; it was a great leap forward, and he got a really good one there."

The most fortuitous convergence of Cash's life, however, wasn't primarily musical, but romantic: his acquaintance with his future second wife, June Carter. The couple first met backstage at the Grand Ole Opry during the late '50s, a good ten years before they were married in 1968. June had been on tour with Elvis Presley, with whom she also shared a manager, Colonel Tom Parker.

June remembers Johnny coming up to her at the Opry (she was a regular on the Prince Albert segment of the show) and saying, "I want to meet you. I'm Johnny Cash." June's response: "Well, I ought to know who you are. Elvis can't even tune his guitar unless he goes, 'Everybody knows where you go when the sun goes down.'" The line was from "Cry! Cry! Cry!," Cash's first hit for Sun; when June was touring the South with Elvis, she recalls the King dragging her into cafes along the way to play Cash's records on the jukebox.

Mother Maybelle and her daughters didn't join Cash's roadshow until the early '60s, but it wasn't long afterward that June found herself falling for Johnny—and dreading it—after discovering he was in the throes of a wicked addiction to pills and booze. She captured the mix of foreboding and desire she felt in "Ring Of Fire," a song she co-wrote with Hank Williams cohort Merle Kilgore and that Cash took to the top of the country charts for seven weeks (#17 pop) in 1963.

June's "Ring Of Fire," which her sister Anita had recorded as "Love's Burning Ring Of Fire" in 1962, was the confession of a woman terrified of her passion burning out of control lest it, or its object, consume her. Johnny's swaggering interpretation of the song could hardly be more different; spurred on by the galloping rhythms of the Tennessee Three, he sounds like he couldn't wait to jump into the flames. "I fell into a burning ring of fire / I went down, down, down / And the flames went higher," he sings, as the mariachi trumpets of Karl Garvin and Bill McEl-hiney fan the blaze.

Cash says he knew what lay behind the lines he was singing; he certainly inhabited them as if he did, abandoning himself to the purifying love he somehow knew would eventually save him from himself. Which, of course, it did. And thus was born one of the most indelible love stories of the past 40 years, one that will be given the big-screen treatment in [*Walk the Line*], a forthcoming biopic to be directed by James Mangold (*Girl Interrupted, Heavy*) and not, as rumored, by Quentin Tarantino.

"As of right now," says Cash, "the number-one contender to play me is Joaquin Phoenix. He's agreed to do the part, and if he and the studio can work it out, I suppose he will. There's a major draft that needs to be done on the screenplay. The version that I have, I didn't approve of at all. There's too much Hollywood junk in it, too much sex and violence for no reason at all—unwanted, unneeded things that just don't work for June and I. So we've got a major rewrite on the screenplay, then if Joaquin Phoenix is still interested, and he can work it out with the studio, he'll play the lead. The girl they're talking about playing June is this girl [Reese] Witherspoon. They say she's perfect for the part."

Indeed, Witherspoon's comedic gifts are likely to do June justice. But perhaps even more crucial than casting the movie will be the ability of the screenwriters to depict the Man in Black as the righteous, irascible, conflicted, utterly complex soul that he is. It would no doubt be tempting, when making concessions to the market, to collapse the tensions that have hounded and driven Cash into a one-or-two-dimensional variant of the persona we've seen during the Rick Rubin era. Again, this isn't to say that the latter-day emphasis on Cash's dark side is mistaken (or that Cash hasn't made worthy records with Rubin)—just that it's incomplete and, as a portrait of so rich and complex a character, woefully inadequate.

Any rendering of Johnny Cash needs to account not just for his pill-popping years, the time he flipped off the camera and the record on which he growled about shooting a man in Reno just to watch him die (a line he hadn't lived but doubtless adapted—from Jimmie Rodgers). It also must address his love of God and family, as well as his fondness for the likes of "Arkansas Traveler"-style hijinx and sentimental weepers— his embrace, as the Carter Family put it, of life's dark *and* sunny sides.

Any treatment of Cash's legacy also must acknowledge how attuned he is to issues of social class. And not just at arm's length, but how he has for decades sustained a vision of justice that compels him to side with all who struggle on the margins—the very thing, in other words, that *makes* him the Man in Black.

"Those are my heroes: the poor, the downtrodden, the sick, the disenfranchised," Cash says. "I just heard a new song by Guy Clark called 'Homeless.' It's really a good song. I'm going to record it. 'Homeless, get out of here,'" Cash intones, his energy flagging. "'Don't give 'em no money, they just spend it on beer.'

"Ain't no end to street people," he adds. "There's no end to the people of the margins. There's no end to the people who can relate to that. People on the margins of economic situations, and of the law. How many people have we got in prison in the U.S.A. now, 1,300,000?" [The figure's more like 2 million.]

It is precisely this prophetic voice—Cash's ability, in "Folsom Prison Blues," to connect the dots between poverty and incarceration, or, in "The Ballad Of Ira Hayes," between racism and disenfranchisement—to which the Americana Music Association and the Nashville-based First Amendment Center paid tribute in September.

Cash said he particularly appreciated the chance "to say a word or two at a time when everyone was waving flags and speaking out for America." Yet, in lieu of making an acceptance speech, Cash surprised everyone in the audience that night, when, in a weakened yet authoritative baritone, he recited an updated version of his 1974 poem "Ragged Old Flag."

Those in the audience who leaned to the left politically, myself included, might have wished Cash had spoken out against the Bush administration's talk of attacking Iraq. Folks on the right probably didn't find the image of a ragged old flag patriotic enough. But, as his comments at the Carter Fold a week later attested, the matter was, very much like Cash himself, more complicated than that, particularly given the way the aggression and injustices perpetrated by the United States have contributed to the sometimes shabby state of our nation's flag.

"You're absolutely right about that," Cash said when I asked him as much. "The raggedness of the flag is due to a lot of things that we've brought onto it ourselves. The fires that we've put it through."

On this day at the Carter Fold, however, it's Cash and his wife who are feeling ragged. "We're a little busted down today," says June, after poking her head into the room to play us a rough mix of the version of the Carter Family's timely "Storms Are On The Ocean" she'd recorded the day before.

"We're just tired," Johnny adds.

No doubt, and not just from recording fourteen songs in two days, but, in Cash's case, from a lifetime of trying to come to grips with his own conflicted self—amid a world of people who, much like his latter-day mythologizers, are too rarely drawn to the light.

INTERVIEW WITH JOHNNY AND ROSANNE CASH

Holly George-Warren | August 2003 | Interview Transcript

Two-time Grammy-nominated writer and editor (and full disclosure: my wife of thirty-three years) Holly George-Warren's August 2003 interview with Johnny Cash is one of the last to which he consented. Though portions of it appear in the PBS documentary *The Appalachians: America's First and Last Frontier* and the accompanying book, coedited by Holly George-Warren, Mari-Lynn Evans, and Robert Santelli, it has never been published in full.

After striking up a professional relationship with both Johnny and June in the 1990s, George-Warren would be invited several times to their Hendersonville home to listen to their stories, and to take note. She always came away profoundly moved and enriched.

Following this last interview with Cash, George-Warren would become a renowned best-selling biographer of Johnny Cash's hero Gene Autry (*Public Cowboy No. 1*, 2007), indie rock godfather Alex Chilton (*A Man Called Destruction*, 2014), and rock 'n' roll icon Janis Joplin (*Janis: Her Life and Music*, 2019), among many other credits. But she counts her time with Johnny and June as some of the most precious moments of her illustrious and charmed career, and her life.

"I first interviewed Johnny Cash in 1996," she says. "It was for a big feature I was doing for *Rolling Stone* on the legends of country music. I'd grown up a fan. The previous five or six years I'd seen him perform for his usual country audience. I saw him at Fan Fair in 1991, at the Tennessee State Fairgrounds in Nashville. His very active fan club—lifelong devotees in their sixties and seventies—had created a replica of a little Appalachian front porch like the Carter Family would've had. Johnny and June sat in rocking chairs, greeting fans. I'd also seen him do his traditional set in some diverse venues—a borscht belt theater and an outdoor festival, both in the Catskills, his Christmas show at The Ritz in New York. I got to see this beautiful interaction between Johnny and June and the other members of his touring ensemble—it was a really cool, family atmosphere.

"I finally met him thanks to my friend Marty Stuart. Johnny was on *The Tonight Show with Jay Leno*. I was in L.A., and Marty invited me to tag along. When we were introduced in the green room, he held out his hand and actually said, 'Hello, I'm Johnny Cash.'

"The 1996 interview was at his office at the House of Cash in Hendersonville. I was really excited. I had this strong feeling we were gonna hit it off, and he's gonna invite me over to his home on the lake.

"We really *did* hit it off. He told some stories about his childhood that I'd never read anywhere. One about a drifter that would come through every year and help bring in the cotton crop. They called him Old Jim George, and he always had this bandanna around his neck. Over supper one night, they asked him about that bandanna. He said, 'When I was a young man, they tried to hang me for a crime I committed, but I didn't die, so they let me go. The bandanna covers up the burn marks on my neck from being hanged.'

"I was a huge Carter Family fan, and I was very interested in June, her family and music. So for part of the interview with Johnny, I went off book. I asked him about her, and he really enjoyed talking about that part of his life, and his love of the Carter Family. The downstairs of the House of Cash had previously been a museum with artifacts from the Carter Family, as well as Johnny's career. It wasn't open to the public anymore, but all of that was still there. Our interview went for quite a while, but he was having a lot of jaw pain, and we had to stop because of that. But he invited me to spend as much time as I wanted in the museum.

"When I was walking around the museum, his assistant says, 'Holly, John's on the phone for you.' So I pick up the phone and he's like, 'I told June about you, and she'd really like to meet ya, why don't you come on over to the house.' I drove over to this breathtaking home sitting next to Old Hickory Lake. As I walk in, he's leaving, and he says, 'June's all ready to meet you. I'm heading over to my little cabin to work on some songs.'

"Sure enough, there was June inside. It was like we were old friends. She had her scrapbooks out. She started telling me all kinds of amazing stories about her life as a young artist performing not only with her mother and sisters, but her years studying acting, performing with James Dean at the Strasberg Institute where Lee Strasberg himself coached them; stories about touring with Elvis. She was an incredible storyteller, delightful.

"When June's first solo album in twenty-four years, *Press On*, was released in 1999, I reviewed it for *Rolling Stone*. After that, I interviewed her for the *Oxford American*. Then I got invited to a party at their Hendersonville home. It was a big picnic, with fried chicken and all the trimmings. I walked in with George Jones and Skeeter Davis. I could not believe I was there.

"Fast forward to summer of 2003. We'd lost June on May 15. I was working with film-maker Mari-Lynn Evans, who was making the PBS documentary *The Appalachians*. I was a writer and editor on the companion book. Because of my past interviews and relationships, she invited me to come back to Johnny and June's home and interview him for the film.

"It was very difficult, but also uplifting. It had been only a few years since I'd last seen him, but it looked like he had aged fifty years. He was very, very frail, nearly blind, and could not get around on his own. The dining room was still set up for the music video for 'Hurt,' one of the greatest music videos ever made.

"It was a very emotional time. I was nervous because I was interviewing him while he was on camera. He was in such a fragile state, but he completely rallied once we got going. It was shocking how strength returned to his body. His mind was like a steel trap, and his sense of humor was intact. He spoke very clearly, even cracked a few jokes. It was a once-in-a-lifetime opportunity to be there with him so close to the end of his life, when he's reflecting on childhood memories, and also musical memories about his beloved wife's family and how much that affected him as an artist.

"And then of course to be joined by his eldest daughter Rosanne . . . the bond between them was so deep, and so obvious. Getting to sit there and listen to them sing together, and tell stories together is something I'll never forget." —Ed.

Holly George-Warren: Mr. Cash, what are your first memories of the Carter Family when you were a boy growing up in Arkansas?

Johnny Cash: When I was a boy in Arkansas, cotton country, every night I would listen to the radio. The first time I heard the Carter Family, I suppose it was on a transcription comin' from XERA, and XERF out of Del Rio, Texas. They were singin' the songs of the Appalachian Mountains. Clinch Mountain, "My Clinch Mountain Home." Fine old songs, sustained all these years, they made a lasting impression on me. It was like old home week hearing these songs again comin' from the younger people. I just recently discovered what a treasure I found in those songs. A beautiful treasure.

George-Warren: What is it about these songs that transcend so many generations, and so many different types of people? Everyone from you, to Bob Dylan, to Gene Autry, who was a huge fan of Mother Maybelle Carter's guitar playing.

Cash: Well, there's a common thread that runs through all of the Carter Family songs, the Appalachian songs, and that is the basic emotions that we all hold and find joy in or suffer from in our lifetime. Joy, sorrow, sickness, health, death, love, hate, resentment, leaving, staying. All of those things you find in these songs that were there before the so-called "new" songs of today. Same thing.

George-Warren: When you went over to the British Isles and Ireland for the first time, did you ever hear any of the old original Irish and Scottish songs where suddenly you recognized the melody or some lines that maybe you'd heard in some of the old ballads of the Carters? Is there a connection that you picked up in that centuries-old music and the music of the Carter Family?

Cash: I found some common lyrics in "Wildwood Flower" and other songs of the Carter Family and some Elizabethan ballads. Yeah, some of the songs are a direct lift from those ballads, and some are inspired by them. Some songs that are so-called Carter family songs are of the British Isles.

George-Warren: What about the role of the women in Appalachian music? Seems they played a very strong role in passing down from one generation to the next. For example, did you learn songs from your mother, and did June talk about learning songs from her mother, and did Maybelle ever talk about learning songs from her mother?

Cash: My mother played the guitar and sang songs to me and taught me my first song. My father was not really interested in music. Was not really musically inclined in any way. My mother was the one around our house who was into the music. I found it's very often the case in country music. The mother will inspire the younger people.

George-Warren: I know you're a history buff. I wonder if you know anything about the history of the autoharp.

Cash: I know absolutely nothing about the autoharp. [*Laughter.*]

George-Warren: It must have come down from outer space. [*Laughter.*]

Cash: Must have.

George-Warren: I guess Maybelle and Sara had it back in the twenties. I was wondering if it was an expensive instrument, did you order it from a catalog like a guitar?

Cash: Yeah, you could order an autoharp from the Sears catalog, in the early thirties you could order a Mother Maybelle Carter autoharp. They were reasonably priced. Satisfaction guaranteed or your money back. Mother Maybelle inspired a lot of people with the autoharp.

George-Warren: Can you talk about Mother Maybelle's trailblazing guitar technique, the Carter Scratch?

Cash: Maybelle inspired me when I first started trying to learn the guitar when I was in the Air Force. I tried to play the licks Mother Maybelle was playing on her guitar.

George-Warren: When Maybelle and Sara reunited at Newport in 1967, what was it like? Do you remember the effect their music had on the young people?

Cash: Well, I had this idea for a historic reunion. Bring Maybelle and Sara together for one last project. They'd been separate for many, many years. They hadn't worked together. I talked Sara into comin' back from California. So they teamed up and it was easy for them to pick up the old thread and sing those old songs together. They were a great inspiration to a lot of people. We did a record: *An Historic Reunion: Sara and Mother Maybelle, the Original Carters* [1966].

George-Warren: In your early tours, you had Maybelle and the Carter Sisters. What was it about their music on the road with you? Did it help to bolster you spiritually as well as musically? Did it have other aspects to it that you want to talk about?

Cash: Well, when I took the Carter Family on the road with me in the early '60s, it was because of a love of their music. Actually, I had my eye on that girl in the middle, the one called June. And I knew if I could get her to workin' with her family on my show, she'd stay. So she did. She stayed and kept her family, and we started workin' closer together until we got very close together, and she became my love, and then she became my wife. That was in '68.

George-Warren: The two of you coming together was such an amazing merger of the history of music, and the families. Is that something that's made this music last so long? The family aspect?

Cash: I think so. Country music has always been family music. Mother/daughter, son/father. Put a whole family onstage, or on record, singin' those songs, it's a surefire winner if they got talent to go with it. And of course the Carter Family had that talent. And they were a great inspiration not only to a lot of other people, but to me as well.

George-Warren: June's *Wildwood Flower* album is wonderful. Seems like the universe, the stars aligned for you and June and John Carter to do that album. Such an amazing legacy for June. Can you talk about what that was like, working with your wife and son on that album?

Cash: My participation in June's album *Wildwood Flower* started as a joke when June called me a Carter Brother. When I started singing with them, I was singing my bass part and hadn't even thought of being part of anything, actually. I was just sittin' in with them, trying to enjoy the music. And I got roped into it. I became one of them. I became a Carter Brother. And June let me stay. And we really had fun. It was a wonderful experience doing that album.

George-Warren: Can you tell me the history of Carter Family?

Cash: Alvin Pleasant Carter, A. P. Carter, he married Sara Dougherty, and Maybelle Addington married Ezra Carter who [would become] my father-in-law. They got together because A. P. Carter was a fruit tree salesman, and he'd cross Clinch Mountain into the country sellin' fruit trees and swappin' food, such as country ham and so forth, for a song. If somebody had a song that A.P. wanted to buy, on occasion he would give 'em a ham for a song. So the story's been told to me. And I don't think he did that but once or twice. There weren't that many country hams for sale. But A.P. and Sara and Maybelle heard about this man that was gonna be in Bristol at a hotel on August 2nd, 1927, listenin' to singers and recording them for the Victor Talking Machine Company.

They went to Bristol and went to this hotel and auditioned for Ralph Peer and Peer International Publishers for the Victor Talking Machine Co. And in a short while they had a record out. They recorded six songs that first day. One of 'em was "Bury Me Beneath the Willow."

George-Warren: Were their records immediately a success among the mountain people?

Cash: Immediately. They were an immediate success among the mountain people. The records were. They played them on the radio constantly.

George-Warren: Were your own mother and father fans of the Carter Family music also?

Cash: Yes. Very much so.

George-Warren: What about your own family background? Where did your grandparents and great grandparents start out?

Cash: They started in Arkansas. My parents came from Arkansas, and I went to Tennessee [in 1954], and they came to Tennessee about 1967. But mainly we lived in Arkansas when I was a kid.

George-Warren: Talk about the government program that gave your father the land to farm.

Cash: There was a government program under President Franklin D. Roosevelt: A farmer, a successful farmer who'd lost it in the Depression and wanted to cut a new trail for himself, could apply for this land. So there was twenty acres, a barn, and a cow. I believe that's what it was. My father was one of those selected, and he got a loan for that first year to make a crop. He was given that property, that house, and he made the crop the first year and started making payments.

George-Warren: Did everybody pitch in?

Cash: Everybody in the family pitched in and worked in the fields. I worked in the cotton fields till I was eighteen years old.

We come from the flat black Delta land . . . and after I got into the music field and started writing and recording and singing songs about the things I knew, I wrote a lot of songs about life as I knew it back when I was a little bitty boy. One of the things I remember most when

I was a little boy was one cold winter night the rain had been fallin', the river kept risin' and all the old folks kept sayin', "The Mississippi River's gonna break that levee!" And one morning, the levee broke over at Wilson, Arkansas, and that black, muddy Mississippi River came right up over the cotton patch, and right up to the front door of our house, and I heard my daddy hollerin', askin' my mama, [*sings*] *How high's the water, Mama? Two feet high and risin'* . . .

Back in that cold winter of 1937, [my father] put us on the bus to take us to the train that carried us down the hills to Pine Bluff to save us from being washed away in the flood. I was four years old at the time, and I can't remember a lot about it, but Daddy said that when we got back home, the house was full of mud, and chickens and pigs and nine bullfrogs. Mama cleaned the house out that winter, and the next spring daddy and my older brother Roy cleared a lot more cotton land, and the cotton grew tall in 1938, and we got a crop that was fair to middlin', which, incidentally, is a grade of cotton.

George-Warren: When you and June got together, did you ever trade stories about your grandparents and her grandparents as far as family get-togethers, family reunions, supper-on-the-ground, those types of things?

Cash: Yeah, we did. We had supper-on-the-ground—it wasn't really on the ground, it was on a table out under a tree. And invariably somebody would take out the guitar and we'd start singin' and playin'. This happened every time we got together.

George-Warren: What year did you first go up to the Carter Fold and walk that ground and see that store A. P. Carter had? What were your impressions when you were in that area for the first time?

Cash: I was up there way before the Carter Fold [performance theater] was built [in 1979]. A.P.'s son Joe built the Carter Fold. He did a really good job. It's still stands exactly the way he built it. There've been some improvements made, but it's still like it was. It's really a wonderful place for the preservation of the Carter Family music.

George-Warren: Can you talk a little about where the Carter Family gospel songs came from? And how gospel has been such an important influence in your own music? I've always read you left Sun because Sam Phillips didn't want you to do gospel.

Cash: Well, first of all, Sam Phillips . . . it wasn't that he didn't want me to do gospel. Sam Phillips loved gospel music. He told me that. But he also told me he didn't know how to sell it. He wasn't set up at Sun Records to market gospel music, and he wouldn't be able to record gospel. That was *one* of the reasons why I went to another record company. I also wanted to be able to expand and spread my wings and do what I wanted to do as far as records go. And as it turned out, I was able to do that my first couple of years at Columbia. I had a hymn album, gospel songs, country gospel [*Hymns by Johnny Cash*, 1959].

George-Warren: Did you record some of the gospel songs the Carter Family had done, or some you'd learned from your church or your mother?

Cash: A.P. brought in songs that were part of the church repertoire. I did the same when I started recording. I started singing songs in the studio seeing what would work on record.

George-Warren: Can you talk about why religion was so important to Appalachian people?

Cash: Religion offers Appalachian people hope, where sometimes there is no hope. Hope from poverty, hope from the cold, from depression. The Carter Family had a song called "No Depression." ["No Depression in Heaven."] They sang about, "I'm going where there's no depression . . ."

[Appalachian people] aren't *religious* people, but they are in one sense. They have faith in God. That's their religion. But they're not into *religiosity*. Not the ones I know. All of A.P.'s descendants . . . I was just up there for vacation. I went to the Carter Family Fold. These people, they're into loving their fellow man. That's what religion is to them. I think that's what I try to make it be for me.

George-Warren: What do you think makes people from Appalachia so unique?

Cash: I think probably living an isolated existence. That has a lot to do with the fact that Appalachian mountain people are so unique in the way they love their fellow man, and the way they treat their fellow man. Because over the next holler there might not be a house, or over the next hill there might be a woman with a sick baby that really desperately needs help and doesn't know how to get it. They reach out to her and they help. Or maybe somebody is broken down and can't get to the doctor, so they take him to the doctor. They take care of each other. They always do that. They take care of each other.

[*Enter Rosanne Cash.*]

Cash: What do you want to sing, dear?

Rosanne Cash: I was gonna tell a story about "Forty Shades of Green."

Cash: You wanna do that one?

George-Warren: [*Jokingly*] I hear "Forty Shades of Green" is a real old ancient Irish song!

Cash: It is? [*Laughter.*] Yeah, I was an old man when I wrote it.

Rosanne Cash: [*To Johnny Cash*] You remember you told me the story about . . . you wrote this gorgeous song called "Forty Shades of Green" after the first time you visited Ireland. And then you went back [to Ireland] and you were singing "Forty Shades of Green." Where were you when you sang it?

Cash: I was in Kildare, I think, at a youth center.

Rosanne Cash: A youth center. And an old man comes up to him afterward the show and says, "Aye, the 'Forty Shades of Green,' 'tis a fine old Irish folk song." You said, "No sir, I wrote that song." And he said, "No, 'tis a fine old Irish folk song." [*Laughter.*]

Cash: He wouldn't have it. It had to be an Irish song. I finally gave in. I said, "OK." But I did write it.

[*Rosanne and Johnny Cash sing "Forty Shades of Green."*]

Rosanne Cash: 'Tis a fine old Irish folk song!

George-Warren: Do you remember the first song your dad ever taught you, Rosanne?

Rosanne Cash: Well, when I went on the road with him after high school when I was nineteen, I was a Beatles fan, I was a rock 'n' roll fan, and I didn't really care for country music. But I liked my dad. And we were on the bus, and they would sing these old songs, and I started to get very interested in the songs. And he saw I was getting interested, and he gave me a list: "100 Essential Country Songs." And he said, "You have to learn these." [*Johnny Cash laughs.*] Do you remember?

Cash: Yeah. I don't remember the list.

Rosanne Cash: I remember part of the list. Part of it was the old protest songs, the old history songs like "The Battle of New Orleans," "This Land Is Your Land," on up to Hank Snow, Hank Williams, and of course Appalachian songs, Carter Family songs. "Banks of the Ohio." [*She would record songs from this list for her 2009 album* The List. —*Ed.*]

Cash: June always loved "Banks of the Ohio." That was her favorite Carter Family song.

Rosanne Cash: That was the first song I learned to play on the guitar. That's how I learned to play guitar.

Cash: Was it really?

Rosanne Cash: Yeah. Helen and June taught me that.

Cash: June's older sister, Helen.

Rosanne Cash: Right. Helen was a great guitar player. She'd learned from Maybelle. She had it down, that Carter Scratch.

George-Warren: Can you describe what the Carter Scratch is?

Rosanne Cash: It's using the thumb for the bass note and the fingers for the rhythm. I don't do it very well [*laughs*], but Helen and Maybelle . . .

[*Rosanne and Johnny Cash sing "The Banks of the Ohio."*]

> *I asked my love to take a walk*
> *Take a walk just a little ways*
> *And as we walked, along we talked*
> *All about our wedding day*

And only say that you'll be mine
In no other's arms entwined
Down beside where the waters flow
Down by the banks of the Ohio

Rosanne Cash: It's one of those songs that has about a hundred verses. And I think [the protagonist] kills her, right?

Cash: He kills her. Plunges a knife into her breast.

Rosanne Cash: "The Merry Golden Tree" was one of our favorites. We were always singing that one. What was interesting is that Aaron Copland used it in one of his pieces [*as "The Golden Willow Tree," part of "Old American Songs, Set 2." —Ed.*] and it was also a Carter family song. Although I think Aaron Copland borrowed it straight from the Elizabethan. They pay off the captain to sink his ship. It's a great story. Dad and I know one verse. [*Laughs.*] We should sing this one verse.

There was a little ship
And it sailed upon the sea
And it went by the name of the Merry Golden Tree
As it sailed upon the low and lonesome low
As it sailed upon the lonesome sea.

Rosanne Cash: And then he calls to the captain and gives him two hundred dollars to sink that ship in the lonesome sea.

George-Warren: [*To Johnny Cash*] Is there any of Rosanne's music that she's taught you, or music that June taught you? Talk a little about the give and take between turning each other on to stuff.

Rosanne Cash: I know one you might not remember.

Cash: What's that, hon'?

Rosanne Cash: I turned him on to Bruce Springsteen's *Nebraska* record. And you ended up recording two songs from that. "Highway Patrolman" and "Johnny 99." That's about all I've given him, actually. [*Laughs.*]

Cash: She wrote a fabulous song that even today, after twenty years, it brings tears to my eyes. Called "My Old Man." A song she wrote for me. So beautiful.

Rosanne Cash: And he and I did "September When It Comes." That was the first time we ever did a duet.

George-Warren: What about Irish music or Scottish music? Do you think there's some kind of genetic memory there, when you hear that music or go to those countries it's like you've been there before?

Cash: I think so. I think so. There's genetic memory all right.

Rosanne Cash: Our roots are in Scotland. Ancient, ancient roots.

Cash: My family came from a little town called Strathmiglo in County Fife, Scotland, several hundred years ago.

Rosanne Cash: The Cash who emigrated was named William Cash. He was a mariner. He settled in Salem, Massachusetts, and then our family had a lot of whalers and sailors around Salem and Nantucket and down into the Chesapeake Bay area.

Let me tell about the song "The Winding Stream," one of the more obscure Carter Family songs. Helen and June and Anita taught it to me when I was a young girl, and I always play it to myself. I never actually heard a recording of it. It's one of Dad's favorite songs. It was one of June's favorites. At June's big birthday celebration in the summer of 2001, we all had to do something, so I sang this song to her. Sometimes now in concert I sing it for June. I have to borrow some of her fearlessness to do it.

[*Rosanne Cash sings "The Winding Stream."*]

George-Warren to Johnny Cash: How does it feel to have all these talented women in your life?

Cash: It feels wonderful.

Rosanne Cash: He's the only guy who had his wife, his mother-in-law, and his daughter in the "40 Greatest Women in Country Music" list.

[*Laughter.*]

Rosanne Cash: My voice is just like his, apparently. A doctor at Vanderbilt told me that we had the same . . . tone.

Cash: The same voice box.

George-Warren: [*To Johnny Cash*] I remember you told me a long time ago about when you were young, and your voice was still high, and you came home one day, and it had changed.

Cash: That happens to boys, you know. It just dropped suddenly. It happened to me when I was seventeen. I'd been cuttin' wood all day long with my father. And I came in and I was singin' a gospel song. [*Sings*] *Everybody gonna have religion and glory / Everybody gonna be singin' a story.* Suddenly my voice dropped and I'm singing way down low in the key of E. My mother said, "Who is that singin'?" She came out the back door and there I was. I said, "That was me, Mama." She said, "Well keep on singin'!" So I kept on singin: *Everybody gonna have religion and glory / Everybody gonna be singin' a story / Everybody gonna have a wonderful time / Glory hallelujah!*

George-Warren: Rosanne, a minute ago you talked about how June was a fearless woman, and I think Maybelle and Sara had to be very fearless to [be professional musicians]. Do you think it was their mountain heritage that made them be that way, to buck society and go out on the road and play music?

Rosanne Cash: June was particularly fearless.

Cash: Mm-hm.

Rosanne Cash: There's a great story of her as a young woman on the road with her sisters and mother. They were on a package show. The band before them, the banjo player didn't show up, so they said, "Anybody around here play banjo?" And June said, "I do!" And she went out and played the whole set with them, and she'd never played banjo in her life. That's how fearless she was. That's a very rare quality.

George-Warren: How old was she when she started performing?

Cash: She was on XERA, the Mexican border station when she was nine. Helen was eleven. Anita was the little one with the high voice. They put her on at the age of six. June sang, "I'm just trying to make a hundred / And ninety-nine and half won't do!" [*Laughs.*]

George-Warren: Can you talk about June's character Aunt Polly? Was that a tradition from her childhood? Was there a real Aunt Polly?

Cash: You got me. I don't know. I don't know where she got that character. She made her up from the country people she met that came backstage and talked to her. They didn't know they were giving her a routine, but they were. This old lady said, "I went into the restroom and looked in the mirror and said, 'Oh you look so sick, you need a banana.' I reached in my purse and I had one. I peeled the banana and offered it to the woman in the mirror who said, 'Oh I already got one.'" [*Laughter.*]

Rosanne Cash: When she stopped performing Aunt Polly, she actually buried the costume. She had a funeral. She said, "That's it, Aunt Polly is over with. I'm never doing Aunt Polly again." Well. Dad had never seen Aunt Polly because Aunt Polly was buried by the time he came along. And he begged her for years and years, "Please let me see just a little bit of Aunt Polly," and June would say, "No, she's gone. I buried her. It's over." And after years of begging, she came out as Aunt Polly on Dad's birthday. We had this little birthday celebration, and everybody put on a show and Aunt Polly came out. It was great.

George-Warren: Was it everything you thought it would be?

Cash: It was wonderful. She was wonderful. She tickled me to death. She was so funny.

George-Warren: I love her stories. That one about the guy riding the horse into the Italian restaurant in New York City [*"Gatsby's Restaurant" from* Press On, *1999. —Ed.*]. Is that another part of the tradition of Ireland and Scotland and the music of the Carters and June and yourself. The great stories . . .

Cash: Mm-hmm. Yeah. Story songs. It comes from the troubadours. Fourteenth, fifteenth, sixteenth century, they'd travel the country, stop at a farmhouse, and write a song for the person who lived there to let them stay overnight. Then they'd give them the song they wrote. The troubadour always paid his way with a song. For an overnight stay in a warm bed with breakfast in the morning.

George-Warren: You've always been a supporter of the underdog. You sang the songs that resonated with people who had hard times. People could really relate to you. Can you talk about the hard times people had in Appalachia and why songs were so important to bring them peace and happiness?

Cash: I can relate to that because that's how I feel about it. When hard times come, if I hear a song I love, it's like therapy. It's healing. The music is very, very healing.

SYLVIE SIMMONS INTERVIEWS JOHNNY CASH

Sylvie Simmons | November 2003 | *MOJO*

"To see him in that state of complete brokenness, but absolutely up for the battle, was quite extraordinary."

So says veteran music writer and musician Sylvie Simmons of her time with Johnny Cash in the late summer of 2003. The five days she spent at his home in Hendersonville, Tennessee, would constitute his last major published interview and provide source material for an acclaimed hardcover liner notes book accompanying the posthumous box set *Unearthed*. Simmons describes the book as her "tribute to a man who struck me as Abraham Lincoln, Joe Strummer, a bottle of pills and a Bible all rolled into one."

Six weeks after their last conversation, Johnny Cash's body would succumb to a wide variety of ailments. "Respiratory failure due to complications from diabetes" was the "official" cause of death. June Carter Cash had passed away unexpectedly four months previously, following heart surgery. They'd been married thirty-eight years. Although "heartbreak" is not listed on Cash's death certificate, the stress of bereavement certainly contributed to his passing at age seventy-one.

Perhaps realizing his time was nigh, three days after June's funeral, Cash surprised everyone by insisting he enter his home recording studio and work—create in the face of loss, as he always had. Document the pain, perhaps as a means of controlling it. That's where Sylvie Simmons would find him.

Simmons, a British expat living in San Francisco, has been interviewing musicians since the 1970s. A shortlist of her subjects: Mick Jagger, Robert Plant, Black Sabbath, Neil Young, the Who, Tom Petty, Lou Reed, Aerosmith, Radiohead, Tori Amos, and Guns

N' Roses, to name a few. Her biographies of Leonard Cohen (*I'm Your Man*, available in twenty-three languages), Serge Gainsbourg (*A Fistful of Gitanes*, available in nine languages), and Debbie Harry (*Face It*, three languages) are widely heralded, as is her fiction. (She is also a renowned singer-songwriter, with two acclaimed albums on which she accompanies herself on ukulele.)

All the above experience, however, didn't completely prepare Simmons for her stay in Hendersonville, about which she also wrote for *MOJO* magazine. While she'd previously inter-viewed Cash several times by phone (easier) and in-person (less so, due to his commanding physical presence), of the Hendersonville visit she says, "I'll never forget his entrance. The Italian housekeeper who adored him and June was nattering and nattering and gossiping, and suddenly a glass elevator came down the wall, and you could see Johnny's head. He was in a wheelchair. Dressed immaculately head-to-toe in black. Black shoes, black socks, black shirt, black pants. White hair. He looked like he'd gone in the ring with Muhammad Ali. His face was beaten up, sunken and swollen at the same time, bruised and red. He was not a well man. But he looked at me with those piercing eyes and held out his hand and said, 'Hello, I'm Johnny Cash.' It was kind of surreal."

Simmons was surprised to be there. "I'd been suspicious it would never happen," she says. "A year before, Rick Rubin got in touch and said he was going to do a ten-year anni-versary box set [of Cash's *American Recordings* albums, all Grammy winners], and Johnny wanted to do a gospel album [for the box set] at his compound. Rick said, 'I was thinking it'd be a good idea to do a hardcover book, maybe another book later. Would you like to do it?' I said, 'Yes, please.'"

The cyclical nature of it was striking. Cash had initially walked into Sam Phillips's Sun Records in 1954 an aspiring gospel singer. Phillips would not allow it, and instead encouraged Cash's original work. The rest is history. But even after Cash became the big-gest thing since Elvis, Phillips would not record the songs Carrie Cash had sung back on the Dyess, Arkansas, farm. Now, in 2003, Johnny Cash could record whatever he wanted. And he was desperate to do an album of solo acoustic gospel songs to include in the box set that would become *Unearthed*.

Soon after Rubin commissioned Simmons for the project, however, June passed away unexpectedly. Simmons assumed it was off. Like anyone who knew details of Cash's frailty, she was waiting for the other shoe to drop.

"I'd thought once June had gone, Johnny was bound to follow soon," she says. "June had kept him alive, not just being his support, but by having online prayer-ins. We were all praying. Anybody who believes in prayer, at least, was praying for Johnny, and he kept going into hospital and coming back out again. It was miraculous. Then June went in for something relatively minor and didn't emerge. Out of the blue, Rick called and said, 'Johnny wants you to go out to his house in Hendersonville.' I thought, 'This is weird.' I've interviewed Johnny before, but he's a man's man. I didn't think he would call for a woman in his last hours."

It had been Rubin's choice. And, as Simmons says, "Johnny was incredibly, incredibly fond of Rick. They'd spoken, and he'd said, 'Let's do it now.' Rick told me Johnny said, 'The only way I'm gonna get through this pain is to work.'"

Because there was no hard deadline, Simmons says, "You're in a different state of mind. You've got a certain amount of time." Even with the palpable grief hanging in the air, the more relaxed vibe allowed Simmons to essentially become part of the household. As Rubin had no doubt ascertained, Simmons's experience around icons, and ease in strange situations, proved invaluable.

"I was just helping out," she says, "being a gofer. Witnessing it, being there and talking to some of the people he was working with. I was part of the family. I didn't get adopted, unfortunately."

Cash told Simmons he probably would not be able to talk for long periods. But that turned out to be inaccurate.

"Every morning we had breakfast together," Simmons says. "It was very lighthearted conversations over breakfast. He said he got up with the chickens, and I told him I kind of went to bed with the chickens, so maybe we could find some middle ground. But I got up early. Rick brought in a couple of people to help him out. One was a chef who was cooking healthy versions of Southern breakfast, lean turkey bacon, grilled tomatoes, things like that. Johnny laughed at that. Rick had also brought in a nutritionist, and a therapist, someone trying to get him out of the wheelchair and walking.

"People were coming by, often a daughter. I recall talking to lovely Rosanne for some time. She was saying she loved Rick for what he was doing for her dad's career after he was kind of kicked into the gutter.

"Every afternoon he was in the studio. I was very welcome to be there with them. It actually was his bachelor bedroom that has the circular bed with animal skin covering over it, which John Carter Cash had inherited as his teenager bedroom. I went and got Coca-Cola from the fridge when his voice stopped. Occasionally these little bits of helping out to the point where he said I should get an album credit.

"One morning, he said, 'Are you married?' I said, 'Are you proposing?' He said, 'No, but I've got a whole lot of sons-in-law that are out of my daughters' lives, take your pick.'

I think [former son-in-law] Marty Stuart was living on the compound. I said, 'I'll have Nick Lowe please.' [Ex-husband of Carlene Carter, June's daughter by Carl Smith.]

"He was trying to make me eat more. He said, 'There's no more to you than a minute.' I'm 105 pounds. It was really sweet.

"He was funny. He was very cheeky when he was around the male friends. He was good at joshing with them. I think he was a bit more circumspect about what he might say to a woman. He'd tell me all these anecdotes, all these people that were over at his house while they were doing *The Johnny Cash Show*. He said he knew a lot about 'this longhaired element.' He called them 'the longhaired element.'"

Simmons came away from the experience with a deepened sense of the profound affection between Rick Rubin and Johnny Cash. The loyalty between the two men was a big reason she was there. Rubin had chosen her; Cash had signed off.

Much has been written about the remarkable work Cash and Rubin produced in this final decade of Cash's life. The unquantifiable core of that relationship, the engine of all that material, was a love the likes of which Simmons had never witnessed.

"They were so close," she says. "To the point where I'd say, 'Get a room' to both of them. When they looked at each other. I told them I could imagine them running in slow motion at each other through the cornfield. Rick's beard flying behind him. Johnny's black coattail. I always laughed about that with them, and they would laugh. They truly were dead close." —Ed.

Twenty miles north of Nashville, a stone's throw from the House Of Cash, a winding road off Johnny Cash Parkway leads to Old Hickory Lake. They have history, Johnny and this lake. There was the time he took the bundle of love letters Elvis Presley sent June, when he had a crush on her, and hurled them into the water. Or the winter when Cash went missing for several days and they found him literally frozen to a tree while the lake lapped at his upturned tractor.

Cash bought this house built into the limestone cliffs in 1967, shortly before he married June Carter. Her imprint is everywhere you look—the ornate, ancient dark-wood furniture, four-poster beds, antique china, chandeliers, silver candlesticks and tureens; Johnny once said his wife had "a black belt in shopping" so he wasn't going to put up a fight. The baronial-gothic, June-decorated dining room downstairs looks exactly as it did when it was used for the setting of the "Hurt" video.

The round room at the far end of the house is a far less majestic affair. It has the same bachelor pad appearance it had when Johnny Cash first moved in. Wooden ceiling, mirrored doors, large windows with a panoramic lake view, hunting trophies, music awards, guitars, and, bang in the middle, a huge circular bed draped with animal hides. This is the room where 36 years ago Johnny Cash went cold turkey, spending the best part of the month on this bed kicking the amphetamine habit that helped cement his reputation as the tough, doomed, dangerous Man In Black. Right now, though, Cash is using it as a recording studio, where he's cutting songs for his next album.

"I'm working on *American V*, hot and heavy," he says. So far, he has around 50 songs in various stages of completion—a variety of material, though predominantly old country, gospel or folk. "I told Rick, 'We've done a lot of work on this and it's costing you a lot of money,'" he laughs. "He said, 'I don't care, do you?' 'No,' I said, 'Let it blow.'" Rick Rubin, his producer and the man responsible for Cash's more unusual covers (Soundgarden, Nine Inch Nails, Danzig, etc.) since signing him to his American Records label in 1993, is at home in Los Angeles working hard on *Unearthed*, the box set of unreleased material he and Cash have been compiling to mark their tenth anniversary together.

"Rick is talking about the next ten years," says Cash, "and I am too. I'm ready for it." He gives a rusty, lopsided smile, the product of a jaw broken too many years ago to remember the details, adding, "I'm ready for the next five anyway." It's July 2003, less than two months since June died, and Johnny Cash is back doing what he does best. "She told me to go on," he says, "and I said, 'I think I will.'"

Running the computer recording programme is Cash's longtime engineer David Ferguson. Pat McLaughlin, a fine singer-songwriter himself, is here to add acoustic guitar. "I still pick up a guitar most days," says Johnny, in spite of the visible tremors in his swollen hands—the outcome of a cocktail of health problems that have hit him these last ten years. Diabetes, autonomic neuropathy, the asthma that causes the breathlessness, the glaucoma that means he needs his lyrics printed out in gigantic type. Luckily his memory is perfect; he remembers the words to almost every song he has ever heard.

"Give me my list," he commands (Johnny Cash is nothing if not commanding in a work situation) and an assistant goes to find it. "Thank you," he smiles when it's handed to him. "I believe in lists." This one has 33 songs written on it. Cash scrolls down it and announces he's going to try "Through The Eyes Of An Eagle," a song written by June's cousin Joe Carter, son of A.P. and Sara of The Carter Family. There's a painting of Joe's uncle and June's father Eck Carter on the wall; Cash dedicated his album *Man In Black* to Eck. The history of this family, in this house, can get a bit overwhelming at times.

Cash's voice may be strained when he speaks, but when he sings, it's mesmerising. Mighty. Very hard to imagine it emanating from the frail, surprisingly shrunken, white-haired man in the wheelchair. When the sweltering Southern summer heat makes the room too hot to bear, he announces a ten-minute air conditioning break (it makes too much noise during the recording) and swigs on an ice-cold bottle of Coke.

There's something surreal about being there listening to the play-backs. Hearing that voice, a template of 20th century music, coming through the speakers while its singer is sitting opposite you, the other side of a circular bed, dressed all in black, like Abraham Lincoln in headphones beamed into an early '70s "home decor for men" magazine. Adding to the weirdness factor are the speedboats that occasionally pass by on the lake. Once in a while one of them will come close and do a double take—circle round and check if that really was the Man In Black they just saw at the window upstairs.

Cash makes a note of the passages where he feels his voice has let him down and tackles them again—he runs a tight ship; Ferguson is right to call him "Cap'n." After a few hours of recording Cash declares, "I'm past my prime. I'm packing it in." Just for this afternoon though. The next day he's back recording again. Among the songs I heard him cut during my five days in Hendersonville were an old spiritual, "Ain't No Grave" (Cash had added some verses he wrote himself. "Everybody else has done that," he says, "so I did too"), a Neil Young song, a Tom Paxton song, and a new song he wrote in his house in Jamaica last winter, "inspired by the words from 1 Corinthians 15:55: 'Death where is thy sting?' It took about a month to write. I mean I just took my time—that's the way to make it work, take your time. You don't do anything in a hurry. If you can do it tomorrow," he chuckles, "you put it off till tomorrow."

I ask him if there is any magic to writing a song and he nods. "Yes, there is a magic to writing. Sometimes when you're trying to get a line that rhymes and it won't come and then all of a sudden it's there, and you want to get up and shout and turn around three times and sit back down. Yes, it's got magic to it."

For someone who has written so many classics—"I Walk The Line," "Folsom Prison Blues," and so on and so on—he's seemed for some time to prefer singing other people's songs to writing his own. I ask if, because he now has a reputation for being able to take the most unexpected contemporary material and reshape it into a Johnny Cash song, it's something he feels he has to keep doing. His dark eyes blaze. "Not at all. I don't feel in any way pigeonholed. Certainly not. I can break loose and get out any time I want to."

He is immensely proud of the four albums he has done with Rubin and is delighted with the box set. He doesn't stop talking about it. *Unearthed* has three albums of some of the best songs they recorded that didn't fit onto the albums at the time. I've heard it and there's some absolutely excellent material. Among the guest appearances are Joe Strummer, Tom Petty and Nick Cave. There's also a fourth album in the box, one that Cash is particularly pleased with—an album of old church songs sung alone with his guitar.

"It felt good, to be able to go straight to the heart of the listener," he says of his records with Rubin. Country music, he says, has lost that ability to go straight to the heart. "I have wondered why everyone got away from it. Why get away from it? I don't hear any people that are really laying it on the line like we did back then—I don't know, maybe they are, maybe I'm just not able to see it, but I don't see anybody on the country music scene whose songs have really moved me all that much. And I think the country fans are losing a lot by the radio stations not playing some of the older, the veteran artists. I think they're cheating them out of their tradition." It took a while for Nashville to warm to Cash's *American Recordings* albums. Fortunately, being too country for country did not mean that Cash was not cool enough for the rest of us.

He chuckles as he recalls a young male fan shouting up at them, during one of their shows, "Mrs Cash, you kick ass."

The songs he has recorded this afternoon will be printed on a CD and sent to Rubin. He'll play them and then they'll talk about what he's done. "I'm talking to Rick on the phone every day. For weeks and months we talk. We talk about what I've done that day in the studio, the session, how I went about it, how it worked out. When I've got four or five songs recorded, he'll listen to them and tell me what he felt about them. Some of them I saw that he was right and I'd drop them from the project. Some of them I'd disagree with him so I didn't drop them from the project. And we'd get along just great with that. We've always got along good with that, that we were going to agree to disagree. We've always just got along good."

Before Johnny heads off for supper and an early night—since his health forced him to give up touring after 42 years on the road, he says he goes to bed "with the chickens." He's usually up around four or five, says "Good morning, God" then potters about, listens to some music (there were a bunch of old gospel CDs littered about the stereo), sings to himself, or takes down one of this vast library of books and slots the page under the magnifying device that projects the words, enlarged, onto a screen. ("I can see," he tells me, "but it's very foggy.") He makes cross-references, takes notes, scribbles out lists of the work he still has to do. "If I'm going to handle this terrible misfortune that's come to me at this time in my life," the death of his wife, "and go on through it," he says, "I'm going to have to work through it. Anyhow, I don't believe in retiring."

Endings are always tough. With the box set finished and mixed, Cash was talking about flying out to Los Angeles to start work with Rick recording *American V*. Then on Friday September 12th his breathing became laboured and he was rushed into hospital. A few hours later he was gone.

I wouldn't dream of claiming that I knew Johnny Cash. I'd interviewed him three or four times in the past and this summer I got to spend five days with him, talking for the liner-note book of *Unearthed*. But what I do know is that he was everything I thought he would be—a gracious, hospitable Southern gentleman with equal measures of gravity and mischief. He was a family man, enormously proud of his children, someone who talked to God but didn't always listen to the reply. Even from a wheelchair he cast a mighty big shadow. And I can definitely confirm that, sartorially speaking and in every other way, he was the Man in Black.

ABOUT THE CONTRIBUTORS

British-born **Patrick Carr** wrote extensively about music through the 1970s and '80s. His byline has appeared in *Country Music* magazine, the *Village Voice*, the *New York Times*, *Rolling Stone*, and *The Illustrated History of Country Music*. The artist he wrote about the most was Johnny Cash, whom he met in 1972. In addition to coauthoring *Cash: The Autobiography*, he is the coauthor of *Gun People* (with George Gardner), *Backstage Passes: Life on the Wild Side with David Bowie* (with Angie Bowie), and *Sunshine State: Wild Times and Extraordinary Lives in the Land of Gators, Guns, and Grapefruit.*

Rosanne Cash is a four-time Grammy-winning singer-songwriter, best-selling author, and activist. A member of the Nashville Songwriters Hall of Fame, she has had eleven number-one country hit singles, twenty-one Top 40 country singles, and two gold records. She is the recipient of the 2021 Edward MacDowell Medal. She's been artist-in-residence at Carnegie Hall, Lincoln Center, San Francisco Jazz, the Minnesota Orchestra, the Library of Congress, and NYU Steinhardt. She is the eldest child of Johnny Cash and Vivian Liberto.

Anthony DeCurtis is a Grammy-winning author, teacher, and widely published music critic. He is the author of *Lou Reed: A Life*; *In Other Words: Artists Talk About Life and Work*; and *Rocking My Life Away: Writing About Music and Other Matters*. He is also the editor of *Present Tense: Rock & Roll and Culture*, and coeditor of *The Rolling Stone Illustrated*

History of Rock & Roll and *The Rolling Stone Album Guide* (third edition). He is a contributing editor at *Rolling Stone*, where his work has appeared for over thirty years. He is a distinguished lecturer in the creative writing program at the University of Pennsylvania. DeCurtis collaborated with Clive Davis on Davis's autobiography, *The Soundtrack of My Life*, which rose to number two on the *New York Times* nonfiction bestseller list.

Nashvillian **Bill Friskics-Warren** is the author of *Heartaches by the Number: Country Music's 500 Greatest Singles* and *I'll Take You There: Pop Music and the Urge for Transcendence*. His writing has appeared in the *Washington Post*, the *New York Times*, *SPIN*, the *Village Voice*, *Nashville Scene*, *Newsday*, *No Depression*, the *Oxford American*, *Rock & Rap Confidential*, and the *Los Angeles Times*. He has also lectured in Church and Society at Vanderbilt University.

Holly George-Warren is a two-time Grammy nominee and the award-winning author of sixteen books, including the *New York Times* bestseller *The Road to Woodstock* (with Michael Lang) and biographies *Janis: Her Life and Music*; *A Man Called Destruction: The Life and Music of Alex Chilton*; and *Public Cowboy No. 1: The Life and Times of Gene Autry*. She has written for numerous publications, including *Rolling Stone*, the *New York Times*, the *Village Voice*, *Entertainment Weekly*, and *MOJO*. She is currently at work on a biography of Jack Kerouac.

As NPR's national political correspondent, **Don Gonyea** travels the country, talking to citizens about issues, man-on-the-street style. He serves as a fill-in host on NPR news magazines *Morning Edition*, *All Things Considered*, *Weekend Edition*, and *Weekend All Things Considered*. He has contributed to PBS's *NewsHour*, the BBC, CBC, AP Radio, and the *Columbia Journalism Review*. He was part of the team that earned NPR a 2000 George Foster Peabody Award for the *All Things Considered* series "Lost & Found Sound."

Terry Gross is an American journalist who is the host and co-executive producer of *Fresh Air*, an interview-based radio show produced by WHYY-FM in Philadelphia and distributed nationally by NPR. Since joining NPR in 1975, Gross has interviewed thousands of guests. She has won praise over the years for her low-key and friendly yet often probing interview style and for the diversity of her guests.

South Dakota Hall of Fame inductee **Glenn Jorgenson** and his wife Phyllis saved and transformed hundreds of lives through their River Park alcohol and drug treatment programs. River Park was South Dakota's first nonprofit, privately funded treatment center for addiction. As a recovering addict and alcoholic, Jorgenson led a movement to change societal attitudes toward addiction, to correct misinformation, and to eliminate the shame and stigma often attached to addiction. He hosted the nationally distributed series *It's Great to Be Alive*, featuring interviews with prominent Americans and celebrities whose lives or families were impacted by addiction. With Phyllis and journalist Terry Woster, he coauthored a book version of *It's Great to Be Alive*.

Before cofounding and publishing *Country Music* magazine, entrepreneur and writer **Jack Killion** helped raise the initial capital for *Rolling Stone*. He authored *Network: All the Time, Everywhere with Everybody*. He also taught at Rutgers University, Montclair State University, and Fairleigh Dickinson University (FDU).

Larry Linderman wrote extensively for *Playboy* and *Penthouse* in the 1970s and '80s. He helped famed operatic soprano Beverly Sills pen *Beverly: An Autobiography*. His article "Undercover Angel," in the July 1981 issue of *Playboy*, was the basis for the screenplay for the 1993 Charlie Sheen movie *Beyond the Law*.

Lyle Lovett is a Texan singer, songwriter, actor, horse enthusiast, and record producer. He has recorded thirteen albums, released twenty-five singles, and won four Grammy Awards. On the family farm in 2002, he saved his uncle from a bull attack, resulting in Lovett's leg being shattered, an injury from which he fully recovered.

Peter McCabe was an editor at *Rolling Stone* and *Oui* magazine, editor-in-chief of *Country Music* magazine, and a widely published music journalist. He coauthored *Apple to the Core: The Unmaking of the Beatles* and *John Lennon: For the Record*, and authored *Bad News at Black Rock: The Sell-Out of CBS News*.

Filmmaker, columnist, film reviewer, and travel and feature writer **Áine O'Connor** achieved renown on Irish television screens as a presenter of *Tangents, P.M.*, and *First House*. She was the host of the popular talk show *Leading Hollywood*. O'Connor was one of the original developers of the Daniel Day-Lewis film *In the Name of the Father*.

Nashville-based music journalist, author, and historian **Robert K. Oermann** is a longtime contributor to the trade publication *MusicRow*. He's written for *Entertainment Weekly*, *Esquire*, *Billboard*, *the Hollywood Reporter*, and *Us*, to name a few. He was the first country music reporter and critic for *USA Today*, and longtime music reporter for *The Tennessean*. He's written liner notes for over seventy-five albums, including the *O Brother, Where Art Thou?* soundtrack. With his wife, Mary Bufwack, he cowrote *Finding Her Voice: The Saga of Women in Country Music*, which won the ASCAP Deems Taylor Award for music-book excellence. He was Dolly Parton's cowriter for *Songteller*. Oermann also has worked in film, television, and radio, primarily as a writer for documentaries and sometimes also as a host. He owns approximately three hundred thousand records.

Red Robinson was the first broadcaster to play rock 'n' roll on a regular basis in Canada. Prior to retirement, he enjoyed a sixty-three-year career as a popular radio and television personality and frequent MC. He's in the Rockabilly and Canadian Broadcast Halls of Fame, and he received the Order of British Columbia for contributions to society. *Red Robinson's Legends*, his trove of vintage audio interviews with music stars, lives on Soundcloud.

Pete Seeger embodied folk music ideals—communication, entertainment, social comment, historical continuity, inclusiveness. The songs he wrote, discovered, and shared helped preserve our cultural heritage. His political activism—from the civil rights movement and anti-McCarthyism to resistance to fascism and the wars in Vietnam and the Middle East—influenced countless musicians and fellow conscientious citizens. These activities also got him blacklisted during the 1950s and '60s. He nevertheless won a Grammy Lifetime Achievement Award, a Harvard Arts Medal, the Kennedy Center Award, the Presidential Medal of the Arts, and membership in the Rock & Roll Hall of Fame.

Sylvie Simmons is a London-born, San Francisco–based music journalist, author, singer-songwriter, and recording artist. She has been interviewing musicians since the 1970s. Her byline has appeared in *MOJO, Q*, the *Guardian, San Francisco Chronicle, Kerrang!, Sounds*, and many other publications. A shortlist of her subjects: Mick Jagger, Robert Plant, Black Sabbath, Neil Young, the Who, Tom Petty, Lou Reed, Aerosmith, Radiohead, Tori Amos, and Guns N' Roses. Her biographies of Leonard Cohen (*I'm Your Man*, available in twenty-three languages), Serge Gainsbourg (*A Fistful of Gitanes*, available in nine languages), and Debbie Harry (*Face It*, three languages) are widely heralded, as is her fiction.

For twenty-nine years, **Christopher S. Wren** was a reporter, foreign correspondent, and editor at the *New York Times*. He headed the *Times'* news bureaus in Moscow, Cairo, Beijing, Ottawa, and Johannesburg; covered the United Nations; and reported from the former Soviet Union, Eastern Europe, the Balkans, the Middle East, China, Southeast Asia, Africa, South America, and Canada. He taught at Princeton University and Dartmouth. In addition to writing "The Gospel Road" and "Jesus Was a Carpenter" for Johnny Cash, he authored the books *Those Turbulent Sons of Freedom, Walking to Vermont*, and *The Cat Who Covered the World*. He lives in Vermont.

CREDITS

I gratefully acknowledge the help of everyone who gave permission for material to appear in this book. I have made every reasonable effort to contact copyright holders. If an error or omission has been made, please bring it to the attention of the publisher.

Johnny Cash and the Tennessee Two on *Town Hall Party*, November 15, 1958. Printed with permission from Tom Ritter / and more bears.

Interview by Red Robinson at Division Street Corral, Portland, Oregon, June 27, 1959. Printed with permission from Red Robinson.

Pete Seeger interviews Johnny Cash and June Carter for *Rainbow Quest*, 1966. Printed with permission from Historic Films Archive LLC / Pete Seeger Estate.

"The Restless Ballad of Johnny Cash," published April 29, 1969, in *Look*. Reprinted with permission from Christopher S. Wren.

"Foreword to Dylan, Cash & the Nashville Cats Exhibition Book" copyright © 2015 by Rosanne Cash, originally published by Country Music Hall of Fame. Reprinted by permission from Writers House LLC acting as agent for the author.

"An Interview with Johnny Cash," published 1973, in *Country Music* magazine. Reprinted with permission from Russell Barnard, editor-in-chief, *Country Music* magazine.

Interview by Larry Linderman in *Penthouse* magazine, published August 1975. Reprinted with permission from Penthouse Global Licensing, LLC.

Interview with Áine O'Connor for RTÉ Ireland, 1975. Printed with permission from RTÉ Archives.

"Cash Comes Back," published 1976 in *Country Music* magazine. Reprinted with permission from Russell Barnard, editor-in-chief, *Country Music* magazine.

Interview by Red Robinson at Pacific Coliseum, Vancouver, BC, August 28, 1976. Printed with permission from Red Robinson.

"Johnny Cash's Freedom," published April 1979 in *Country Music* magazine. Reprinted with permission from Russell Barnard, editor-in-chief, *Country Music* magazine.

Interview by Don Gonyea at Monroe County Fair, Michigan, August 8, 1981. Printed with permission from NPR correspondent Don Gonyea.

Johnny Cash press conference, Norrköping, Sweden, November 3, 1983. Public domain.

Interview by Glenn Jorgenson for *It's Great to Be Alive*, 1983. Printed with permission from Avera Health.

"Superstar Cash Still Speaks for the Hearts of Americans," published Sunday, April 26, 1987 in the *Nashville Tennessean*. Reprinted with permission from Robert K. Oermann.

"'Biggest Party Ever' Opens New Cash Exhibit," published Wednesday, March 23, 1988 in the *Nashville Tennessean*. Reprinted with permission from Robert K. Oermann.

Interview by Red Robinson at Queen Elizabeth Theatre, Vancouver, British Columbia, July 9, 1988. Printed with permission from Red Robinson.

Johnny Cash's Rock & Roll Hall of Fame induction, January 15, 1992. Printed with permission from Joel Peresman / Rock & Roll Hall of Fame Foundation.

Robert K. Oermann interviews Johnny Cash and June Carter, March 1995. Reprinted with permission from Robert K. Oermann.

"Rosanne Cash Interviews Johnny Cash" copyright © 1996 by Rosanne Cash, originally published in *Interview*. Reprinted by permission of Writers House LLC acting as agent for the author.

Terry Gross interviews Johnny Cash on *Fresh Air with Terry Gross*, November 4, 1997. Printed with permission from *Fresh Air with Terry Gross*.

Anthony DeCurtis interviews Johnny Cash, October 2000 and February 2002. Printed with permission from Anthony DeCurtis.

"The Man in Black and White . . . and Every Shade In-Between" published November 2002 in *No Depression* magazine. Reprinted with permission from Bill Friskics-Warren.

Holly George-Warren interviews Johnny Cash and Rosanne Cash for *The Appalachians*, August 2003. Printed with permission from Holly George-Warren.

"Sylvie Simmons Interviews Johnny Cash," published November 2003 in *MOJO* magazine. Reprinted with permission from Sylvie Simmons.

INDEX

All songs and album titles by Cash unless otherwise attributed

ABC (TV network), xxvi, 37, 41, 163–164
Acuff, Roy, 89
addiction, 125–133. *See also* drug use
Addington, Maybelle. *See* Carter, Maybelle
advice, to young country singers, 75
African American ancestry, xviii(n)
Ahern, Brian, 116–117, 118
"Ain't No Grave," 252
Ain't No Grave (American VI), 188
Air Force service, xxii, 12, 22, 31, 73–74, 181
air sickness bag mail, 162
alcohol abuse, 48, 126, 128, 131–132, 135
"All Over Again," 5
All-Star Tribute to Johnny Cash, An, 188, 196, 203
"Always Alone and Born to Lose," 99
American II: Unchained, 154–155, 167–170, 188, 199–202
American III: Solitary Man, 173, 188, 190, 197–198
American IV: The Man Comes Around, 29, 188, 190, 211, 213, 215, 220
American V: A Hundred Highways, 188, 251, 254
American VI: Ain't No Grave, 188
American Oil commercials, 50–51
American Recordings, xv–xvi, 153–154, 155, 167–168
Anderson, Pink, 151
Angola State Prison, 121

"Any Old Wind That Blows," 47
"Apache Tears," 24
Appalachian music and people, 233–234, 239, 241
Appalachians, The, 231, 232
arrests, 32, 63–64
"As Long as the Grass Shall Grow," 25
Asbury Park, NJ, 118
At Folsom Prison, xxiv, xxvi, 36, 139, 168, 221
At Madison Square Garden, 28, 221
At San Quentin, xxiv, 29, 36, 86, 139
Aunt Polly (character), 245
autoharps, 234–235
Autry, Gene, 165, 234

Baez, Joan, 225
Ball, Earl, 120
"Ballad of Barbara, The," 139
"Ballad of Ira Hayes, The," 13–14, 64–65, 78, 137, 229
"Ballad of the Talking Leaves, The," 24
"Banks of the Ohio, The," 191, 241–242
"Bar with No Beer, A," 99
Bare, Bobby, 112
Baron, The, 110, 111–112
"Battle of New Orleans, The," 241
Beck, 168
"Before My Time," 200
Believer Sings the Truth, A, 98
Betty Ford Clinic, 116

"Big Iron," 211
"Big Mouth Woman," 206
"Big River," 151, 157, 160, 225
Billy Graham Crusades, 97
Bitter Tears: Ballads of the American Indian,
    13, 14, 24–25
Black, Bill, 196
black clothing, xviii–xix, 73, 112, 137, 157,
    170–171, 184, 248
Blackburn, Rick, 135, 136
Blaine, Hal, 118
Blake, Norman, 53
"Blue Yodel," 225
Bob Dylan (Dylan), 225
boogie-woogie sound, 86
Bootleg Vol. III: Live Around the World, 28
"Both Sides Now" (Mitchell), 163
"Bottom of a Mountain," 183
"Boy Named Sue, A," xv, xxiv, 29, 36,
    112–113, 168, 221–222
"Boy Named Sue, A" (Silverstein), 163
Bragg, Charlie, 79, 82, 101
breakfast conversations, 249
"Bridge over Troubled Water," 220
Brunet, Robin, 93
Buckingham, Lindsey, 168
Burton, James, 118
"Bury Me Beneath the Willow" (Carter
    Family), 237
Butler, Larry, 97, 99

Campbell, Glen, 37, 78
Cannon, Gus, 178
capital punishment, 203
car accidents, 62, 63, 64
"Careless Love," 99
Carnegie Hall, 33, 40, 57, 154
Carr, Patrick, 77–78, 80–92, 97–109, 173–175
Carruthers, Bill, 164
Carryin' On with Johnny Cash & June Carter,
    190, 206
Carter, A. P. (Alvin Pleasant), 15, 18, 20–21,
    166, 214, 216–217, 236–237, 239
Carter, Anita, 139, 227, 243, 244
Carter, Carlene, 120–121, 143
Carter, Ezra "Eck," 98, 214, 236
Carter, Helen, 139, 241, 243, 244
Carter, Jimmy, 90–91, 92, 106

Carter, Joe, 214, 238, 252
Carter, June
    Aunt Polly routine, 245
    banjo playing, 16–17, 26–27, 244
    on Carter Family, 18–21, 159
    on charisma, 166
    death, 247, 248–249
    Elvis Presley and, 166, 227, 250
    fearlessness of, 244–245
    first meeting with Cash, 158–159, 226–227
    "Gospel Road" and, 42–44
    influence of, 94
    interventions by, 46–47, 49, 63, 129–130,
        192–193
    Jimmy Carter's relationship to, 90–91
    Kristofferson and, 161–162, 226
    love for, 87, 247
    performing with, 64, 120, 184–185, 215,
        235–236
    personality, 17–18, 232
    relationship with, 33, 206
    Springsteen and, 119
    support for Johnny, 248–249
    support of, 128, 152
Carter, Maybelle, 15, 18–19, 27, 73, 108, 216,
    217, 235, 244
Carter, Rosie, 121
Carter, Sara, 15, 18–19, 20, 98, 235, 236, 244
Carter Family
    appeal of, 15, 159–160
    history, 236–237
    influence of, 73, 74, 216–217
    June Carter on, 18–21, 159
    memories of listening to, 158, 233–234
    touring with Cash, 221, 227, 235–236
Carter Family Fold, 212, 214–215, 239
Carter Scratch, 235, 241
Cash, Carrie Rivers (mother), xix, xxi–xxii,
    21–22, 73, 149, 171, 177, 178, 184, 234,
    244
Cash, Cindy (daughter), 121, 139, 143
Cash, Jack (brother), xxii, xxiii
Cash, John Carter, 48–49, 54, 59, 118–119,
    120, 138, 147, 236
Cash, Johnny
    acting career, 10, 10n, 69, 96, 97, 139–140,
        142, 159
    ancestry, xviii(n), 243

birth and childhood, 22, 29, 31, 58, 232, 237–238
birth name, xxi–xxii
charisma, 79
as collector, 143, 147, 172, 192, 216–217
darker side, 216, 218–219, 228
death, 247, 254
on doing a weekly TV show, 69, 78, 194, 221
fame and, 87, 137, 180–181
as fan of music, 146–147
on fearlessness of Carter women, 244
as film producer, 94, 96
on friendships, 196–197 (see also Jennings, Waylon)
on healing power of music, 246
on his destiny, 70–71
on hit records, 83
images of, xv–xvii, xxii–xxiii, xxiv, 193–194, 213, 218–219 (see also Man in Black persona)
influences on, 74–75, 114, 151–152, 156–158 (see also Carter Family; Dylan, Bob)
injuries suffered, 11, 62, 63, 135
intelligence, 174–175, 189
jobs held, 32, 58, 85, 178
largesse, 34, 121, 140
on listening to his own music, 205–206
on not compartmentalizing music, 60
as performer, 8, 30, 54–55, 58–59, 184
personality traits, xxii, 34, 60, 98–99, 155, 250
physical features, 33, 58, 248
self-awareness, xv, xxiii, 62–63, 86–87
on sex education, 170
singing voice, 74, 171, 176–178, 244, 252
suicide attempt, 127–129
teenage years, xxi, 29–30, 31, 176
on voting, 91
Cash, June Carter. See Carter, June
Cash, Ray (father), xix, xxi, xxii, xxiii, 31, 58, 66, 175–176, 221
Cash, Rosanne (daughter), 111–112, 120–121, 142, 169–172, 191
on family stability, 36
interviews, 38–40, 240–245
"My Old Man," 138, 243

reunion with father, 57
on Rick Rubin, 167–168
on Walk the Line, xvi
Cash, Roy, Jr. (nephew), 2, 138
Cash, Tara (daughter), 120, 121
Cash, Tommy (brother), 221
Cash, William (ancestor), 243
Cash Cabin Studio, 200
Cash: The Autobiography (Cash and Carr), 173–175
Cash: The Life (Hilburn), 8, 14, 42, 72, 77, 135, 149
Cave, Nick, 197, 203, 220, 253
CBS/Columbia, 153, 223
Ceciliani, Richard, 9
Cherokee alphabet, 24–25
Cherry, Hugh, 89
"Children," 44
Christian faith, xxii, 41–42, 63, 68, 97, 106–108, 126–127, 144, 175, 207. See also religion
"City Jail," 86
Clark, Guy, 136, 139, 228
Clark, Roy, 95
Class of '55: Memphis Rock & Roll Homecoming, 145, 146
Classic Cash: Hall of Fame Series, 142
Clement, Jack, 2, 80, 83–84, 99–100, 102–103, 123, 142, 151, 196, 223
CMA Awards, 29, 90, 95, 98, 105–106
"Cocaine Blues," 219
Cohen, Leonard, 154
Collins, Larry, 2
Collins, Lorrie, 2, 7–8
Colt pistols, 143
Columbia Records, xxiv, 1–2, 13, 29, 37, 72, 79, 81, 110, 135, 220
"Committed to Parkview," 79, 80, 84, 86, 156
Composed (R. Cash), 36
Copland, Aaron, 242
Corbijn, Anton, 154
Costello, Elvis, 136, 139
cotton songs, xx, 15, 75, 160
country music
appeal of, 155–156
changes in, 88–89, 104–106, 113, 253
influence on, 28–31, 49–50, 57–58, 224
June Carter on, 119–120

love of, 120
popularity of, 95
tradition in, 165, 236, 241, 253
Country Music Association (CMA). *See* CMA
Awards
Country Music Hall of Fame, 134, 141–144,
147, 148
"Country Trash," 200–201
County Fife, Scotland, 243
"couth" book, 33
cover songs, 217, 253
"Coyote, My Little Brother" (Seeger), 23
"Cripple Creek" (Seeger), 27
crossover appeal, 59–60
crossover records, xxi, 89–90, 112–113
Crow, Sheryl, 203
Crowell, Rodney, 100, 101, 218
"Cry! Cry! Cry!" xx, 150, 179, 180, 182
Cunningham, Walt, 54
"Cyclone of Rye Cove, The" (Carter Family),
20

"Daddy Sang Bass," xv, 29
daily devotional recordings, 198
Daniels, Charlie, 106
Danzig, Glen, 154
"Dark as a Dungeon," 137, 183
"Daughter of a Railroad Man," 80
Davis, Clive, xxiv
Davis, Don, 83
Davis, Jimmie, 6
Davis, Skeeter, 233
Davy Crockett (character), 142
Davy Crockett: Rainbow in the Thunder, 142
Day, Dennis, 176
DeCurtis, Anthony, 188–189, 190–211
"Delia's Gone," 154, 168, 177, 187, 218
Denny, Jim, 88
"Desperado," 220
"Dirty Old Egg-Sucking Dog," xv
disc jockey training, 32
Division Street Corral, 7, 8, 9
"Don't Take Your Guns to Town," 2, 4
"Don't Think Twice, It's All Right," 225
Door to Door Maniac (1961), 139
Dougherty, Sara. *See* Carter, Sara
Drake, Guy, 66, 78
Driftwood, Jimmy, 168

"Drive On," 154
drug use, 8, 48–49, 61–63, 75
cycle of, 32, 181
deception of, 126–127, 129, 132
family interventions on, 129–130, 192–193
quitting, 32, 46–47
relapses into, 86–87, 116, 135
Dyess Colony, AR, xxi–xxii, 29–31, 58, 237–238
Dylan, Bob
admiration of, 224–226
on Cash's voice, xiii
duet with, 38–40, 113–114
as guest on Cash's TV show, 163, 194–196
influence of, 69–70, 196, 209
meeting, 162–163, 225–226
Dylan, Cash, and the Nashville Cats (exhibit), 38

Eagles, the, 220
Eat the Document (1972), 39
Edmunds, Dave, 113
Ehrlichman, John, 57, 68
Elfstrom, Robert, 42, 45
Elliott, Jack, 160
emotionality, 86, 218, 233
Essential Johnny Cash, The, 205–206
Evans, Mari-Lynn, 231, 233
Everybody Loves a Nut, xv, 219

Fabulous Johnny Cash, The, 2, 190, 206, 220
"Falling Star" (Newman), 113
family
gatherings, 238
interventions, 129–130, 192–193
love of, 138, 152, 217–218
singing with, 159, 185
"Fate of Dewey Lee, The" (Carter Family), 20
Feller, Dick, 50
Ferguson, David, 251, 252
Fez Café (New York City), 154
"Field of Diamonds," 200, 203
Finding Your Roots (TV series), xviii(n)
finger picking, 53–54
First Amendment Center, 229
"First Time Ever I Saw Your Face, The," 211,
220
Fisher Body Company, 85, 176
"Five Feet High and Rising," xix, 9, 11, 22, 75,
137, 160

Flack, Roberta, 211
Flea (Red Hot Chili Peppers), 168
Fleetwood, Mick, 168
"Flesh and Blood," 83
Fogerty, John, 145
folk music, 21, 119–120, 159–160, 234
Folsom Prison, 183
"Folsom Prison Blues," xxi, xxiv, 35, 36, 137, 157, 168, 182–183, 229
Ford, Gerald, 57, 90
"Forty Shades of Green," 72, 75–76, 240
Foster, Stephen, 197, 200, 218
Frank, J. L., 21
"Frankie's Man Johnny," 5
Franklin Electronics, 198
Freewheelin' Bob Dylan, The (Dylan), 39, 119, 225
Friskics-Warren, Bill, xv, 212–213

"Gambler, The" (Rogers), 97
gardening, 172
Gates, Henry Louis, xviii(n)
Gatlin, Larry, 44, 163
George-Warren, Holly, 231–233
"Get Rhythm," 151
"Ghost Riders in the Sky," 116
Gift. The Journey of Johnny Cash, The (2019), xviii
"Girl from the North Country," 37, 38, 110, 113, 225
"Give My Love to Rose," 5
Glastonbury Festival, 154
Glen Campbell Goodtime Hour, The, 37
"Golden Idol, The," 162
Gone Girl, 97, 98–102
Gonyea, Don, xix, 109–115
Goodman, Steve, 101
gospel music, 2, 43, 47–48, 64, 75, 133, 206–207, 238–239
"Gospel Road, The," 28, 44
Gospel Road: A Story of Jesus (1973), 42–46, 93, 96
Graham, Billy, xviii, xxvii, 41, 43, 56, 78, 219
Grand Ole Opry appearances, 88–89, 157
Grant, Marshall, xx, 1, 8, 11, 14, 19, 77, 78, 196, 216. See also Tennessee Three; Tennessee Two
Gressett, Floyd, 183

"Greystone Chapel," 60
Gross, Terry, xiv, 173, 175–187
Grossman, Albert "Al," xxvi
"Guess Things Happen That Way," 225
guitar pulls, 70, 163
guitars, 22, 31, 34, 39, 122–123, 142, 235
Gunfight, A (1971), 140
Guthrie, Woody, 21

Haden, Josh, 168
Haggard, Merle, 48–49, 156, 183–184, 200–201. See also "Okie from Muscogee" (Haggard)
Haldeman, H. R., 57, 67–68
Hale, Jack, Jr., 120
Hall, Tom T., 49, 100, 101, 226
"Hard Times Come Again No More," 197, 200
"Hardin Wouldn't Run," 193
HarperCollins, 94, 173
Hayes, Ira, 13
health issues, 86, 116, 140, 142, 146, 153, 173, 201–202, 212–213, 233, 249, 251
"Heartbreak Hotel," 8
helicopter story, 161–162
Hello. I'm Johnny Cash, 28
"Help Me" (Kristofferson), 44
Hendersonville guitar pull, 163
Hendersonville home, 250–251
Hensley, Jerry, 86
"Hey Porter," xix, xx, 58, 179, 180
"Highway Patrolman," 117, 118, 242
Highwaymen, the, 79, 203, 209–210
Hilburn, Robert, 8, 14, 42, 72, 77, 135, 149
Hill, Smilin' Eddie, 74, 156
Historic Reunion: Sara and Mother Maybelle, the Original Carters, An, 235
Holiday Inns, 144
Holiff, Saul, 37
Holland, W. S "Fluke," 79, 115, 120
"Homeless," 228–229
Hootenanny (TV show), 159
Hootenanny Hoot (1963), 159
House of Cash, 50, 79, 136, 141, 232
Howard, Jan, 99, 100
Hundred Highways, A (American V), 188, 251, 254
Hurst, Jack, 46

"Hurt," xvi, 29, 189, 211, 213, 233, 250
Husky, Ferlin, 105, 106, 113, 159
Hymns by Johnny Cash, 2, 190, 206–207, 224, 239
Hymns from the Heart, 2

"I Am a Pilgrim," 16
"I Got Stripes," xxiv, 9, 11–12, 137
"I Hung My Head," 211, 220
"I See a Darkness," 202
"I Still Miss Someone," 2, 39, 221
"I Threw It All Away" (Dylan), 38
"I Walk the Line," 2–3, 5, 32, 60, 114, 181–182, 219
   as crossover hit, 89, 112
   Lyle Lovett on, 150
"I Was There When It Happened," 2, 5
I Was There When It Happened (Grant), 8, 14, 78
"I Will Rock & Roll with You," 102
"I Wish I Was Crazy Again," 84
"I Won't Back Down," 201
"I Would Like to See You Again," 97
"I'd Rather Have You," 139
"If I Were a Carpenter," 160–161
"I'm Leaving Now," 200
"I'm So Lonesome I Could Cry," 220
In His Steps (Sheldon), 106–107
In Other Words: Artists Talk About Life and Work (DeCurtis), 189
Ireland trips, 72, 75–76, 234, 240
Irish music, 176, 234, 243
Israel trip, 42–46
"It Ain't Me Babe," 225
"It Was Jesus," 2, 5
"It's All Over," 81
It's Great to Be Alive (TV show), 124–125
"I've Been Everywhere," xv
Ivey, Bill, 141, 144

James, Sonny, 112
jaw pain, 63, 149, 153, 232
Jefferson, Blind Lemon, 151
Jennings, Waylon
   friendship with, 84, 107, 140, 145–146, 209–211
   Highwaymen reunion and, 203
   music by, 89–90

   in "Outlaw" movement, 77–78, 157–158
   working with, 84, 99, 103–104
"Jesus Was a Carpenter," 28, 44
John R. Cash, 56
"Johnny 99," 242
Johnny 99, 116–117
Johnny Cash and the Holy Land, 42–46
Johnny Cash and the Tennessee Three, 79–80, 115
Johnny Cash and the Tennessee Two, 1, 2–6, 73
Johnny Cash at Madison Square Garden, 28, 221
Johnny Cash Children's Album, The, 56
Johnny Cash Exhibit (Country Music Hall of Fame), 134, 141–144, 147
Johnny Cash Is Coming to Town, 136, 139, 140
"Johnny Cash on Campus" (episode), 134, 155
Johnny Cash på Österåker (Johnny Cash at Osteraker), 116, 121
Johnny Cash Show, The (TV show), xxvi, 37–38, 41, 78, 93, 163–164, 194, 221. See also "Johnny Cash on Campus" (episode)
Johnny Cash Sings Precious Memories, 56
Johnny Cash! The Man, His World, His Music, 42
Johnny Cash with His Hot and Blue Guitar, 5
Johnson, Diana, 144
Johnston, Bob, xxiv–xxv, 36–37, 223
Jones, Fern, 2
Jones, George, 233
Jorgenson, Glenn, 124–133
Jorgenson, Phyllis, 124, 125

"Keep on the Sunny Side," 19, 216, 219
Keller, Helen, 147
Kilgore, Merle, 192, 227
Kindred Spirits, 225
Klein, Gary, 81–82
Krementz, Jill, 40
Kristofferson, Kris, 43, 44, 107, 161–162, 163, 165–166, 175, 226. *See also* Highwaymen, the
Ku Klux Klan, 34, 137–138

LaFarge, Peter, 14, 23, 25, 65
Lane, Red, 53–54
Lansky Brothers (store), 151
Las Vegas Hilton appearances, 56, 58–59
Last Deejay, The (Brunet), 93
"Last Night I Had the Strangest Dream," 221
Law, Don, 223
"Lay, Lady, Lay" (Dylan), 163
"Legend of John Henry's Hammer, The," 193
"Let the Train Blow the Whistle," 154
Leventhal, John, 38
Levi's jeans, 122
Lewin, Bob, 120
Lewis, Jerry Lee, 145, 146, 157, 223, 224
Liberto, Vivian (wife), xviii(n), 1–2, 62, 219
Life Is Strange, 205
Light Crust Dough Boys, 156
Linderman, Larry, xviii, 56
Lindfors, Lars, 116, 122
List, The (R. Cash), 241
"Little Birdy" (Seeger), 26
Little House on the Prairie (TV show), 96, 97
Little Richard, 152
"Loading Coal," 149–150
Lollapalooza, 167
"Lonesome Death of Hattie Carroll, The"
    (Dylan), 226
long-haired element, 134, 250
"Long Legged Guitar Man," 206
Look at Them Beans, 56
Los Angeles Times, xix
Louvin Brothers, 74, 156
Love, God, Murder, 190, 198, 204–205, 218
"Love Has Lost Again" (R. Cash), 79
Lovett, Lyle, 148, 150–151
Lowe, Nick, 113, 121, 154, 218
"Lucky Old Sun," 177

MacColl, Ewan, 220
"Maggie's Farm," 209
"Mama, You Been on My Mind," 225
Man Comes Around, The (American IV), 29,
    190, 211, 213, 215, 220
"Man in Black," 112, 134, 155
Man in Black (Cash), xiv, 56, 126
Man in Black persona, xiv, xviii–xix, 112, 137,
    139, 218, 228, 251
Man in White (Cash), 94, 139

Mangold, James, xv, 227
marijuana legislation, 61
"Marrakesh Express" (Nash), 163
Martin, Dean, 168, 197
Martin, Steve, 194
Matthews, Vince, 163
McCartney, Paul, 142
McLaughlin, Pat, 251
"Me and Bobby McGee" (Kristofferson), 163,
    226
media coverage, xxiii, xxv–xxvii, 87
"Memories Are Made of This," 168, 177
Memphis, TN, lure of, 156
Mercury/Polygram, 135, 136, 142, 185, 223
"Mercy Seat, The," 197, 202, 203
"Merry Golden Tree, The," 242
Million Dollar Quartet (2010), xvii
Mississippi Flood. *See* "Five Feet High and
    Rising"
Mitchell, Joni, 163
Moman, Chips, 145
Morning Edition (NPR), 110
Mount Vernon Cemetery, 19–20
"Mountain Dew," 225
"Mr. Garfield," 193
murder ballads, 191–192, 220. *See also*
    "Delia's Gone"
Murder in Coweta County (TV movie), 117
Murray, Larry, 165
music-magazine ads, 31
"My Best Friend" (Orbison), 207
"My Clinch Mountain Home" (Carter
    Family), 233
My Life Story (Keller), 143, 147
"My Old Man" (R. Carter), 138, 243

Nash, Graham, 163
Nashville Skyline (Dylan), 37–39, 225
Nashville sound, 39–40, 89, 224
National Public Radio (NPR), 109, 110
Native American ancestry, xviii, 23, 34, 65
Neal, James, 67
Nebraska (Springsteen), 118–119, 242
Nelson, Willie, 77–78, 79, 88, 105, 106,
    157–158, 165–166, 203
New York City trip, 99–100
Newbury, Mickey, 163, 226
Newman, Jimmy, 113

Newport Folk Festival, 30, 39, 162–163, 225, 226, 235
Nickajack Cave, 127–129
"Night Hank Williams Came to Town, The," 136
Nine Inch Nails. *See* Reznor, Trent
9/11 attacks, 208
"No Depression in Heaven" (Carter Family), 239
"No Expectations," 99–100
"Nobody," 197

O'Connor, Eine, xviii–xix, 72–76
O'Donnell, Red, 195–196
Oermann, Robert K., xix, 134–136, 141, 153, 155–163, 165–166
"Okie from Muscogee" (Haggard), 66, 78, 221, 222
Ol' Blue Suede Shoes Is Back (Perkins), 104
"Old Apache Squaw," 24
"Old Fishhawk," 48
Old Golden Throat (1968), xiv
Oldham, Will, 202
"One," 199–200
"One on the Right Is on the Left, The," xv
"One Piece at a Time," xv, 77, 79, 83, 85
One Piece at a Time, 77, 79, 80–81, 84
"Oney," 47
Orange Blossom Special, 205, 206, 209, 225
"Orange Blossom Special" (Rouse Brothers), 164
Orbison, Roy, 93, 145, 146, 163, 196
"Orphan of the Road," 50
Österåker prison, 116, 121
"Outlaw" movement, 77–78, 88, 157–158

Parkinson's disease misdiagnosis, 173
patriotism, xxii, 66, 208
"Peace in the Valley," 54
Perkins, Bertie, 2
Perkins, Carl, 12, 29, 66, 94, 104, 108, 145, 146, 181, 221, 222, 225
Perkins, Luther, xx, 1, 2, 4, 115, 216
Petty, Tom, 201, 253
Phillips, Dewey, 156
Phillips, Sam, xix–xxi, 2, 123, 151, 157, 178–179, 181, 207, 216, 223, 239, 248. *See also* Sun Records

Phoenix, Joaquin, xvi, 228
Physicians' Desk Reference, 132
piano lessons, 53–54
"Pickin' Time," 22–23, 75, 160
Pierce, Webb, 105
"Pilgrim, Chapter 33, The" (Kristofferson), 175
Planned Parenthood, 170
Plantation Dinner Theater, 79
political views, 51–52, 78, 90–92, 106, 137–138, 170, 229
Polygram. *See* Mercury/Polygram
Pond, Steve, 149
Popovich, Steve, 135, 144
Presley, Elvis, 2, 123, 156–157, 180
    Cash's parody of, 8, 11
    death of, 98, 108
    at Grand Ole Opry, 88
    and June Carter, 166, 227, 250
Pride of Jesse Hallam, The (1981), 140
Prine, John, 101
Prior, Anna, 9
prison concerts, xxiv, 34, 116, 182–183, 221
prison reform, 34, 52–53, 60–61, 140

radio stations, 89–90, 156–157, 233, 253
"Ragged Old Flag," 67, 137–138, 229
Rainbow Quest (TV show), xviii, 13–14
Ramblin' Jack, 160–161
"Rebel—Johnny Yuma, The" 72
record production, 50, 222–223
recording sessions, 78–82, 84, 100–102, 201, 204
"Red Hot & Blue," 151, 156
"Red Robinson's Legends," 7
religion, 43, 47, 63, 114, 239. *See also* Christian faith
Resurrection of Johnny Cash: Hurt, Redemption, and American Recordings, The (Thomson), 136
Reznor, Trent, 189, 211, 213
Richards, Keith, 149–150
Ride This Train, 96, 190, 206
Ride This Train (TV show segment), 122, 165
"Ring of Fire," 14, 192, 227
Ring of Fire: The Best of Johnny Cash, 72
River Park, 124–125
Robbins, Marty, 105, 106, 211

Robin, Lou, 116, 174, 183, 185, 198
Robinson, Red, xxiii, 7, 9–12, 93–96, 145–147
Rock & Roll Hall of Fame, 148–152
Rockabilly Blues, 115
rockabilly music, 149, 193
Rodgers, Jimmie, 74, 191, 228
Rogers, Kenny, 97
Roosevelt, Franklin D., 31
Rouse Brothers, 164–165
Routh, Jack, 200
"Rowboat," 168
Rubin, Rick
    artistic vision, xv–xvi, 168–169
    compared to Sam Phillips, 223
    DeCurtis on, 189
    relationship with Cash, 154–155, 169, 185–186, 199, 205, 248–249, 251, 254
    Rosanne Cash on, 167–168 (see also *American Recordings*)
"Rusty Cage," 169, 189

"Sam Hall," 220
"San Francisco Joy" (Newbury), 163
"San Quentin," 183
San Quentin concerts, 183
Saul of Tarsus, 94
Scheff, Jerry, 118
Schoemer, Karen, 149
Seeger, Pete, xviii, 13–27, 164, 194
Seoul, Korea, tour, 17–18
September 11 attack, 208
"September When It Comes," 243
Sequoia, 24–25
Shelton, Robert, 225
Sherley, Glen, 60–61
Sherrill, Billy, 110
Shindig, 159
Shy-Drager syndrome misdiagnosis, 173, 202
Silver, 116
Silverstein, Shel, 163
Simmons, Sylvie, xxiii, 247–250
singing lessons, 177–178
"Sixteen Tons," 177
slapback, 80, 82, 102
Smith, Carl, 105
Smith, Joe, 44
Snow, Hank, 74, 89, 105, 114, 151, 157

"So Doggone Lonesome," xxi
social issues, concern for, 228–229
"Sold Out of Flagpoles," 86
Solitary Man (American III), 173, 188, 190, 197–198
"Someday My Ship Will Sail," 84
song collecting, 216–217
song lists, 241, 252
Songs of Our Soil, 220
songwriters' parties, 70, 163
songwriting, 22, 31, 73, 75, 86, 155–156, 160, 197, 198–199, 253
Soundgarden, 218
South, Joe, 44
South by Southwest, 154
"Southern Accents," 168
"Spiritual," 168, 190
spiritual strength, 63, 91–92, 125–126, 152, 190–191. *See also* Christian faith; *Gospel Road: A Story of Jesus* (1973)
Spotify, 189
Springsteen, Bruce, 117, 118
"State Trooper" (Springsteen), 119
Statler Brothers, 101, 221
steel guitars, 122–123
Stewart, Jay, 3–6
Sting, 220
stories and storytelling, xvii, xix, 31, 245–246
"Streets of Laredo, The," 220
Strummer, Joe, 253
Stuart, Marty, 118, 120, 168, 218, 232
Sun Records, 2, 32, 58, 123, 178–179, 223–224. *See also* Phillips, Sam
Sun Records sound, 60, 79–80, 81, 216
"Sunday Morning Coming Down," 86, 162
"Suppertime," 6
Sweetheart of the Rodeo (Byrds), 39
synthesizers, use of, 142, 154

tank prank, 14
"Tennessee Flat-Top Box" (R. Cash), 142
Tennessee State Prison, 61
"Tennessee Stud," 168
Tennessee Three, 79–80, 115
Tennessee Two, xx, 2–6, 58, 73
Texas State Prison, 34, 182
Thaddeus Rose and Eddie (TV movie), 97
Tharpe, Sister Rosetta, 98, 151, 156

"That Old Wheel," 142
"There Ain't No Good Chain Gang," 84, 97
"There's a Mother Always Waiting," 21–22
Thomson, Graeme, 136
"Through the Eyes of an Eagle," 252
Tittle, Jimmy, 120
Tom Petty and the Heartbreakers, 168, 201
Tonight Show with Jay Leno, The, 232
touring
    behavior while, 33, 34–35
    with Carter Family, 221, 227, 235–236
    Cash on, 111, 171–172
    with Elvis Presley, 180
    Ireland, 72, 75–76, 234, 240
    Korea, 17–18
    love of, 11, 53
    Vietnam, 65–66, 78
Town Hall Party, 1–2
"Train of Love" (Dylan), 225
Travis, Merle, 90, 139, 165
Tricky Dick and the Man in Black (2018), xvii
Tubb, Ernest, 74, 105

U2, 154, 199
Unchained (American II), 154–155, 167–170, 199–202
Unearthed, 247, 251–254

Vanderbilt University, 134
Vietnam tour, 65–66, 78
Vietnam War, 51–52, 134, 155, 219

Wagnon, William B., Jr., 1
Wagon Train (TV series), 10n
Waits, Tom, 154
Walk the Line (2005), xvi, 213, 227–228
"Wanderer, The," 154
"Wanted Man," 70
Water from the Wells of Home, 142
Watergate, 56, 66–68

"Watermelon Wine" (Hall), 49
Wayne Newton Theatre, 154
"Ways of a Woman in Love, The," 5
"Welfare Cadillac" (Drake), 66, 78
"We'll Meet Again," 220
Wells, Kitty, 90
"Were You There When They Crucified My Lord?," 64
"What Is Truth," 43, 78, 137
White House performances, 66
Wilcox-Gay recorder, 181
"Wildwood Flower," 234
Wildwood Flower (J. Carter), 236
Williams, Burt, 197
Williams, Charlie, 12
Williams, Hank, 57, 151, 220
"Winding Stream, The" (Carter Family), 243
"Wings of a Dove" (Husky), 113
Winners Got Scars Too (Wren), 28
Winston, Nat, 129, 130
Witherspoon, Reese, xvi, 213, 228
"Without Love," 113
WMPS (Memphis radio station), 74
Wootton, Bob, 79, 115, 118, 120
Worldwide Pictures, 96
"Worried Man Blues," 19
Woster, Terry, 125
Wounded Knee, 65
Wren, Christopher S., xviii, 28, 29, 44

XERA (radio station), 158, 216, 233, 244

Yoakam, Dwight, 135
"You Wild Colorado," 193
Young, Faron, 105
"Young Love" (James), 112
"You're Right, I'm Left, She's Gone," 84–85
"You're the Nearest Thing to Heaven," 4

Zooropa (U2), 154